Criminal Justice
Issues and the
African-American
Community

Dedicated to my close friend, former student and colleague—
Prof. Ernest Miller who passed away suddenly on MLK day

———————————————

© 2008 Komanduri S. Murty

Published in the United States by
Beckham Publications Group, Inc.

ISBN 10: 0-9802380-2-1
ISBN 13: 978-0-9802380-2-0
10 9 8 7 6 5 4 3 2 1

Library of Congress Cataloging-in-publication data: 2007941421

Criminal Justice Issues and the African-American Community

Edited By

Komanduri S. Murty, Ph.D

The Southern Center for Studies in Public Policy
Clark Atlanta University, Atlanta, GA

PUBLICATIONS GROUP, INC.

Silver Spring

CONTENTS

FOREWORD

In 1895, Atlanta University inaugurated a series of investigations into the condition of African Americans, which resulted in annual conferences at the university and the publication of a series of monographs based on data collected. Under the leadership of W. E. B. Du Bois, Atlanta University became one of the first institutions in the South to engage in scientific sociological research. Scholars and teachers in colleges and universities across the nation are still using the Atlanta University conference monographs and other publications by W. E. B. Du Bois. The series of conferences and annual reports referred to as the Atlanta University Publications received great attention from scholars throughout the nation and provided a foundation for constructive efforts in social betterment for African Americans.

To recreate this tradition, Clark Atlanta University, in partnership with the Andrew Mellon Foundation has instituted a research program that seeks to increase research in the social sciences. The goal of the program is to ensure that social science research on African-American issues done by W. E. B. Du Bois during the first half of the 20th century is continued in the 21st century.

Established in 2001, the Du Bois Institute of Clark Atlanta University commits to regain its historic and significant leadership role in the development of a research agenda on historical and contemporary issues relating to African Americans and people of African descent. The Institute's focus is on generating relevant research, teaching and social change by strengthening faculty research, particularly in the social science departments. The Institute addresses regional, national and international issues that impact African Americans.

This monograph on *Criminal Justice Issues and the African-American Community* is one such attempt. I am happy to acknowledge Dr. Komanduri S. Murty, Professor and Chairman of the Department of Sociology and Criminal Justice for undertaking the editorial responsibility of this important document. Hopefully, the issues discussed in this document find their way to active research agenda and public policy.

Ron Finnell, D.P.A.
Director
Southern Center for Studies
in Public Policy and
WEB Du Bois Institute

PREFACE

In the beginning of the 20th Century, under the aegis of W.E.B. Du Bois, the Atlanta University conducted a ten-year cycle of conferences to study the African-American community in terms of physical conditions of life, social organization, economic activity, education, religion, and the important matter of Negro crime. The proceedings of these conferences were published as *The Atlanta University Publications.* A century later the Du Bois Institute of Clark Atlanta University began the Du Bois Annual Spring Conferences on various topics—starting with Health (2002), Housing (2003), Education (2004) and the present focus is on Criminal Justice Issues (2005). Keeping with the tradition, these issues aim at the betterment of the African-American community.

This monograph contains 17 articles organized under six categories: felon disfranchisement; death penalty; domestic violence; community policing; impact of incarceration, imprisonment, and police contact; and, criminal justice reforms. Experts in the chosen areas including academicians, law enforcement officials, and judges wrote these articles. The discussant reports are included at the end under the category of discussions.

The monograph opens with a background article entitled *The African-American Perspective: W.E.B. Du Bois and the American Criminal Justice System.* This paper delves into Du Bois' contributions in revealing the issue of crime and African Americans. The authors provide detailed descriptions of the methodology he used in his Negro crime studies, his view on the causes and effects of African-American crime and the reasons for the disproportionate number of black Americans in prisons.

Two articles are included in the first category of felon disfranchisement. The first one, Sampson Ike Oli's *Felon Disfranchisement is Unconstitutional and Unjustified* supports the belief that the disfranchisement of felons is unconstitutional. The author maintains his position that the principle behind rehabilitation is to reform. This reformation includes allowing ex-convicts to vote. The second article, written by Ryan Scott King, *Felony Disfranchisement: The Political and Social Impact of an Exclusionary Policy* calls attention to the problems of the disfranchisement of felons in the United States. The author points out "the act of voting is a shared experience and is an opportunity for a community to come together publicly and express their political will."

The second category is death penalty. There are two articles addressing this issue. Michael Mears in *A Strategy for Confronting Racial Discrimination in the Use of the Death Penalty in Georgia* elaborates on the unjust application of the death penalty in the case of African-Americans. He draws on previous research findings of racial discrimination and the disproportionate number of black executions. The second article, written by Komanduri Murty and Vandana Murty is entitled *Capital Punishment: Helping or Hurting?* The paper addresses the ever-present national dilemma.

The third category is domestic violence. *Domestic Violence, Law Enforcement and African Americans*, written by Joanne Rhone, is a comprehensive work displaying the cause and effects of domestic violence in African-American families along with illustrating the role of law enforcement in these matters.

The fourth category included in this monograph is community policing. The first article in this category is *Community Policing in the African-American Community: A Perspective by Chief Thetus A. Knox*. This piece is a view on the effects of community policing as an effective measure to control crime in the community. The author draws from her personal experience as the Chief of the Zone Four precinct. Alan J. Dreher in *Successful Community*

Policing Strategies within the Atlanta Police Department provides another view of community policing and its effects. The author recognizes the important role the community has in controlling crime. He expresses the philosophy behind this proposed method of control and lays out its principles and goals.

The fifth category, impact on incarceration, imprisonment and police contact, contains three articles. *The Effects of Crime and Imprisonment on Family Formation*, written by Obie Clayton and Joan Moore, expands on the effect of imprisonment of family members on the family itself. It reveals the perpetual damage to family life that unintervened imprisonment may cause. It is important to try to help those African Americans that are misguided as a result of media and members of the criminal justice system unwilling to provide aid. The second article, *The Impact of Race, Police Experience, and Feeling of Safety on Attitudes Towards the Police*, written by Sutham Cheurprakobkit, reflects on research indicating that positive police-citizen interaction and feeling safe in the neighborhood produce positive ratings of police performance. The author states the need for increased efforts and resources to be spent to create safe and friendly neighborhoods, especially in the black community. The last article, *The Impact of Massive Incarceration on the African-American Woman, Her Family, and the Community,* is written by Gale "Sky" Edeawo. Edeawo discusses the difficulties of discrimination the African-American woman faces in the criminal justice system. The paper explores the impact massive incarceration has on the women's families and well-being and cites specific examples to illustrate the troubles that an African-American woman undergoes.

The largest category, criminal justice reforms, contains six articles. Michael Blain, in *Sentencing Reform and the African-American Community*, raises the question of whether the war on drugs has been effective. Blain further investigates the success of the U.S. policies implemented to stop the drug problem and also questions the unbalanced number of minority (namely African-American) users imprisoned as a result of these policies. The next article written by Helen Brantley, Lucinda Barron and George E.

Hicks, is *Training Pre-service Teachers to Work with Juvenile Delinquents: from Theoretical Implications to Practical Applications*. In this paper, the authors provide a four-strand model to training pre-service teachers. The paper emphasizes the need for professional development and training programs of pre-service teachers to recognize and rectify the incongruence and inconsistencies of serving a diverse student population including those at-risk for violence and juveniles in other settings. Amy Howell, in her paper entitled *Trying Children and Adults in Georgia: Can the Seven Deadly Sins be Forgiven?,* questions the competence of the juvenile court judge to determine whether to children cases should be, under the rule of SB440, automatically pushed into the adult system. She presents several juvenile cases in the context of some criminal justice policies of trying juveniles as adults. The remaining three articles in this category are written, respectively, by the Honorable Judges M. Yvette Miller, Thelma Wyatt Cummings Moore, and Lynn Sherrod. Judge Miller, in *The Criminal Justice System in Georgia: Issues in the African-American Community*, states the issues in the criminal justice system as a result of keeping recidivists in contact with one another for long periods of time. She provides an overview of the Georgia Criminal Justice system and accentuates the importance of instilling values in youth as they grow to become productive citizens. Judge Moore's article, *Creation of an Urban Family Court,* expounds on the need for a family court that can adapt to the unique needs of families in trouble. The prolongation of child custody, support, and visitation disputes could be resolved by the creation of the family court. She continues to state the family court offers therapeutic justice where it is most needed. Judge Sherrod draws on her experiences to reveal the effects of drugs, alcohol, and violence on whole families in her article, *Treatment Courts of Madison County, Alabama.* She reveals the seeming indifferent attitude of youth about to be incarcerated and their preference to go to jail than home due to the dysfunctional and disorganized family structures.

The last section, discussions, includes the remarks and comments made by three discussants namely, Saliba Mukoro, Ali

Al-Taie, and Dianne A. Williams. The purpose of these reports is to provide first-hand accounts of the scholars in the audience.

I express my deep appreciation to Dr. Ron Finnell, the Director of WEB Du Bois Institute, for choosing me to edit this monograph; and, to Mr. Jeffrey Williams, Research Associate of WEB Du Bois Institute, for his efforts in coordinating between me and the contributing authors by securing manuscripts, following up on updates and requirements, and always being available when needed. It is a pleasure for me to acknowledge the contributing authors for their scholarly and original work included in this monograph. I love to acknowledge the assistance provided by my daughter, Vandana Murty. Her enthusiasm, despite her college studies, especially meticulous attention to all the facets of preparing the manuscript for publication, was an enormous benefit to the successful completion of this monograph. Finally, thanks to Ms. Toni Fanning for introducing me to the publisher, Beckham Publishing Group, Inc.

Komanduri S. Murty, Ph.D

The African-American Perspective: W.E.B. Du Bois and the American Criminal Justice System

Komanduri S. Murty and Vandana Murty

"Crime is a phenomenon of organized social life, and is the open rebellion of an individual against his social environment."

–W.E.B. Du Bois

The above quotation made by Dr. Du Bois in *The Philadelphia Negro: A Social Study* aptly describes the situation most African Americans face. As the third major ethnic group to populate the United States, after the Native Americans and the whites, African Americans are the only group to ever be enslaved. Though slavery ended over one hundred years ago, its effects still remain engrained in the foundation of this nation's criminal justice system. The person to first explore this institutionalized discrimination is Dr. W.E.B. Du Bois. Although a social science Renaissance man of sorts, Dr. Du Bois had a distinct interest in American criminology. His most well known writing on crime is a social study entitled *The Philadelphia Negro*. In this study and in the other literature he authored about this subject, Du Bois outlines his thoughts about the causation of African-American crime and the reason for the disproportionately high number of blacks in prisons.

Born on February 23, 1868 in Great Barrington, Massachusetts, W.E.B. Du Bois showed an ardent concern for the development for his race since childhood. Surprisingly, he did not have to deal with overt racism in the community he lived. At the time Great Barrington had very few black people (about 50 out of a population of 5000). Despite this, the vindictive attitudes of the white residents towards the black residents did not go unnoticed by Du Bois. The outgoing and good-natured boy became sullen and withdrawn. When in high school, Du Bois became the local correspondent for the *New York Globe.* As correspondent, Du Bois took it as his duty to help advance his race by impressing upon the black people the need for them to be more politicized. While describing a specific event that happened in his hometown, Dr. Du Bois wrote:

> *The Citizens of the town are forming a Law and Order Society to enforce the laws against liquor selling which have been sadly neglected for the past year or two. It would be a good plan if some of the colored men should join it. (Du Bois, W.E.B, 1883/1986, p 1)*

This passage clearly illustrates that even at a young age Du Bois was aware that there was a serious problem brewing in the institutions of this nation. He also understood that in order to make a difference, people must unite.

Du Bois was an intelligent student and effortlessly surpassed his classmates in academic and other pursuits. Though his first choice of college was Harvard, through financial aid from family and friends and a scholarship, Du Bois ended up in Fisk College (now Fisk University). When Du Bois traveled to the South for school, his knowledge of the race problem in America became more defined. The discrimination and overt racism he witnessed solidified his resolve to help accelerate the freedom of his people. While at Fisk, Du Bois pursued a career in writing and editing and developed his oratorical skills. Du Bois realized that if he was to understand the race problem in America completely, he would have to spend more time in the South. He spent two summers teaching in a community school and became further acquainted with the people in Tennessee. Du Bois observed firsthand the poverty, infertile lands, ignorance, and prejudice that controlled and severely limited the advancement of his people in the South. Most impressive was the obvious desire of the black people to pursue and obtain an education.

Du Bois obtained his associate degree and then attended Harvard University as a junior. As a student he was very drawn to the social sciences. While Du Bois's primary focus was philosophy, he steered away into history by one of his mentors, the esteemed psychologist William James. It slowly turned to economics and social problems. He graduated from Harvard with honors and immediately set out to obtain his masters and doctoral degrees. Shortly before the completion of his Master's degree in 1891, Du Bois received a grant to study abroad at the University of Berlin in Germany. During the two years he spent in Germany, Du Bois noticed that race problems were not unique to America. He saw similar problems throughout Europe and read about more problems in Africa and Asia. Upon returning to the United States, Du Bois decided to make a career by combining his social science studies into a scientific approach of social research. His doctoral dissertation entitled, *The Suppression of the African Slave Trade in America*, is the seminal work on this subject.

Du Bois received his doctoral degree at the age of twenty-six. He later accepted a fellowship at the University of Pennsylvania to conduct a research project in Pennsylvania's slums. The work that resulted from this study, *The Philadelphia Negro*, unearthed more scientific knowledge about the color prejudice than any other study. "It revealed the Negro group as a symptom, not a cause; as a striving, palpitating group, and not an inert, sick body of crime; as a long historic development and not a transient occurrence." Nearing the end of his tenure in Philadelphia, Du Bois, at the 1897 Academy of Political and Social Sciences conference, presented his plan for the scientific study of African-American problems. He spoke of the lack of scientific studies about African-American crime and of the double standard in the American criminal justice system. On this point, he wrote:

It is extremely doubtful if any satisfactory study of Negro crime and lynching can be made for a generation or more, in the recent condition of the public mind, which renders it almost impossible to get at facts and real conditions. (Du Bois, W.E.B, 1898/1982, p 49)

After completing the special fellowship with the University of Pennsylvania, Du Bois accepted a position at Atlanta University to progress with his studies in sociology. During the thirteen years he spent at Atlanta University, Du Bois studied African-American morality, urbanizations, business, college-bred black Americans, churches, and African-American crime. He became the leader of the "Atlanta School" of social scientific research. Because of his enthusiastic involvement in the race problem while at Atlanta University, it has been said that "there was no study made of the race problem in America which did not depend in some degree upon the investigations made at Atlanta University."

Du Bois Methodology to Study African-American Crime: In an attempt to create a scientific basis for studying crime, Du Bois adopted an empirical methodology with the hope that if other cities like Boston in the east, Chicago Kansas City in the west and Atlanta, New Orleans, and Galveston in the south followed, a fair basis of induction as to the condition of the American Negro could be constituted. His methodology involved analysis of crime at three levels. First, Du Bois examined the history of Negro crime in Philadelphia tracing back to the earliest advent of the Negro and legislations passed through the approval of various governors, councils, mayors, and other authoritative figures. Second, he analyzed data from the reports of the Eastern Penitentiary and Moyamensing Prison covering the period of 1829 to 1854 in terms of total commitments by race and kinds of crime by race. Then, Du Bois focused on Negro crime since the Civil War because he expected a parallel increase in Negro crime corresponding to the rapid raise of the white crime, which has been the general characteristic since the war, especially in urban America. Another conjecture Du Bois made was that following the emancipation of slavery, many blacks migrated to cities and consequently there would be an increase in Negro crime, as in the case of all lower classes. Here, he looked at annual arrests and percentage of Negro arrests in Philadelphia from 1864 through 1896. The trend analysis also included prisoners in Moyamensing Prison, inmates of the House of Correction where mild cases and juveniles were sent and convicts committed to the Eastern Penitentiary. Following these three levels of analysis, Du Bois conducted a special study in crime consisting of 541 Negro prisoners during a ten year period (1885-1895). The variables included in this special study were: chief crimes for which these prisoners were convicted, conjugal condition (gender and marital status) of convicts, illiteracy, age, prior criminal record, length of sentence, and selective case studies.

Such a comprehensive methodology, which Du Bois formulated at the time that no reliable study of Negro crime was ever present, provided a benchmark for subsequent researchers in the field.

Du Bois' Findings: In reference to the question of the cause of crime, Du Bois recognized the role of "social revolution". Following the emancipation of slaves, thousands of rural black Americans migrated to the North (the Union) in hopes of employment and education opportunities. But being thrust into unfamiliar surroundings and growing metropolises led to a number of conditions for the African Americans, including crime. Faced with blatant use of discrimination in employment, the black people were in a way forced into crime in order to survive. Still, there were a significant disproportional number of African Americans in prisons compared to white Americans. He noted this about the black man:

> *He was arrested for less cause and given longer sentences than whites. Great numbers of those arrested and committed for trial were never brought*

to trial so that their guilt could be proven or
disproven. (Du Bois, W.E.B, 1899b/1973, p 235)

Additionally, Du Bois pointed out the average length of
sentencing for black Americans was longer by a year. He observed
that in courts there were obvious disparities:

The rich are always favored somewhat at the expense
of the poor, the upper classes at the expense of the
unfortunate classes, and whites at the expense of
Negroes. (Du Bois, W.E.B, 1899b/1973, p 249)

He also directed readers' attention to the inconsistent treatment
of certain crimes. So-called white-collar crimes including
embezzlement are treated less severely than petty theft and robbery,
especially if that crime is committed by a person of color.

We know for instance that certain crimes are not
punished in Philadelphia because the public opinion
is lenient, as for instance embezzlement, forgery, and
certain sorts of stealing; on the other hand a
commercial community is apt to punish with severity
petty thieving, breaches of the peace, and personal
assault or burglary. (Du Bois, W.E.B, 1899b/1973, p
249)

In the report Du Bois edited, *Some Notes on Negro Crime*
Particularly in Georgia, presenters at the Ninth Atlanta
Conference concluded results that were in concordance with Du
Bois' previous research conclusions. Several social scientists of
the day including M.N. Work, H.H. Proctor, and A. G. Coombs
deduced certain causes of African-American crime and classified
them into two categories: faults of the Negroes and faults of the
whites.

Faults of the Negroes:

1. Abuse of their new freedom and tendency toward idleness and vagrancy.
2. Loose ideas of property, petty pilfering.
3. Unreliability, lying and deception
4. Exaggerated ideas of personal rights, irritability and suspicion.
5. Sexual looseness, weak family life and poor training of children; lack of respect for parents.
6. Lack of proper self-respect; low or extravagant ideals.
7. Poverty, low wages and lack of accumulated property.
8. Lack of thrift and prevalence of the gambling spirit.
9. Waywardness of the "second generation."
10. The use of liquor and drugs.

Faults of the whites

1. The attempt to enforce a double standard of justice in the courts, one for Negroes and one for whites.
2. The election of judges for short terms, making them subservient to waves of public opinion in a white electorate.
3. The shirking of jury duty by the best class of whites, leaving the dealing out of justice to the most ignorant and prejudiced.
4. Laws so drawn as to entangle the ignorant, as in the case of laws for labor contracts, and to leave wide direction as to punishment in the hands of juries of petty officials.
5. Peonage and debt-slavery as methods of securing cheap and steady labor.
6. The tendency to encourage ignorance and subservience among Negroes instead of intelligence, ambition and independence.

7. *The taking of all rights of political self-defense from the Negro either by direct law, or custom, or by the "white primary" system.*

8. *The punishment of crime as a means of public and private revenue rather than a means of preventing the making of criminals.*

9. *The rendering of the chastity of Negro women difficult of defense in law or custom against the aggression of white men.*

10. *Enforcing a caste system in such a way as to humiliate Negroes and kill their self-respect. (Du Bois, W.E.B, 1904, p 55-57)*

While they claimed the studies they performed were still too incomplete to lead them to many definite conclusions, the causes listed above were ones they were certain contributed to the cause of African-American crime.

Frank B. Sanborn describes crime as generally "the portion of human depravity and passion which is regarded and punished by human laws." Du Bois had a similar outlook on crime, but he also believed there were those who were criminals, not because of the depravity they suffer, but solely because of their nature. In *The Philadelphia Negro*, Dr. Du Bois divided the population into four classes he referred to as four grades.

Du Bois' Typology of African-American Society: Grade one consists of "families of undoubted respectability earning sufficient income to live well." In this group the woman remains a housewife. The children's only object is education and the family lives in a "well-kept home." These families form the "aristocracy of the Negro population in education, wealth and general social efficiency." They represent the possibilities for the colored population yet do not mingle very much with the other classes. This lack of merging also presents a lack of communication that increases the difficulty of other African Americans to rise as this group has. Du Bois believed that the groups only had blood and color prejudice to bind them together. The upper classes are slow to realize that their duty is to serve the lower classes. However, comparatively, in the white world, these families are still considered poor, so they do not have many faculties with which to assist the lower classes.

The second grade is the respectable working-class. The younger children are in school and there is more or less steady income for the household. These are the "Negroes; the mass of the servant class, the porters and waiters, and the best of the laborers." This class works hard is honest, faithful, fair, and have some economic foresight in terms of owning land and property. The drawback to this class, according to Du Bois, is the lack of congenial occupation among the young men and women and the consequent discontent and complaint. The majority of this class is literate and ambitious; they have at least common school training. The main motivation in their life is the African-American church; it is the center of their social life and the place of guidance and closure.

Grade three is the poor. There is no steady income and although not always thrifty, these people are honest. They compose the casual laborers who have failed to find an assured place in life in the city. Though honest, these people are not reliable and spend money recklessly. This class includes the sick, the maimed, widows, orphans, deserted wives, and those who have suffered from accidents. While those in this class may regularly interact with criminals and live in the slums with them, they do not adapt criminal behavior and try as much as possible to stay on the right side of the law. However, ignorant and easily influenced, they do not always succeed.

There is a fine line between the third grade and fourth grade of society. Du Bois defined the fourth grade as the "submerged tenth," a distinct criminal class. This class generally includes those of the third class who have sunk below and become influenced by illicit actions. These people involve prostitutes and loafers; they tend to be involved in "shrewd laziness, shameless lewdness, and cunning crime." His description continued,

Their nucleus consists of a class of professional criminals, who do not work...and migrate here and

there...these are a set of gamblers and sharpers who seldom are caught in serious crime, but who nevertheless live from its proceeds and aid and abet it. The headquarters are usually the political clubs and pool rooms; they stand ready to entrap the unwary and tempt the weak. Their organization, tacit or recognized, is very effective, and no one can long watch their actions without seeing that they keep in close touch with the authorities in some way. (Du Bois, W.E.B, 1899b/1973, p 312)

He recognized that the people in this grade "are no fools, but sharp, wily men who often outwit both the Police Department and the Department of Charities." While the size of this grade is not particularly large, the population is large enough to characterize the slum districts. The younger generation of the city population is attracted by the idleness and seeming excitement of the lowest grade. This is how the influence of the criminals expands and the slums persist.

While Du Bois's first scientific studies were conducted in the North, primarily Pennsylvania, Du Bois also noticed key factors involved in the festering status of African Americans in the South. While slavery may be the initial cause for the black man's current position in society today, emancipation was the catalyst for his current economic status. While finally free, the former slave was still subject to his former master's rule. Du Bois noted that the South was determined to retain its slave labor; it enacted:

Elaborate and ingenious apprentice and vagrancy laws (Black Codes)... passed, designed to make the freedmen and their children work for their former masters at practically no wages. (Du Bois, W.E.B, 1901, p 111)

The Black Codes described above were laws enacted in 1865 primarily by southern states to serve as a way to inhibit and control the freedom of former slaves. While every state had different codes, the goal was the same: to regulate the civil and legal rights of African Americans. Commonly, codes compelled freedmen to work. In many situations, if unemployed, blacks were arrested or fined. For those who did have work, the codes regulated hours, wages, and behavior for the agricultural workers. Self-sufficiency was also discouraged. The Black Codes prevented African Americans from raising their own crops. In some states, black people were restricted from renting or leasing any land outside of cities or towns, in other states, they needed permission from employers to enter and reside in a town. These codes served the purpose they intended for nearly a century.

In his first publication devoted to black crime ("The Negro and Crime"), Du Bois sketched four causes:

1. The Convict-Lease System
2. The attitude of the courts towards black Americans
3. Lawlessness and barbarity of mob-action of white Americans
4. The unnatural separation of the races—Segregation

The Convict-Lease System: The Convict-Lease System was a method of continuing slavery under a different name. In this system the state could lease convicts (former slaves) to the highest bidder with no oversight of the state. Generally, former slaves were bought back by former owners. Once the convicts returned to the fields, the daunting threat of being reported to the police and returning to jail kept the former slaves "out of trouble." Du Bois also tells how the convicts, some innocent and some guilty, and "depraved men, women, and children were turned over to irresponsible men who were out to make as much as possible." The establishment of the Convict-Lease System made the innocent look bad and the guilty were made to look worse. Women and children were raped and abused. Though not officially recorded, Du Bois believed that the death-rate from cruelty, exposure, and overwork rose to higher percentages. This system was an effective arrangement that greatly decreased any motivation black Americans would have had to rebel.

The attitude of the courts: A second proposed cause of the disproportionate number of African Americans in prisons is the encouraging attitude of the courts. In the South, all authorities, political and justice, were white Americans. Even though federal government interventions such as the Freedmen's Bureau somewhat slowed the effect of the state-enforced Black Codes, the process was gradual and unsteady. In essence the state courts and correctional authority solely represented the majority of white Americans in the area; and thus, reflected their racist attitudes. Du Bois was convinced enough in his convictions to state that,

> *The state became a dealer in crime, profited by it so as to derive a net annual income for her prisoners. The lessees of the convicts made large profits also. (Du Bois, W.E.B, 1901, p 112)*

Du Bois also observed that the "careless and untrained Negroes" received severe penalties, much more retribution than for what the crime actually called. He remarked that,

> *The courts and jails became filled with the careless and ignorant, with those who sought to emphasize their new-found freedom, and too often with innocent victims of oppression. The testimony of a Negro counted for nothing in court, while the accusation of white witnesses was usually decisive. (Du Bois, W.E.B, 1901, p 111)*

Lawlessness and barbarity of mob-action of white Americans: The third cause was the lawlessness and barbarity of the mob. There was a dramatic increase in lynching of blacks during the post-reconstruction period. This was an open invitation for blacks to retaliate; thus they were thrown into prison. Dr. Du Bois at the beginning of this article fittingly describes this injustice:

> *Let a Negro be simply accused of any crime from*
> *barn-burning to rape and he is liable to be seized by*
> *a mob, given no chance to defend himself, given*
> *neither trial, judge nor jury, and killed. Passing over*
> *the acknowledged fact that many innocent Negroes*
> *have thus been murdered, the point that is of greater*
> *gravity is that lawlessness is a direct encouragement*
> *of crime. It shatters the faith of the mass of Negroes*
> *in justice; it makes race hatred fiercer; it discourages*
> *honest effort; it transforms horror at crime into*
> *sympathy for the tortured victim; and it binds the*
> *hands of those race leaders who are striving to*
> *preach forbearance and patience and honest*
> *endeavor to their people. It teaches eight million*
> *wronged people to despise a civilization which is not*
> *civilized. (Du Bois, W.E.B, 1899a/1982, p 50)*

The unnatural separation of the races—Segregation: The fourth and arguably the most obvious cause is segregation. By physically keeping people separate from one another so that one group may not 'pollute' the other, the state is leading to the growth of a belief more dangerous than racism—acceptance. This acceptance was believed by both groups. This "was just the way things are." Mutual acceptance of superiority and acceptance of inferiority on opposing ends of the equation lead to stagnation in advancement. This is the primary reason the South is the part of the nation that is dealing with the most inequality. Stagnation in advancement leads to retention of unjust laws and practices. Also, after such a long period of stagnation, progression is opposed by both sides. Change is not a natural human trait. So, as a result, the people are locked in an unfortunate truce that is hard to break. Thus, the disproportional penalties and sentences continue.

After conducting a study in 1890 recorded in the *Notes of Negro Crime, Particularly in Georgia* regarding the number of colored prisoners, the offenses they were charged with, their sex and geographical divisions, the average age of the prisoners, and the ratio of crime and illiteracy, Dr. Du Bois concluded the following:

1. *That eight-tenths of the Negro prisoners are in the South where nine-tenths of the Negroes dwell. This is further emphasized by the fact that Negroes in the North furnish 60 to 75 prisoners for every 10,000 of population, while those in the South furnish about 30. This discrepancy is largely explained by the difference in urban and rural populations, and the migration northward.*

2. *While 60% of the prisoners are in State prisons and Penitentiaries, this excess of dangerous criminals is apparent and not real and is due to the census method of computing crime.*

3. *Half of the Negro prisoners are between the ages of 20 and 30 years, a fifth, 10-19 years, and another fifth, 30-40 years. This shows a lower criminal age than among whites.*

4. *Nearly half of the Negro prisoners are confined for crimes against property. If commitments were tabulated, undoubtedly pilfering would be found to be pre-eminently the Negro crime. This is due to imperfect ideas of property ownership inseparable from a system of slavery.*

5. *One-fourth of the Negro prisoners are confined for crimes against the person. This consists of fighting and quarrelling, ending at times in homicide, and also the crime of rape. Fighting is to be expected of ignorant people and people living under unsettled conditions. Of 1,392 persons confined for rape in 1890, 578 were Negroes. These figures exaggerate the apparent guilt of Negroes because the Negroes received an average sentence of 14.04 years while whites received an average of 12.72 years, and probably a still larger disproportion in life sentences*

> *existed. Negroes too are more easily convicted of this crime to-day, because of public opinion. Notwithstanding all these considerations there is no doubt of a large prevalence of sexual crime among Negroes. This is due to the sexual immorality of slavery, the present defenselessness of a proscribed cast, and the excesses of the undeveloped classes among Negroes.*

6. *One-sixth of the criminals in jail were charged with crimes against society—gambling, drunkenness, adultery, etc.*

7. *The age statistics show that among both whites and blacks the younger criminals steal; among Negroes, crimes against society and the person claim the next older set, while crimes against the government and the person come next among whites.*

8. *The illiterate Negroes furnish more of the criminals than those who read and write. The difference in education between the great number who can just barely read and write and the wholly illiterate is not great, so that this does not really illustrate the full degree in which ignorance causes Negro crime. There has been so much dispute and misapprehension on this point. (Du Bois, W.E.B, 1904, p 15-16)*

Today, there are many sociologists influenced by W.E.B. Du Bois who have expanded on his findings of the status of African Americans and contributed to them. For example, Sutherland cites *The Philadelphia Negro* in his text *Criminology* to demonstrate the patterns of Negro crime. Sellin also refers to Du Bois's publications in this light. In his text, *An American Dilemma*, Gunnar Myrdal relies on Du Bois's writings to discuss African-American involvement in the justice system. Franklin Frazier also reviews literature on Black crime and points out that Du Bois's thinking was along the same lines as the Chicago School scholars. Many agree the original cause of African-American crime is slavery. It is significant to this situation that the African-American group is the only major ethnic group to ever be in slavery America. This has placed them in a persistent status of subordination. Slavery in essence dehumanized the Negro. To the white people he was perceived as merely property, while he saw himself as forever trapped. His culture was diluted by the white man and did not permit him to develop completely. Slavery encroached upon the development of three key characteristics for normal group life: stable family relations, stable economic organization, and stable community life. Without these essential components to establish the foundation for normal group life, the African American was unable to maintain a stable domestic life in the forthcoming years. Slavery also nurtured a set of habits and attitudes that still trouble African Americans today: lack of self-respect, lack of self-confidence, distaste for hard work, dependence on white friends, and lack of regard for others property, feeling that white people owe them a living, distrust of white man's law, and an indifference to the future. Though emancipation was seemingly the solution to this problem, it could not erase hundreds of years of established attitudes. It still did not allow for Negroes to compete on level ground with whites. While the white man had to, fundamentally, learn he was not as high up in the social order as he thought; the black man had to learn to break the barriers placed on him by the color bar and fly up to equal status of the white man.

Black Americans had to overcome cultural retardation, social, and economic shortcomings. Hard enough by itself, this experience was exponentially difficult with the strong resisting force of the majority of the population. Not only was there a strong backward movement, there was a significant group in the population that was indifferent or ignorant to the race situation at all. The black man was on his own.

There is general agreement that economic factors and crime causation are related. As an underprivileged economic class, African Americans contributed to the total amount of delinquency because it was the only option for survival. During Du Bois's time, and in some parts even today, the bulk of a black man's wages barely accomplish to fulfill the bare necessities; food, clothing, shelter, and education. When every part of the country has some amount of racial prejudice and the black man and his needs are, at best, second priority, law-breaking is inevitable. Dr. Du Bois stated if white Americans choose to continue blatant discrimination, then they also choose to accept the likelihood of black criminality.

These unconcealed bigotries were allowed to continue because, in the case of the North, the blasé attitude of the Courts, and in the South the supportive attitude of the Courts. The penalties for crimes that African Americans committed were, and still are, on the average, higher than those of which a white offender would receive. Even the definition of crime is different where race is concerned. white collared crime such as embezzlement is seen as less severe than petty theft and robbery, especially if that crime is committed by a person of color. Capital punishment is executed at a greater frequency on African Americans than white Americans. The black man's chance of access to bail, to efficient legal counsel, to payment of cash fines instead of jail terms, to appeals, and to all other legal advantages is much lower than the chance of the white man.

Furthermore, the status of the black man has exposed him to the danger of becoming a scapegoat and pawn in several crimes committed by white people. Well known situations in which this is the case occurred by the bushels in the South. A white person may commit a crime in such a fashion that the circumstantial evidence would point to some African-American. Deceit was also involved, a white criminal often colored his face black or wore a black mask to trick any supposed witnesses. Also, many accusations of rape by compromising white women after the sexual act were brought onto many African Americans. Even immaterial courtesies, those that should not have been enforced after emancipation (forgetting to say "Mister" to a white man, "looking at" a white woman), proved severe consequences.

In addition to the increased severity implemented by the courts, police mistreatment is a significant factor in unjust sentencing as punishment. The police have a unique position in the administration of justice. Variations in their activities and testimonies can prove very different results in arrests and in punishments. Police brutality has always been aimed to the lower sects of the community and because the history of the nation has caused the economic degradation of the African-American population, by the transitive property, police brutality is primarily aimed at black Americans. The black American is more exposed to the misuse of police power than any other ethnic group. They are arrested on slight suspicion and too quickly subject to the use of guns and clubs. They are therefore keyed to a desperate "shoot first or get shot" policy. Police mistreatment provokes bitterness among the underprivileged and actually stimulates crime. Ironically, the police let criminal activities occurring in black neighborhoods pass under their noses. The seeming general thought is that criminality among the blacks is condonable as long as it does not seep into the white communities and disturb the residents there. This mode of thinking causes regression the progression of a safer society and causes the growth and development of new criminals every day. Feelings that the law is unjust contribute highly to the real and the apparent criminality of black Americans. Corruption in politics also results American male votes being traded for jobs. These votes are generally for politicians that petition for policies that keep many African Americans unjustly in jail. This triggers an unbreakable cycle in which the African Americans are, again, at the disadvantage.

Though much ameliorated, institutional racism and prejudice still exists and there are many policies that must change in order to come to at least a partial solution to the race problem. In this context, Dr. Du Bois drew up two lists of suggestions, one for black Americans and one for white Americans, to follow in order to eradicate and reestablish justice in the justice system.

The "duty of the Negroes" according to Dr. Du Bois is to primarily learn self-advancement. He goes on to say that "simply because the ancestors of the present white inhabitants of America went out of their way barbarously to mistreat and enslave the ancestors of the present black inhabitants, gives those blacks no right to ask that the civilization and morality of the land be seriously menaced for their benefit." The African-American has a right to demand freedom for self-development and aid that is required for said development. While relief and protective agencies should help as much as they are able, "the bulk of the work of raising the Negro must be done by the Negro himself." (Du Bois, W.E.B, 1899b/ 1973, p 389)

1. **Efforts must be made to stop crime-** While the crime rate among African Americans is exaggerated; it is still strongly prevalent and acts as a significant detriment to the development of the race. These efforts must begin in the home. Black homes must cease to be "breeders of idleness and extravagance and complaint." If the problem is stopped at the source from the beginning, there is greater chance of success in eliminating the problem.

2. **Work should be impressed upon-** Regardless of the kind of work, hard work should be promoted and impressed upon black children as "the road to salvation."

3. **Virtues must be enforced-** Honesty, truth, and chastity should be held as high virtues and the way to gin self-respect. Without self-respect a man will not go very far. Self-respect must be taught as the surest way to gain the respect of others.

For now nearly twenty years we have made of ourselves mudsills for the feet of this Western world. We have echoed and applauded every shameful accusation made against 10,000,000 victims of slavery. Did they call us inferior half-beasts? We nodded our simple heads and whispered "We is." Did they call our women prostitutes and our children bastards? We smiled and cast a stone at the bruised breasts of our wives and daughters. Did they accuse of

*laziness 4,000,000 sweating, struggling
laborers, half-paid and cheated out of much of
that? We shrieked: "Ain't it so?" We laughed
with them at our color, we joked at our sad past,
and we told chicken stories to get alms. (Du
Bois, W.E.B, 1914, p 24)*

4. **Encouragement should be given to ambitious
    children-** African-American children should be ever
    encouraged to rise as high in the world "as their ability
    and just desert entitle them." Still, they should always
    remember crime and idleness are below the lowest
    menial labor. Successful black Americans should always
    try to help the children rise and help to supply better
    opportunities for them.

5. **Rational means of amusement-** Methods of
    amusement are important in a developing mind. The elder
    generation should try to understand that prayer meetings
    and church socials have their place but do not hold the
    entire attraction of the dance halls and billiard tables.
    Amusement should be "a means of education,
    improvement and recreation." The type of amusement,
    such as dancing and billiards, the young people enjoy
    should be brought out of the clubs and bawdy-houses
    and encouraged in clean environments. Then the young
    people will not have a chance to look for these
    amusements and consequently be subject to influence
    of crime, disease and death.

6. **Preventive and rescue work-** There is so much the
    African-American community can do in an effort to
    protect the young:

*...keeping little girls off the street at night,
stopping the escorting of unchaperoned young
ladies to church and elsewhere, showing the
dangers of the lodging system, urging the*

buying of homes and removal from crowded and tainted neighborhoods, giving lectures and tracts on health and habits, exposing the dangers of gambling and policy-playing, and inculcating respect for women. (Du Bois, W.E.B, 1899b/1973 p 391)

By making it a habit to follow certain precautions, the chance for exposure to crime is decreased and the safety of the community is increased. The African-American attention should be directed towards safe entertainment and secure homes.

7. **Special attention should be given to spending of money-** Money is wasted on unnecessary decorations and entertainments. Money would be better put to use in buying homes, educating children, bettering the community, and in saving for emergencies.

8. **Enthusiasm for education should be rekindled-** There is a general neglect among children and adults alike for the importance of education. Education is the strongest weapon a man can hold, rich or poor. Regular attendance in school should be enforced and every effort to excite children about school should be implemented.

9. **The better classes of African Americans should recognize their duty towards the lower classes-** People should not forget from where they have come. The upper classes should make genuine efforts to encourage and provide aid to their fellow African Americans. "So hard has been the rise of the better class of African-American that they fear to fall if now they stoop to lend a hand to their fellows." This attitude must change.

10. **Finally, the African Americans must cultivate a spirit of calm, patient persistence in their attitude toward their fellow citizens-** Strong calmness and patient persistence will eventually triumph and prove

time and again to be the smart, mature way to address a social problem.

Du Bois points out the "tendency on the part of many white people to approach the Negro question from the side." They feel it unimportant and maybe even inexistent. It is the immediate duty of the whites to change these attitudes and the consequential mindsets that come from having these attitudes.

1. **Discrimination in the workplace should be stopped-** "Industrial freedom of opportunity has by long experience been proven to be generally best for all." It is practical to keep a criminal off the road by giving him enough money to do a job he is capable of doing well. The same opportunities should be given in light of capability and not color.

2. **Recognize the existence of the better class of African Americans and gain their active aid and cooperation by polite conduct-** While the better class of African Americans may not need pity, it does need an acknowledgement of the difficulties it had endured and the sacrifices it has made. If there is a social sympathy between the best of both races, together they will be able to bring up the lowest of the races and help them to make better choices.

3. **The white people must remember that "Much of the sorrow and bitterness that surrounds the life of the American Negro comes form the unconscious prejudice and half-conscious actions of men and women who do not intend to wound or annoy"** (Du Bois, W.E.B, 1899b/1973, p 396-397) - A consciousness among the general public should arise that the African-American is an American citizen who should be treated with as much respect as any other. It is not necessary to sneer or be unkind to unruly children, to stare at a black woman walking down the street, or

to avert one's eyes if one sees a familiar black face in public. Civility is the key to a better society.

Obviously many of Dr. Du Bois's proposed remedies have already been implemented; American society is moving in the right direction, given not at the desirable degree of speed.

W.E.B. Du Bois's work and discoveries are still in relevance in society today. Though Du Bois was elemental in bringing about change in the African-American community, his sullen nature turned angry in the later days of his life. He was very interested in encouraging black Americans to relate back to their true motherland, Africa. While he did not agree with Marcus Garvey's "Back to Africa Movement," characterizing Garvey as "a hard-working idealist, but his methods are bombasts, wasteful, illogical, and almost illegal," Du Bois still planned two Pan-African movements. He planned on raising awareness of the problems Africans faced around the world with the support of the NAACP. However as the NAACP was headed by white men at this time, his efforts were not as recognized. Contrarily, Garvey was able to gain mass support and his ideas held fantastic appeal. Although not as popular, Du Bois still held his conference in 1923. When the conference concluded, Du Bois set sail to visit Africa for the first time. Upon returning to the United States Du Bois became very discouraged by the one-step-forward-two-steps-back motion America was set in regarding the race issue. As a left-wing member of the American Labor Party he expressed his thoughts on America at the time, "Drunk with power, we (the U.S) are leading the world to hell in a new colonialism with the same old human slavery, which once ruined us, to a third world war, which will ruin the world." In the end, feeling utterly despondent about the American situation, Du Bois returned to Africa and spent the rest of his days there until he breathed his last on August, 1963 in Ghana. Du Bois's visions for the African Americans were revolutionary. The progress made by American society up to today would not have been possible without W.E.B. Du Bois and his dedication to improve mankind.

References

Du Bois, W.E.B. (1883, April 10). (Reprinted in *Newspaper columns by W.E.B. Du Bois (Vol. 1 1883-1944)*, p. 1 by H. Aptheker, Ed., 1986, White Plains, NY: Kraus-Thomson Organization)

Du Bois, W.E.B. (1898). The study of Negro problems. *Annals of the American Academy of Political and Social Sciences, 11* (January), 1-23. (Reprinted in *Writings in periodical literature edited by others vol 1(1891-1909)*, pp. 40-52, by H. Aptheker, Ed., 1982, Millwood, NY: Kraus-Thomson Organization)

Du Bois, W.E.B. (1899a) The Negro and crime. *The Independent, 51* (May), 1355-1357.

Du Bois, W.E.B. (1899b/1973). *The Philadelphia Negro: A Social Study.* Millwood, NY: Kraus-Thomson Organization.

Du Bois, W.E.B. (Ed.). (1904). *Some Notes of Negro crime, Particularly in Georgia.* Atlanta, GA: Atlanta University Press.

Du Bois, W.E.B. (1914, May). *The Crisis.* 24.

Du Bois, W.E.B. (1986). *Writings.* New York, NY: Literary Classics of the United States, Inc.

Frazier, E.F. (1949). *The Negro in the United States.* New York: The Macmillan Company

Gabbidon, S. L. (1996). An Argument for the Inclusion of W.E.B. Du Bois in the Criminology and Criminal Justice Literature. *Journal of Criminal Justice Education, 7*(1), 99-111.

Gabbidon, S. L. (1998). W.E.B. Du Bois on Crime: Rethinking the Beginnings of American Criminology. *The Criminologist, 23*(6), 1, 3, 21.

Gabbidon, S. L. (1999). W.E.B. Du Bois on Crime: American Conflict Theorist. *The Criminologist, 24*(2), 2, 3, 20.

Gabbidon, S. L. (2001, May). W.E.B. Du Bois: Pioneering American Criminologist. *Journal of Black Studies, 31*(5), 581,599.

Johnson, G.B. (1941, September). The Negro and Crime. *Annals of the American Academy of Political and Social Science. 217*, 93, 104.

Myrdal, G. (1944). *An American Dilemma: The Negro Problem and Modern Democracy.* New York: Harper and Brothers Publishers.

Sellin, T. (1928). "The Negro Criminal: A Statistic Note," *The Annals of the American Academy of Political and Social Science,* CXXX: 52-64.

Sutherland, E. (1924). Criminology. Philadelphia: J.B. Lipincott Company.

FELON DISFRANCHISEMENT

Felon Disfranchisement is Unconstitutional and Unjustified

Sampson Ike Oli

Each year in this country, approximately three quarters of a million prisoners are released from prison and jails into the community. The usual expectation, of course, is that such persons have learned a lesson from their incarceration and will now become law abiding and productive members of society. Unfortunately, such expectation is often misplaced because majority of such persons enter prison uneducated and with little or no job skills and leave prison no better than when they entered. A large proportion of such persons entered prison with several other attendant problems such as alcohol and drug addiction and lack of skills for coping with various frustrations in community life. They leave prison with all of these problems virtually intact. As if to make matters worse, their efforts at successful reintegration are made almost impossible by the "ex-con" label. It should therefore come as no surprise that many of such persons recidivate.

Ex felons are statutorily prohibited from holding several jobs, including some in government and the armed services.[1] But one of the most serious civil penalties that often attend a felony conviction is a restriction on the right to vote, which is generally referred to as felon disfranchisement. This restriction follows the convict into prison

---

[1] U.S. Department of Justice, *Civil Disabilities of Convicted Felons: A State by State Survey* See http/www.usdo.gov/pardon/collataral consequences.pdf

and continues to stay with him or her even after they have served their time and paid their penalty. Their good behavior while in prison does not always affect this disability. Neither does the fact that they are serving their time outside the prison as probationers. The denial of the right to vote resulting from a felony conviction continues to be one of the most socially and legally wrenching problems of our time.

To present a seasoned discussion of the above subject, it is necessary to provide an explanation of the important words that constitute the term "Felon Disfranchisement." First we must determine what we mean by "felon". The word felon neither refers to every person that commits an offense, nor every person that has been convicted of an offense. There are three major classifications of offenses, Felonies, Misdemeanors and Simple offenses or infractions. Felonies are offenses that attract a punishment of one year or more and up to the death penalty. Misdemeanors are offenses that attract punishment of less than one year. Simple offenses or infractions are offenses that attract little or no incarceration. These are usually punished with fines, probation or some form of restitution. It is the law that determines whether an offense is a felony, misdemeanor or infraction, not the punishment that is imposed after conviction. A felon therefore, is someone who has not only engaged in a conduct, which is defined by law as a felony, but has been tried and convicted, for that misconduct.

Enfranchise and Disenfranchise are more complex terms to explain. Several dictionaries simply repeat the words, after depicting how they are pronounced. They do not provide any explanation of the meaning of the terms. To decipher the terms therefore, we must go back to the word "franchise". Franchise is "...a privilege of a public nature conferred on an individual or body of individuals by a governmental grant."[2] Franchise is also defined as '...a special privilege to do certain things conferred by government on an individual or corporation and which does not belong to citizens

---

[2] *Random House Dictionary of the English Language*, 1996 Random House Inc, New York. Jess Stein, Editor In Chief.

generally of common right; e.g. right granted to offer cable television services."[3]

Blacks Law Dictionary goes on further to define the word enfranchise as "...the act of conferring the privilege of voting upon classes of persons who have not previously possessed such." This definition seems to indicate that franchise is a privilege and enfranchise is the granting of such privilege by government to persons, in order to enable them do things that they could not do without such franchise. It follows therefore, that governments do not have the power to grant the right to vote to native-born citizens, because those citizens already possess that right under the *15th Amendment*. Since to enfranchise is not the same as to grant citizens the right to vote, the government cannot and should not continue to arrogate to itself the power to determine whether felons should or should not vote, especially when such felons are native-born U.S. citizens.

The United States government can grant citizenship to classes of immigrants and thereby confer upon them the privilege to vote. The government thereby retains the power to revoke such privilege, if such persons are convicted of some specified offenses.

But whereas the government can enfranchise and thereby grant voting privileges to naturalized citizens, it does not have an equivalent power to enfranchise native-born U.S. citizens. Because it does not have such powers, it cannot disenfranchise what it cannot enfranchise, and felon disfranchisement of native-born citizens is therefore both illegal and unconstitutional.

In the United States, proper logic makes it obvious that the government did not grant native-born citizens the right to vote, because the constitution already conferred such rights on native-born citizens; the 1965 Federal Voting Rights Act notwithstanding. The 15th Amendment to the U.S. Constitution states very clearly that "The right of citizens of the United States to vote shall not be denied or abridged by the United States or by any State on account of race, color, or previous conditions of servitude." In 1971 the 26th Amendment was added to the Constitution as follows: " The right

---

[3] *Blacks Law Dictionary,* West Publishing Co. St. Paul MN 1991. Henry Black

of citizens of the United States, who are eighteen years of age or older, to vote shall not be denied or abridged by the United States or by any state on account of age.

When these two Amendments are read together, the obvious interpretation should be that "The right of citizens of the United States to vote shall not be denied or abridged by the Federal or any State legislature on account of race, color, previous conditions of servitude or age (which the 26th Amendment sets at eighteen)." Unfortunately many academicians do not seem to want to accept the obvious meaning of the 15th Amendment. The U.S. Constitution already confers upon native-born citizens the inalienable right to vote. Attempts by government and Constitution bashing individuals, to arrogate to itself, the power to enfranchise and or disenfranchise native-born citizens is *ultra vires* its powers under the constitution and therefore void.

Unfortunately this subject continues to attract debate among academicians, because the courts have avoided taking any direct stand on the issue, except to render tunnel vision opinions on peripheral issues, brought before it by litigants. This is understandable since under our judicial system, courts do not initiate litigations, plaintiffs do. Therefore, the courts can only rule on the true interpretation of the provisions of the 15th Amendment, if and when someone initiates an action that would require exclusive direct interpretation, of the provisions of that Amendment.

One group of academicians favor the dictionary interpretation, arguing that since enfranchisement is a governmental function, and since under such interpretation the privilege to vote derives from the government, then the privilege to vote may be withdrawn at the government's pleasure. The other group cites the constitution and argues that voting is not a privilege but a right conferred upon citizens by the constitution. If that is true, then the government cannot pretend to withdraw what it did not confer. Moreover, current studies are replete with data that indicate that no country in the free world comes close to the U.S. scale of felon disfranchisement. Recent estimates disclose that 4.7 million Americans, or one in forty-three adults, have currently or permanently lost their voting rights as a result of felony convictions.[4] Yet the U.S. continues to parade herself around the world as the champion of democracy.

Proponents of governmental powers have succeeded in muddying the field by avoiding any direct reference to the 15th Amendment, preferring instead to emphasize the term "franchise" as if it means the same thing as "right to vote." By so doing they have succeeded in diverting attention from using the correct term "denial of the right of felons to vote" by substituting it with the term "felon disfranchisement." Currently, the argument has shifted from constitutionality of the original right, to a struggle between the states and the federal government as to who should have the power to exercise peripheral powers on the issue. If the language of the 15th Amendment were the issue, the question about enfranchisement and disfranchisement would not arise. Unfortunately like most issues that contain some racial underpinnings in this society, felon disfranchisement continues to attract vociferous but inconclusive arguments, because the courts have consistently avoided addressing the words of the 15th Amendment as it stands.

Between 1870 when the 15th Amendment was ratified and 1974 when the case of *Wolf v McDonnell* came before the Federal Supreme Court,[5] the courts have consistently struck down laws that attempted to restrict qualification to vote by excluding any particular class or race, but it did not specifically deal with the rights of felons to vote. It steered clear of the issue by maintaining what was referred to at that time, as the "hands-off doctrine." Typifying the prevailing view about prisoner's rights in this country, the Virginia Court of Appeal in *Ruffin v. Commonwealth* described prisoners as "slaves of the State." The court went on to observe that prisoners had no rights, and any rights they may once have had were forfeited as part of the price they had to pay for their crimes.[6] Most courts do not express their views on prisoner's rights so blatantly; they

---

[4] Bureau of Justsice Statistics, *Sourcebook of Criminal Justice Statistics 2000,* US Department of Justice, Kathleen Maguire & anor eds., Washington D.C. 2000.pp.500-501. See also: http/www.sentencingproject.org

[5] Wolf v. McDonnell 418 U.S. 539 (1974)

[6] Ruffin v. Commonwealth, 62 Va. 790 (1871) 152

prefer instead to steer clear of the issue by maintaining that while inmates might have rights, it was the responsibility of the legislative and executive branches of government to enforce such rights when necessary.

The courts gave some reasons to justify their "hands-off doctrine" in matters affecting prisoners, amongst which are:

a.   That judicial enforcement of inmates' rights would interfere with the operation of prisons by the legislative and executive branches of government.

b.   That judicial enforcement of inmates' rights would unduly encroach on the authority of the states to run their prisons.

c.   That judicial interference in the operation of prisons might jeopardize institutional security and frustrate the goals of incarceration.

d.   That judicial enforcement of prisoner's rights would result in the courts being inundated with prisoners' complaints many of which would be frivolous.

e.   That correctional decisions were guided by rehabilitative goals, were therapeutic in nature, and thus did not need, or were inappropriate subjects for, judicial review.

In 1974, the Supreme Court in a surprising move in *Wolff v. McDonnell,* announced that "there is no iron curtain drawn between the Constitution and the prisons of this country."[7] That decision coincided with an earlier circuit court decision in Jackson vs. Godwin in 1968, and seemed to signal a willingness by the courts to entertain some changes on the entire issue of prisoner's rights, including the right to equal protection and the right to vote. Unfortunately the hopes of some, who had dared to hope that felon disfranchisement would become a thing of the past, were soon dashed. They had hoped that those persons, who had paid their dues to society for wrongs they had committed, would at the least, among other things,

---

[7] Wolf v. McDonnell, 418 U.S. 539 (1974) 280

be allowed to exercise the right to vote. Since the fact of incarceration did not deprive them of their citizenship, they therefore, retained the right to vote under the 15th Amendment.

Unfortunately, the Supreme Court recently reaffirmed in *United States v. Lopez (1995),* "...that because The Constitution creates a Federal Government of enumerated powers." no power exists for Congress to pass any law banning felon disfranchisement by the states.[8] Many scholars carrying the torch for state felon disfranchisement, have seized on this decision and padded onto it the unsavory clause - that congress is impotent to act on any laws passed by states, even when such laws are designed to perpetuate felon disfranchisement.

Although proponents of felon disfranchisement would want us to accept the need to isolate race as one of the factors that propel states to enact felon disfranchisement laws, the history of the United States provides sufficient evidence of the need to consider racism whenever states attempt to tinker with laws that guarantee rights to citizens (whites and blacks) generally. History has taught us to be wary each time states pass laws that are disguised as creating more rights, when in fact they are designed to stifle the ability of an identifiable segment of their citizens to enjoy those rights.

The problem with felon disfranchisement is that it seems to deal a heavier blow on African Americans who make up a disproportionate number of disenfranchised felons in this country. The Bureau of Justice Statistics (1999) estimates that 1.4 million or 13 percent of African-American men are disenfranchised a rate that is seven times the national average.[9] Because disfranchisement is aimed at persons who have committed felony offenses, and because African Americans make up a disproportionate number of felony clients of our criminal justice system, they end up bearing the brunt of the impact of these laws. Current figures from the

---

[8] United States v. Lopez, 490 (1995)

[9] Bureau of Justice Statistics, *Sourcebook of Criminal Justice Statistics (1999).* US Department of Justice, Kathleen Maguire & anor, eds., Washington D.C. 1999 p.518-519. See also: dmacallaire@cjj.org.

Bureau of Justice Statistics indicate that African Americans are more likely to be arrested, more likely to be convicted and more likely to be sentenced to longer terms for committing the same or similar crimes as their white counterparts.[10] Various intervening variables may be responsible for this disparity. It is therefore, necessary to identify and discuss the ramifications of this issue, so that we can produce a clearer understanding of the impact of felon disfranchisement laws.

It seems only fair to document the fact that governments and some philanthropic groups and altruistic individuals, have tried to solve some of the problems of black overrepresentation amongst clients of our criminal justice system. Unfortunately these efforts have not been successful because they shy away from confronting a major, albeit unpalatable factor. Almost all of these efforts have avoided any direct reference to the likelihood that black offending, may be one of the major factors that sustain black overrepresentation in our criminal justice system. We have always avoided any reference to the possibility, that blacks may themselves be unwitting contributors, to some of the factors that precipitate their proclivity for involvement in anti social behavior.

Factors that contribute to black overrepresentation: United States society has practiced and continues to practice various forms of discrimination against African Americans. Racism continues to exist in our society. Racial differences and racial profiling will continue to exist so long as we continue to allow color classifications to remain the norm in our society. But acknowledging the existence of these factors should not detract us from confronting other plausible contributors to the problem, if we are to find lasting solutions to African-American overrepresentation in the U.S. crime statistics.

---

[10] Bureau of Justice Statistics, Sourcebook of Criminal Justice Statistics 2000. US Department of Justice, Kathleen Maguire & anor. Eds., Washington D.C. 2000 pp.457 & 460 See also: www.hrw.org/backgrounder/race

Biological factors as explanations: For many years black offending was waived off by social scientists, as another evidence of the impact of biological inferiority on blacks. In other words, that some inherited inferior characteristics propelled blacks to engage in criminal behavior. Travis Hirschi and Michael Hindelang (1977) observed, "...IQ is a better predictor of delinquency than is father's social class, especially among black boys".[11] Marvin Wolfgang and Franco Ferracuti (1967) coined the term "subculture of violence" to refer to lower class southern groups that demonstrate favorable attitudes toward the use of violence as a means of resolving inter personal grievances. They noted that in such subcultures, violence is viewed as a necessary measure, to uphold one's masculinity.[12] Although the subculture of violence theory is closer to a socio-psychological perspective than the pure biological, the inferences are obvious. Luckily, we now know that these explanations are untenable in so far as they are applied exclusively to blacks. But studies such as the above have left the problem dangling, and as a result, many people in some respectable quarters continue to believe, that African Americans are criminogenic.

Political, historical and economic factors as explanation: United States social system seems to be designed to ensure that African Americans are permanently incapacitated. While other ethnic groups can, if they wish, blend into the mainstream of society, African Americans, because of their easily identifiable skin color and other physical features, have in spite of their many contributions to, and achievements in society, continued to find it difficult, if not impossible, to overcome the disadvantages and handicaps that society attaches to the black color.

Another major problem confronting African Americans in the United States is economic. They are economic because slavery and other historical facts have severely limited the opportunities

---

[11] Hirschi, T. and M. J. Hindelang, "Intelligence and Delinquency: A Revisionist Review" American Sociological Review 42 (August) 1977. pp. 571-87.

[12] Wolfgang, M.E. and F. Ferracuti, The Subculture of Violence: Towards an Integrated Theory in Criminology. (London, Tavistock Publications 1967) p.189.

and abilities of majority of African Americans to rise above financial
dependence. Africa-Americans were until late in United States
history, deprived educational opportunities, denied land ownership
and refused the right to vote. These factors stultified efforts by this
segment of society to fully assimilate and attain any meaningful
economic positions. As a result, many African Americans have
developed such cultural paranoia that they now seem unwilling to
accept at face value, some social programs that are designed to
solve, or at least make the situation more palatable. They trusted
the United States society and their government at one time, but
were let down. Now they are hesitant to accept overtures from the
same society and its government that reappears with what seems
to be another Trojan horse.

It seems that because of these factors, African Americans
have developed a retreatist subculture by resorting to drug use and
other anti social behaviors, as a means of gaining "bad rep" or
prestige. Richard Cloward and Lloyd Ohlin (1960) in their
"Differential Opportunity" theory, define retreatist subculture as
being made up of "double failures." They maintain that "... Unable
to succeed either in the legitimate or illegitimate opportunity structure,
such individuals reject both the legitimate means and ends and simply
drop out; lacking criminal expertise, they seek status through "kicks"
and "highs" of drug abuse, and resort to visible crimes to support
that status.[13] Inability of these individuals to succeed was not
because they did not try; it is because the legitimate opportunity
structure is not equally available to everyone in this society.

Social factors as explanation: A few years ago, Florida's
Racial and Ethnic Bias Study Commission (1989) devoted most of
its two reports to lack of proportionate representation of minorities
among employees of the juvenile and adult criminal justice systems.
The Commission assumed that there was a link between lack of

---

[13] Cloward, R. and L. Ohlin, *Delinquency and Opportunity: A Theory of Delinquent Gangs*, (New York: The Free Press 1960) See: Hagan, Frank, Introduction to Criminology 1994 . Nelson Hall Publishers. P.72

blacks and Hispanics in decision-making positions in the criminal justice system, and disproportionate number of blacks and Hispanics being arrested and incarcerated. Such findings are however, not supported by evidence from previous and current national research. Nor are they supported by realities of either our social structure or our socialization processes. A closer examination of these factors seems to indicate that offending offers a more plausible explanation than representation.

Increasing the representation of blacks among correctional staffers, police, prosecutors and judges will not by itself reduce black criminality. It may reduce arrest and conviction rates, but it will not stop blacks from committing crime. In fact, as observed by William Wilbanks (1986), black representation among decision-makers in the criminal justice personnel has increased over the years, but black participation in crime did not reduce. In fact, it continues to increase.[14]

Perhaps, bringing African Americans back into this society's mainstream will provide a solution to their over involvement in crime. It certainly will, but only to a limited extent. African Americans have really never left the mainstream. They advocate and practice, albeit to some varying degrees, mainstream ideologies and values. Unfortunately, attempts by that segment of society to cross the bridge that separates the two streams, have been consistently thwarted. What exists now is a feeling of frustration. Until the forces that fecundate this feeling of frustration are identified, isolated and extirpated, problems posed by African American over involvement in crime and delinquency will continue to plague our society.

Frustration as explanation: Since racism and offending seem to occupy polar positions on the spectrum, introducing less radical but more central reasoning would seem to be more appropriate. That reasoning is frustration. For more than two centuries, African Americans have been subjected to all forms of

[14] Wilbanks, W., *Myth of A Racist Criminal Justice System*, (Thompson Learning College Publications 1986) p. 87

discrimination in this society. Much of the discrimination against this segment of society has been made possible by their unique and easily identifiable physical characteristics. It is not surprising therefore, that the persistent existence of this situation has given rise to frustration amongst this group. Since frustration breeds discontent and discontent breeds anti social behavior, the link between frustration and anti social behavior becomes clearer when causal factors that breed discontent are examined.

Frustration as a major precipitator of criminality stems from the fact that when legitimate grievances are ignored, aggrieved parties, in frustration, often resort to civil disobedience and later to more serious anti social methods to obtain redress. In black offending, frustration is evidenced by the fact that most black crimes are visible crimes. Very often, people who engage in visible crimes do so because they are frustrated and do not care about getting caught. This is explained by rationalizations from statements of some ex-offenders who were interviewed for this paper. During the interview, a majority pointed to social injustices and discriminations they and or their intimates experienced in the United States prior to offending.

Precipitators of frustration: For frustration to set in, at least six essential prerequisites must exist:

1. The frustratee must believe the much-peddled idea in this society that one can always achieve desired ends through legitimate means
2. The frustratee must have become discontented because they attempted but failed to achieve their desired ends through legitimate means
3. Factors that blocked such attempts must be existent and identifiable
4. The frustratee must have tried to draw the attention of some person or persons in authority to his/her plight
5. Such person or persons in authority must have ignored the frustratee's efforts to gain their attention.

6.   The frustratee is left with no viable positive alternatives

Data from various sources also suggest that there seems to be a direct positive relationship between the degrees of frustration experienced by blacks in this society and their involvement in particular crimes. Since such relationship can be subjected to empirical measurement, the result of a more detailed study can provide useful information on black offending. Such information will enable policy makers to devise programs that will reduce discontent and ultimately eliminate frustration. To do so it will be necessary to understand how frustration begins and what sustains the persistence of frustration, especially frustration that results from inability of blacks to draw attention of the majority to injustices and privations they have suffered, and continue to suffer.

It seems from the above, that dealing with frustration is not as difficult as it seems, if society is willing to pay special attention to its attendant features. Frustration results from a real or pretended lack of understanding by the majority in a society, of the privations experienced by any of its minority segments. It persists when society neglects or refuses to pay attention to the plight of such societal segment, or fails and or refuses to find solutions to their privations. Resort to crime such as drug use, and later to more serious visible crimes such as robbery, by a significant number of members of that social minority segment, are obvious signs of the existence of frustration in that social group.

The link between frustration and propensity for crime has been discussed in academe but has not been fully explored. It is different from the link between frustration and aggression, because most crimes engaged in by African Americans, are not motivated by aggressive behavior.[15] The thesis of this work is not that frustration causes aggression; but that frustration is an essential and integral component of the factors that fuel involvement in aggression manifesting conducts that are defined as felonies.

---

[15] Rose, S. M., *The Betrayal of the Poor*, Cambridge, Massachusetts, (Shenkman Publishing Company, Inc. 1972) pp. 176-179

Inquiring about the factors that precipitate frustration in African Americans is not the same as inquiring about factors that generate frustration among members of other ethnic groups. Admittedly, the factors are highly related, but they are not highly identical. Whereas all ethnic groups in the United States experience social pressures, and some engage in antisocial behavior due to various criminological factors. African Americans, because of their unique physical features, have experienced and continue to experience social pressures in excess of those experienced by any of the other identifiable minority ethnic groups in our society. To deal effectively with crime, drug use and other antisocial behavior by African Americans therefore, society must first discover the factors that contribute to their frustration, and devise programs that will totally eliminate such factors. This is important because these factors may be responsible for their overrepresentation among clients of the criminal justice system, and ultimately their overrepresentation among disenfranchised felons.

Type of crime as explanation: An examination of existing data seem to support the view that when African Americans are involved in crime, they are more likely than others, to engage in visible crimes. According to recent figures from the U.S. Department of Justice, of all offense types charged, African Americans were over represented in robbery, a crime which is primarily visible by 9.0 percent, as against 6.5 per cent for whites. The same holds true for black females at 4.9 as against 2.8 percent for white females.[16]

For drug use in the month prior to the offense, African Americans reflected the highest with 58.3 percent. Again the same conclusions holds true for females who were slightly lower than their white counterparts by approximately two percent. This seems to suggest that a link exists between black offending, type of offense, rate of incarceration, and their number among disenfranchised felons. The report further indicates that when blacks use drugs, the

---

[16] U.S. Department of Justice, Federal Bureau of Prisons, Sourcebook of Criminal Justice Statistics, 2000, US Department of Justice, Kathleen Maguire & anor. Eds., Washington D.C. 2000 p.526

drug of choice seems to be Marijuana/Hashish followed closely by Crack Cocaine, a felony offense that attracts a heavier punishment than powdered cocaine, which is preferred by their white counterparts.

Public perception as an explanation: Experiments by social scientists have shown that people's judgments on such matters as social issues, aesthetic preferences, and religious questions are influenced by what they experienced, what they are told, or what they believe to be the majority view of groups to which they belong. Armed with information deduced from such sources, people will reconstruct and determine their own beliefs, their convictions and explanations about crime, and eventually, their reaction to crime and criminals.

Perception studies of US citizens indicate that Americans have not only become increasingly crime conscious, but a large majority believe that they are more likely to become victims of crime, and that the most likely offender is a stranger with a black face. Acting on this fear, legislators and criminal justice practitioners have begun to urge a redirection of emphasis on treatment of criminals. The result has been the creation of several laws that were designed to target repeat violent offenders and thus reduce violent crime. Examples are the "three strikes you are out" and laws that distinguish crack and powdered cocaine for purposes of punishment. Unfortunately such laws have resulted in putting more blacks behind bars due to the use of profiling and unfettered exercise of discretionary powers by criminal justice professionals. Current racial distribution of the United States correctional population points directly to this disturbing situation. According to the Bureau of Justice Statistics (2000), at yearend 1999, there were approximately 6,000 black male inmates per 100,000 black adults in U.S. jails and prisons, compared to 900 white male inmates per 100,000 white adult residents.[17]

---

[17] Bureau of Justice Statistics, Sourcebook of Criminal Justice Statistics, 2000. U.S. Department of Justice, Kathleen Maguire & anor. Eds., Washington D.C. 2000 pp. 500-501

Several attempts have been made by social scientists to provide explanations for criminal behavior and by doing so produce a solution to the black overrepresentation among clients in the criminal justice system. Unfortunately, such attempts continue to be stultified by faulty public perception of crime, criminality and criminalization. The situation is made more complex because several variables impact each criminal conduct. In addition, many violent criminals were either under the influence of alcohol or some other drug, had a disturbed personality, were psychopathic or schizophrenic at the time they committed the crime. Since each social group portrays a different view of any social problem depending on how it perceives that problem, attempts to fashion an applicable comprehensive explanation of crime and offending continue to evade us.

The quest for an explanation of crime and criminalization reminds one of the fable about the four blind philosophers confronting an elephant for the first time. The one who felt the elephant's ear thought the animal resembled the leaf of a banana plant. The philosopher who grasped its tail described an elephant as something like a rope. The one who felt the animal's legs believed that the elephant resembled the trunk of a tree. The one who felt the elephant's flank thought the animal was like a mud wall. As can be seen, none of these views taken in isolation describes an elephant. But when taken together, they present a close fit of what an elephant looks like.

Because of the existence of this divergence in our understanding of crime, it continues to be difficult to fashion a comprehensive format for solving either the crime problem or the overrepresentation problem. Preliminary studies indicate, however, that fashioning a procedural format for distribution of all national social perquisites will help to alleviate the problem. A viable procedural format should be such as will rely solely on names of individuals, not physical appearance and or presence of applicants. This will eliminate face-to-face interviews and thus reduce the possibilities of confrontations and discriminations. Except in few instances, an individual's name in the US, does not by itself disclose a racial profile of the individual who bears that name. It is therefore possible to grant entitlements through the mail, or by lottery, without personal contact with the individual candidate. By the time the official who grants the entitlement becomes aware of a candidate's racial classification, it becomes too late to discriminate against that candidate. This will help to reduce the frustration experienced by African Americans in this society and consequently eliminate their overrepresentation in U.S. crime statistics.

How to improve interactions during initial contacts between offenders and law enforcement officials, remains another major defiant problem. This stage in the criminal justice process is the major source of data for overrepresentation of African Americans in the population of clients of our criminal justice system. This is because at this stage the law enforcement officer decides whether or not to arrest a suspect, depending on how the suspect reacts during initial confrontation with the officer. Yet this stage receives very little attention in our attempts at crime control. Very little coverage is given to this vital stage either in law enforcement academies or colleges, except to emphasize the need for officers to sharpen their ability to reciprocate, out of concern for officers' personal safety. Further and more detailed studies need to be undertaken to discover what can be done to make this initial officer/ suspect confrontation stage less stressful, and therefore, less likely end in arrests.

Having discussed what generates the overrepresentation of blacks as clients of our criminal justice system, it becomes a little easier to understand why African Americans

exhibit more concern about felon disfranchisement laws. When we take a closer look at majority of those states that were at the forefront of the proclivity towards enactment of felon disfranchisement laws, the inference becomes obvious that they constitute the majority of the states that championed slavery and racial discriminations. They are also predominantly the very same southern states that our history books consistently identify, as breeding grounds for the KKK (Ku Klux Klan), skinheads, white supremacists and other anti black organizations.

Scholars such as Roger Clegg, of the Center for Equal Opportunity, present some compelling but porous argument to justify the continuing existence of Felon Disfranchisement laws. They maintain that because Article One, Section Two of the Constitution says that electors for the House of Representatives – "shall have the qualifications requisite for electors of the most numerous branch of the State legislature, – the Constitution by implication gives authority for determining elector qualifications to the states." Referring to the issue of race, Clegg maintains that – "laws which have a mere "disproportionate effect" or "disparate impact" on the basis of race – but not discriminatory intent - do not violate the 14th and 15th Amendments. That may indeed be so, but there still remains the need to explain the real purpose of such laws. The terms "disproportionate effect" and "disparate impact" are often associated with the terms "unequal" and "discriminatory". Use of the word "mere" to preface the terms, suggests an obvious attempt by proponents of felon disfranchisement, to mellow the impact of both terms, and make them less offensive, in order to disguise their real intent.

So far, the issue of constitutionality of felon disfranchisement laws has escaped direct challenge under the 15th Amendment. Suits that seek to enforce enfranchisement rights have either come under the provisions of section Two of the Fourteenth Amendment, or the Due Process clause of the Fifth and 14th Amendments. The result is that the Supreme Court has continued to skirt a direct reference to the 15th Amendment, thus leaving interpretation of the true force of that Amendment to be kicked around by scholars.

For example, in *Richardson v. Romirez* the plaintiffs contended that curtailment of their right to vote would only be constitutional if the curtailment was necessary to the promotion of a compelling governmental interest. They also argued that abridgement of their voting rights violated their 14th Amendment right to equal protection of the law. No reference was made to the right to vote, which is specifically conferred to native-born citizens by section One of the 15th Amendment. The Supreme Court avoiding the 15th and 26th Amendments, referred to section Two of the 14th Amendment, and held, that it specifically contemplates and condones the disfranchisement of individuals convicted of crimes. It also disagreed that a compelling governmental interest has to be furthered in order to justify placing a restriction, on the voting rights of ex-felons.[18]

Another porous argument advanced by champions of felon disfranchisement, is that voting is both a right and a privilege. The major reason advanced by this group in support of this argument, is that we do not want people voting who are not trustworthy and loyal to our republic. Obvious elementary definitions indicate, that a right and a privilege are not the same. Whereas a right cannot be denied at will, a privilege is either earned or conferred, and may be withdrawn at will. Moreover, persons we so gleefully classify as felons, are only felons because they were unlucky to be detected, arrested and convicted. Many persons who now point accusing fingers at these felons, would themselves be in their numbers, but for good luck. This unfortunate situation is perpetuated because our perception of crime continues to be skewed in the direction of continuing to view ourselves as victims, who are preyed upon by those repeat deviants.

Furthermore, to continue to deny ex offenders the right to vote seems to run counter to our professed Christian ethics. Good Christians would forgive persons who repent and successfully complete punishments meted out to them for their misdeeds. Also, one of the declared major purposes of incarceration is "…providing for the opportunity for rehabilitation of those convicted…" [19] If the principle behind rehabilitation is to reform and return offenders to a better position than the one in which they were before their offense, then felon disfranchisement laws constitute undeniable evidence of both our failure to rehabilitate our offenders, and our unforgiving and unchristian nature.

---

[18] Richardson v. Romirez, 259, U.S. (1974)
[19] Florida Criminal Code, 2004.

Felony Disfranchisement:
The Political and Social Impact
of an Exclusionary Policy

Ryan Scott King

Despite the fact that the United States was founded upon principles of freedom, liberty, and equality, those promises rang hollow to many citizens who were denied the franchise and the right to participate in the political process. Over the ensuing 200 years, significant progress was made to extend the right to vote to many groups that had once been silenced, and in doing so, the United States took important steps to fulfill the promises of the founding fathers. The passage of the 15th Amendment in 1870 extended the right to vote to newly freed slaves, the 19th Amendment granted the franchise to women, the 24th Amendment outlawed poll taxes, and the 1965 Voting Rights Act provided additional protections to minority voting rights.

Despite the national trend to extend the franchise, the practice of disfranchisement for persons convicted of a felony remains a policy in nearly all states. The contemporary practice of disfranchisement remains inextricably linked, in many cases, to its historical roots of racial discrimination and political exclusion. Whereas in the past disfranchisement served to suppress the political voice of newly freed slaves, the modern day practice continues to disproportionately impact communities of color. The contemporary arguments underlying support for felony disfranchisement echo unconstitutional limitations on voting such as poll taxes and literacy tests. In addition, the consequences of disfranchisement are profound, and include vote dilution, political alienation, and barriers to prisoner re-entry. Finally, the manner in which states enforce the policy, from inaccurate voter purges to infrequently exercised restoration processes, serves to exacerbate its exclusionary impact.

Disfranchisement and who it affects: Nearly five million American are prohibited from voting as a result of a felony conviction.[1] More than 1.5 million of these persons have completed their sentence but live in one of 13 states in which a felony conviction can result in lifetime disfranchisement.[2] Forty-eight states and the District of Columbia prohibit voting for persons currently incarcerated, 35 states deny the right to vote to persons on parole, and 31 states do not allow probationers to vote.[3]

It will come as no surprise to persons familiar with the criminal justice system in the United States that this policy has had a disproportionate impact on the African-American community. Approximately 1.8 million African Americans are disenfranchised, with an acute impact on black males. Nationally, 1.4 million African-American males, or 13 percent of the population, are prohibited from voting due to a felony conviction.[4] In six states, more than one-quarter of the population of black males is not permitted to vote.[5]

Compounding the impact on the African-American community is the concentrated spatial distribution of persons with felony convictions. Although more than 47 million Americans have some type of criminal record, and 13 million adult Americans (six percent)

---

[1] Uggen, C. and J. Manza., "Democratic Contraction? Political Consequences of Felon Disfranchisement in the United States." American Sociological Review. 67 (December, 2002): 777-803.

[2] Uggen, C. and J. Manza., *Ibid.*. p 797.

[3] See Appendix A for a listing of categories of felons disenfranchised by state.

[4] *Losing the Vote: The Impact of Felony Disfranchisement Laws in the United States.* (New York and Washington, DC: Human Rights Watch and The Sentencing Project, 1998) 9.

[5] Fellner, J. and M. Mauer., *Ibid.*. p 9.

have been convicted of a felony, the distribution of these persons is not uniform.[6] Urban, low-income, minority communities experience felony convictions and incarceration at a much higher rate than the general population. For example, 20 percent of Ohio's prisoners are from Cuyahoga County (12 percent of the state's general population), while approximately three percent of the county's census block groups comprise 20 percent of the state's prisoners.[7] In Brooklyn, 35 separate blocks send enough people to prison that the state is spending in upwards of one million dollars per block on annual incarceration.[8] As people continue to cycle through the system, these numbers will remain constant. The fact that black males born today have a one in three chance of spending time in prison at some point in their lives illustrates the prevalence of incarceration in many communities.[9] As the number of felony convictions grows, it is critical to keep in mind that this increase is unevenly distributed.

The Origins of Felony Disfranchisement: Prohibiting persons to vote based on a conviction for a crime is a policy with roots in ancient Greece and Rome.[10] The United States imported the practice from Europe, modeling felony disfranchisement laws on the concept of "civil death," which removed all of an individual's civil rights for the commission of certain crimes.[11] Disfranchisement was written into a number of state constitutions at their founding,

---

[6] Travis, J., "Invisible Punishment: An Instrument of Social Exclusion." *In Invisible Punishment: The Collateral Consequences of Mass Imprisonment*, Marc Mauer and Meda Chesney-Lind (eds), (New York: The New Press, 2002) 18.

[7] Lynch, J.P. and W. J. Sabol. *Prisoner Reentry in Perspective*, (Washington, DC: The Urban Institute, 2001) 16.

[8] Gonnerman, J., "Million-Dollar Blocks: The Neighborhood Costs of America's Prison Boom." *Village Voice*, 16 November 2004.

[9] Bonczar, T. P, "Prevalence of Imprisonment in the U.S. Population, 1974-2001," (Washington, DC: Bureau of Justice Statistics, 2003) p 8.

[10] Ewald, A., *Punishing at the Polls: The Case Against Disenfranchising Citizens with Felony Convictions*, (New York: Demos, 2003) 17.

[11] Ewald, A., *Ibid.*. p 18.

but the practical impact was limited because voting was already restricted along gender, race, and class lines.

As the franchise was extended over time, the effect of disfranchisement became tangible. In the wake of Reconstruction a number of Southern states, fearful of the voting power of newly freed slaves, sought to increase the applicability of felony disfranchisement laws as a means of suppressing the black vote. The 1890 constitutional convention in Mississippi constructed a limited disfranchisement law designed to target "furtive offenses" that were perceived to be most likely committed by blacks, while excluding those "robust crimes" that were judged to be more common for white offenders.[12] This created a curious state policy in which a conviction for burglary, theft, or obtaining money under false pretenses would result in the loss of voting rights, while persons convicted of murder were not similarly disenfranchised.[13] This same approach of narrowly tailoring disfranchisement policy to target "black offenses" was undertaken in South Carolina, and is indicative of its discriminatory intent.

Although states currently claim that modern-day policy cannot be judged by its historical origins, the thread over time should not be ignored. Some historians argue that the writing was on the wall with the passage of the 13th, 14th, and 15th Amendment: the post-Reconstruction Supreme Court was going to subject any exclusionary state policies to strict constitutional scrutiny. For this reason, one historian notes that felony disfranchisement may have been seen as "insurance if courts struck down more blatantly unconstitutional clauses."[14] To be sure, that is exactly what has occurred. While poll taxes, literacy tests, and grandfather clauses have all been struck down as overbroad restrictions on voting, felony disfranchisement has withstood constitutional challenge and remains in place in one form or another everywhere but Maine and Vermont.

---

[12] Shapiro, A. L., "Challenging Criminal Disfranchisement Under the Voting Rights Act: A New Strategy." *The Yale Law Journal* 103 (1993): 537-566 and 540-1.

[13] Shapiro, A. L., *Ibid.*. p 541

[14] Kousser J. M., cited in Shapiro, p 538.

The Rationale for Disfranchisement Policy: The fact that disfranchisement policy has its origins, in many states, in the 19th Century, means that current justifications for disfranchisement may differ from the original intent. This argument has been made by states such as Florida, Alabama, and Mississippi, which claim that one cannot draw a link between the historically discriminatory foundation of the policy and the current rationale for continuing the practice. Although claims are made that original intent and current practice are different, an examination of the justification that underlies today's policy demonstrates that there may be more continuity than many proponents concede.

There are a number of arguments offered in support of restricting the right to vote for persons who have a felony conviction. These include protecting the purity of the ballot box, fear of a "criminal voting bloc," and protecting against voter fraud. The belief is that someone who has broken the law should not have a voice in making the law. The commonality that links all of these justifications is a belief that the personal characteristics of people with a felony conviction render them unfit to express their political choice. By virtue of having a felony conviction, a person is presumed to have demonstrated a lack of trust and responsibility, and these traits should not be embodied in the body politic. However, it is at this point where the underlying goals of disfranchisement run afoul of constitutional principles.

National Review Editor Jonah Goldberg commented in an editorial for the *Los Angeles Times* that "voting should be harder – not easier."[15] He argues, as do many other proponents of disfranchisement, that there are "types" of voters who should participate, and there are those whose voice is unwelcome. The fundamental problem with this argument is that Goldberg is arbitrarily defining who should be able to vote based on one's behavior or how one may vote. This is tantamount to a character test, a restriction that is patently unconstitutional. Efforts by post-Reconstruction states to restrict the vote based on race were framed by the same

---

[15] Goldberg, J., "The Cellblock Voting Bloc." *Los Angeles Times*. 8 March 2005.

belief that who you are and what you believe should determine your voting eligibility. Thus, to this degree, modern arguments in favor of disfranchisement remain linked to a discriminatory past.

For a punishment to be just, it must achieve certain goals, which are traditionally defined as deterrence, rehabilitation, and retribution. A state's ability to punish as it sees fit is often given wide latitude, as long as the policy can be demonstrated to have some link to these functions. Felony disfranchisement policy has not been demonstrated to have any deterrent effect on future criminality. As for rehabilitation, not only does disfranchisement fail in this realm, but its exclusionary process may work at cross-purposes with a successful reentry process. Law professor Pamela Karlan argues that disfranchisement only meets the standard for retribution, but the uniform manner in which it is applied (equally for first-timers convicted of a low-level crime and serious career offenders) renders it disproportionate.[16]

Short of a very tenuous link to retributive goals, the core justification for disfranchisement is the belief that a felony conviction is a proxy for persons who have proven themselves to be unworthy of the right to vote. Karlan notes that "the [Supreme] Court has consistently rejected restrictions on the franchise as a reasonable means of promoting intelligent or responsible voting" and have "also barred denying the right to vote to citizens who could not establish that they 'possess good moral character.'"[17] As noted above, many of the past efforts to restrict the vote for newly freed slaves were rooted in a belief that African Americans lacked the responsibility and moral character to vote. Current arguments have simply replaced "race" with "felony conviction" as a proxy for fitness to vote, but in practice, the impact on the African American community is still substantial.

---

[16] Karlan, P. S., "Convictions and Doubts: Retribution, Representation, and the Debate over Felon Disfranchisement." Stanford Public Law and Legal Theory Working Paper Series. Research Paper No. 75.

[17] Karlan, P. S., *Ibid.*. p 8.

The Impact of Disfranchisement Policy: The growth in the numbers of persons disenfranchised, particularly in communities of color, has had significant consequences that touch on issues ranging from political participation to public safety. In communities that experience high-density incarceration, the resultant impact on the political voice is devastating. The effect is felt in two ways: on the individual and on the community. At the individual level, neighborhoods with high levels of incarceration will have substantial numbers of persons absent from the voting rolls. This figure is multiplied significantly in the 35 states that disenfranchise persons on probation and/or parole.

Because high-density incarceration is most often felt in African-American communities, these are the people who experience the most substantial impact on their political voice. A recent analysis of the localized impact of disfranchisement on neighborhoods in Atlanta illustrates this disproportionate effect. In Atlanta, one in every seven black males is disenfranchised (14%).[18] Black males are 11 times more likely than non-black males to be disenfranchised, and one-third of this rate is due to drug convictions.[19] Disfranchisement is so widespread among African-American males that, in Atlanta, more than two-thirds of the gap in registration rates between black males and non-black males can be attributed to this policy.[20] These results suggest that efforts to explain lower voter turnout in the black community must focus on structural impediments rather than individual apathy.

In Atlanta, 11 of the 20 neighborhoods in the analysis had a disfranchisement rate of 10,000 per 100,000 black males, while no neighborhood had a rate higher than 4,000 per 100,000 non-black males.[21] The ratio of disfranchisement rates for black males to that of non-black males in this study ranged from a low of 6.5 to a high

---

[18] King, R. S. and M. Mauer., " The Vanishing Black Electorate: Felony Disfranchisement in Atlanta, Georgia." (Washington, DC: The Sentencing Project, 2004), 5.

[19] King, R. S. and M. Mauer., *Ibid.* p. 3.

[20] *Ibid.* p 6.

[21] *Ibid.* p 10.

of 26.5.[22] In 9 of the 20 neighborhoods, the disfranchisement rate
for black males was at least 10 times higher than the rate for non-
black males.[23] In short, as the population in a community becomes
more densely populated with African-American males, the
disfranchisement rate rises accordingly.

This impacts the individual, but the effect on the community is
no less profound. The direct and strong correlation between the
proportion of a neighborhood's population that is African-American
and disfranchisement rates is an indicator of a suppressed, or diluted,
political voice in those communities. When a significant portion of a
community is prohibited from voting, those remaining persons who
are permitted to vote will experience a diminished representation in
the electorate. For example, a neighborhood in Atlanta that has .37
percent of its population disenfranchised will have a greater impact
on an electoral outcome than a community that has more than six
percent of its neighborhood disenfranchised. There are more eligible
voters in the former neighborhood, so its political impact is presumed
to be more substantial. The role of race, not surprisingly, plays a
critical role in this scenario, as the former neighborhood is two percent
African-American, while the latter is 92 percent African-American.

Thus, disfranchisement exacerbates inequalities that already
exist in society. Urban African American communities tend to be
some of the most disadvantaged, and access to scarce resources
for development are critical in an effort to fight the impact of
economic destabilization. Traditionally, this means that in local and
state politics, these communities are in direct competition with
suburban neighborhoods and downtown enterprise zones, and a
localities' ability to voice its demands will define its success. The
fact that these distressed communities face additional obstacles
through the dilution of their political voice via disfranchisement
furthers a downward spiral. At a time when politicians must be
responsive to the neediest areas, those very areas are being

---

[22] *Ibid.* p 11.

[23] *Ibid.* p 11.

devastated by over incarceration and are losing the political voice necessary to demand constructive change.

As noted above, one-third of the disfranchisement in Georgia can be attributed to drug convictions, a policy that is rooted in discretionary approaches to law enforcement. While African Americans do not use drugs at a rate disproportionate to their representation in the general population, they are impacted by arrest and incarceration for drug violations at a much higher rate. This is primarily due to law enforcement patterns that choose to pursue the "war on drugs" in communities of color. Thus, the growth in more punitive sentencing for drug violations has had its most substantial impact on the African-American community. As a result, many leaders in the black community have struggled for changes in sentencing. Members of neighborhoods that have been devastated by the consequences of the "war on drugs" are desperate for some type of reform. Nevertheless, at a time when we need to consider input from the people most directly affected by drug sentencing policies, felony disfranchisement silences and alienates their political voice.

Disfranchisement also damages the fabric of political culture in a neighborhood. The act of voting is a shared experience and is an opportunity for a community to come together publicly and express their political will. It is the defining act of a democracy, and being such, is commonly characterized by neighborhood-level activity such as candidate forums in local institutions and individual-level discussions over important issues. In communities in which many people are prohibited from voting due to disfranchisement, these discussions are less likely to occur and a culture surrounding electoral politics unlikely to form. If you cannot vote, why would you be interested in the issues or candidates?

In addition to the fundamental questions of fairness that are raised when voting eligibility is linked to felony conviction status, there is also a notable impact on the prisoner reentry process through the stigmatization of being labeled "unfit" to vote. Being denied the right to participate in the political process highlights that a person remains outside of society, making that person "an alien in [their] own country" and sending a message to society "that former offenders are impure."[24] This governmentally sanctioned stigmatization is part of a larger group of collateral consequences that create legislative hurdles to accessing employment, housing, and education. All of these policies are incongruous with a commitment to rehabilitation, perhaps voiced most clearly by President Bush in his 2004 State of the Union address when he said "America is the land of second chance, and when the gates of the prison open, the path ahead should lead to a better life."

Felony disfranchisement is not a policy that assists people in achieving a better life. To the contrary, it alienates people at a time when they are most in need of society's acceptance. Voting, in addition to its practical application, is also symbolic. It is a sign that a person belongs to a larger social collective. When a person chooses to spend the time to learn about issues, study candidates, and vote, that person is reaffirming his or her commitment to the political structures of American society. This is a remarkable indicator of a person's desire to be accepted by society, and to prohibit someone from making that personal statement is counterproductive.

Moreover, the empirical evidence suggests that there is a quantifiable link between voting and future recidivism. Sociologists Christopher Uggen and Jeff Manza have documented a link between political participation and future criminal behavior. They have found "consistent differences between voters and non-voters in rates of subsequent arrest, incarceration, and self-reported criminal behavior."[25] Between 1997 and 2000, only five percent of voters were arrested, compared with 16 percent of non-voters.[26] Looking at the link between voting and recidivism, Uggen and Manza found that 12 percent of voters with a previous arrest were re-arrested,

---

[24] Harvard Law Review. "Note: The Disfranchisement of Ex-Felons: Citizenship, Criminality, and 'The Purity of the Ballot Box.'" *Harvard Law Review.* 102 (April 1989): 1300-1317;. 1313

[25] Uggen, C. and J. Manza., "Voting and Subsequent Crime and Arrest: Evidence from a Community Sample." *Columbia Human Rights Law Review* 36 (2004): 193-215; 213.

[26] Defined as someone who voted in the 1996 election.

compared with 27 percent of non-voters.[27] Thus, there appears to be a measurable correlation between voting patterns and future criminal behavior, and intuitively, as noted above, this makes sense. For this reason, statutorily proscribing voting for those persons who seek to participate in the process is of questionable merit regarding public safety.

The disproportionate impact of disfranchisement policy on the African-American community has begun to draw attention from the Federal court system. In the case of *Farrakhan v. Washington*, the Ninth Circuit ruled that the "totality of the circumstances" clause of the Voting Rights Act "requires courts to consider how a challenged voting practice *interacts with* external factors such as 'social and historical conditions' to result in denial of the right to vote on account of race or color."[28] The Ninth Circuit has ruled that if Farrakhan can demonstrate that the policy of linking voting eligibility to conviction status interacts in such a way so as to discriminate against African Americans, he may be able to demonstrate that the policy violates Section 2 of the Voting Rights Act. Although the Ninth Circuit has given permission for the *Farrakhan* case to proceed, a recent decision in another case in the Southern District of New York ruled that Section 2 was not applicable. The disagreement surrounds the legal question of whether the intent of the law at its time of passage determines whether it violates Section 2, or if the results of implementation can be taken into consideration. This fundamental difference in interpretation may lead one of these cases to be heard in front of the United States Supreme Court in the near future.

Practical Problems with Disfranchisement Policy: In addition to the impact of disfranchisement on individuals and the community, the manner in which states implement their policies serves to intensify inherent problems.

In every state but Maine and Vermont, when a person receives a felony conviction, it is the responsibility of state agencies to remove,

---

[27] Uggen, C. and J. Manza., *Ibid.* 205.

[28] *Farrakhan v. Washington*, 338 F.3d 1009, 1011-1012 (2003).

or purge, those names from the voter rolls. The process varies from state to state and requires the coordination of multiple state and local agencies, which may include the Secretary of State, the Department of Corrections, and local Boards of Election. This procedure can be very convoluted depending on the state law. In states that disenfranchise persons under community supervision, a voter purge list will require collecting data from the Departments of Corrections and Probation and/or Parole, and matching that up with electoral data from the Secretary of State's office. Matching corrections data with locally managed voter files is a cumbersome process, and with a verification procedure that is far from systematic, inaccuracies abound.

This process becomes even more difficult in the 14 states in which persons can lose their right to vote even after completing community supervision. This is perhaps best illustrated by the experience in Florida in the summer of 2004. Florida law disenfranchises all persons for life as the result of a felony conviction, and the right to vote may only be restored through a gubernatorial pardon. In the summer of 2004, the Florida Division of Elections sent out a list of 47,000 persons for local election boards to purge as a result of their status of being convicted of a felony. An investigation by the *Miami Herald* discovered that more than 2,000 of those people on the purge list were identified incorrectly as being ineligible to vote due to a felony conviction.[29] The state was unable to accurately verify the names of the persons who were supposed to be on the list, and in an effort to make sure that eligible voters were not being improperly prohibited from voting, they withdrew the purge list.

The story in Florida is common in other states, and is a result of complicated laws and outmoded databases that cannot accurately sync up information. Some states, such as Maryland, Wyoming, and Nebraska have a statutorily prescribed waiting period before certain individuals can seek to have their rights restored. In

---

[29] Bolstand, E., J. Grotto and D. Kidwell, "Thousands of Eligible Voters are on Felon List." *Miami Herald.* (02 July 2004.)

Maryland, there is a three-year waiting period for some offenders prior to their being able to restore their right to vote. However, the state has no protocol in place to "count" the elapsed time, and the person seeking to restore his or her rights is never notified when they are eligible to register. This creates a confusing scenario in which many people are unaware of their status as it pertains to registration.

A recent report by the American Civil Liberties Union analyzing purge processes in 15 states concluded that the compilation of purge lists is not systematic and is fraught with inaccuracies.[30] In addition, none of the states has a standardized criteria to verify the eligibility on its list. Finally, two-thirds of the states in the study were not even required to notify individuals when they had been purged, which prevents an appeal by those who have been incorrectly identified.

Each of the 13 states that can restrict voting rights for the remainder of a person's life has in place some type of process in which persons can have their rights restored. This is usually through a pardon by the governor of the state, although specific mechanisms will vary by state. Despite having this restoration protocol in place, a recent study by The Sentencing Project concluded that the process was often cumbersome and there is insufficient assistance available for those seeking to apply.[31] For these reasons, the study found that in 11 of the 14 states, less than 3% of disenfranchised persons have had their rights restored.[32]

It is apparent that in addition to fundamental questions of fairness and equality that are raised by the practice of disfranchisement, there are practical questions about the ability of the states to accurately pursue the policy. The difficulty of linking data across agencies (and states), the confusing nature of the laws, and the onerous and limited availability of recourse for a person

---

[30] American Civil Liberties Union. *Purged! How a Patchwork of Flawed and Inconsistent Voting Systems Could Deprive Millions of American of the Right to Vote*, (Washington, DC: American Civil Liberties Union, 2004).

[31] Mauer, M. and T. Kansal, *Barred for Life: Voting Rights Restoration in Permanent Disfranchisement States.* (Washington, DC: The Sentencing Project, 2005); 1-3.

[32] Mauer, M. and T. Kansal, *Ibid.*. p 2.

who has lost the right to vote raise serious questions about the viability of disfranchisement.

Recommendations: The act of a state stripping a person's right to vote due to a felony conviction is an archaic process, rooted in exclusionary law and inextricably linked to an American legacy of racial discrimination. As the correctional system has grown to more than 2.1 million people, the consequences of this policy have become graver for those low-income, communities of color that experience its impact most acutely. The inability of the states to guarantee the accuracy of the purging process and their infrequent use of the restoration processes available place an undue burden upon many who seek to exercise their right to vote. State legislatures, depending on the current state of the law of each, should consider the following recommendations as a response to these issues:

- Reconsider Basing Voting Eligibility on Felony Conviction Status
- Expand Voting Rights to All Persons Not Incarcerated
- Increase the Use of Pardons to Restore Voting Rights
- Provide Notification and Education to Persons Leaving Supervision
- Provide Standardized Training for Corrections and Elections Officials
- Ensure Transparency in the Voter Purge Process
- Provide State Assistance for Persons Seeking to Restore Their Right to Vote

Categories of Felons Disenfranchised Under State Law
(as of July 2005)

State	*Prison*	*Probation*	*Parole*	*Ex-Felons*	
				All[33]	*Partial*
Alabama	X	X	X	x	
Alaska	X	X	X		
Arizona	X	X	X		X (2nd felony)
Arkansas	X	X	X		
California	X		X		
Colorado	X		X		
Connecticut	X		X		
Delaware	X	X	X		X (5 years)
District of Columbia	X				
Florida	X	X	X	X	
Georgia	X	X	X		
Hawaii	X				
Idaho	X	X	X		
Illinois	X				
Indiana	X				
Iowa[34]	X	X	X		
Kansas	X	X	X		
Kentucky	X	X	X	X	
Louisiana	X	X	X		
Maine					
Maryland	X	X	X		X (2nd felony, 3 years)

---

[33] While these states disenfranchise all persons with a felony conviction and provide no automatic process for restoration of rights, several (Alabama, Kentucky, and Virginia) have adopted legislation in recent years that streamlines the restoration process.

[34] In July 2005, Iowa Governor Vilsack issued an executive order restoring the right to vote for all persons who have completed supervision. However, the lifetime prohibition on voting remains Iowa law.

State	Prison	Probation	Parole	Ex-Felons	
				All[33]	*Partial*
Massachusetts	X				
Michigan	X				
Minnesota	X	X	X		
Mississippi	X	X	X		X (certain offenses)
Missouri	X	X	X		
Montana	X				
Nebraska	X	X	X		X (2 years)
Nevada	X	X	X		X (except first-time nonviolent)
New Hampshire	X				
New Jersey	X	X	X		
New Mexico	X	X	X		
New York	X		X		
North Carolina	X	X	X		
North Dakota	X				
Ohio	X				
Oklahoma	X	X	X		
Oregon	X				
Pennsylvania	X				
Rhode Island	X	X	X		
South Carolina	X	X	X		
South Dakota	X				
Tennessee	X	X	X		X (post-1981)
Texas	X	X	X		
Utah	X				
Vermont					
Virginia	X	X	X	X	
Washington	X	X	X		X (pre-1984)
West Virginia	X	X	X		
Wisconsin	X	X	X		
Wyoming	X	X	X		X (5 years)
U.S. Total	49	31	35	4	9

DEATH PENALTY

A Strategy for Confronting Racial Discrimination in the Use of the Death Penalty in Georgia[1]

Michael Mears

In 1994 the United States of America ratified the International Convention on the Elimination of All Forms of Racial Discrimination.[2] This international treaty provided, in part, that the parties to the treaty would:

condemn racial discrimination and undertake to pursue by all appropriate means and without delay a policy of eliminating racial discrimination in all its forms and promoting understanding among all races, and, to this end: (a) Each State Party[3] undertakes to

---

[1] A paper presented to the W.E.B. DuBois Institute of Clark Atlanta University as part of the Institute's Annual Spring Conference, April 7-8, 2005, "Criminal Justice and the African-American Community." I would like to thank my wife, the Reverend A. Coile Estes, for her invaluable editorial help and assistance with this paper.

[2] The International Convention on the Elimination of All Forms of Racial Discrimination, Ratified by the United States of America on October 21, 1994, with reservations.

[3] Vienna Convention on the Law of Treaties, Article 2, paragraph (g); (a State Party is defined as a State which has consented to be bound by the treaty and for which the treaty is in force).

engage in no act or practice of racial discrimination against persons, groups of persons or institutions and to ensure that all public authorities and public institutions, national and local, shall act in conformity with this obligation.[4]

However, the ratification by the United States was made with specific reservations and declarations.[5] Specifically, the United States refused to acknowledge the need for any additional laws in order to protect U.S. citizens from racial discrimination. The reservations which accompanied the signing of this international treaty stated, in part, that

The US Constitution provides enough protection to citizens with regard to racial discrimination; therefore, no new laws are needed for the US to meet its obligations under the International Convention on the Elimination of All Forms of Racial Discrimination.[6]

In 1999, Amnesty International issued a report on racial disparity in the imposition of the death penalty, "*Killing With Prejudice: Race and the Death Penalty in the USA.*" This 21-page report cited statistics, case summaries, and other facts to document the racial disparity of the death penalty in the United States.[7] The report concluded that the criminal justice system in

---

[4] Op. cite. at Article 2.

[5] Article 2 (1)(d) of the Vienna Convention on the Law of Treaties (1969). This article defines a "reservation" as: "a unilateral statement, however phrased or named, made by a State, when signing, ratifying, accepting, approving or acceding to a treaty whereby it purports to exclude or modify the legal effects of certain provisions of the treaty in their application to that State."

[6] Reservations submitted by the United States of America to The International Convention on the Elimination of All Forms of Racial Discrimination, Reservations and Declarations (1994).

[7] "Killing with Prejudice: Race and the Death Penalty in the USA," Amnesty International Report Number 51/52/99, May, 1999.

the United States (including Georgia) is infected with prejudice against minorities, particularly African Americans. Unfortunately, very little has changed in the past six years since the issuance of that report.

Since 1976, the State of Georgia, thirty-seven other states, and the federal government have executed 320 African Americans, 60 Hispanics, 547 whites and 22 persons classified as either Oriental or other.[8] Of those numbers, Georgia accounts for 13 African Americans and 24 whites executed during that time.[9] According to the most recent reports from the Georgia Department of Corrections, there are currently 54 whites, 54 African Americans, and three Hispanics awaiting execution on death row at Jackson, Georgia.[10] These statistics are even more dramatic in light of the census data on race which, over the past three decades, has consistently remained the same. In the 2000 census the population of the United States was 75.1 per cent white, 12.3 per cent black, 3.6 Asian, 0.9 American Indian and Alaska Native, and other 8.2 per cent.[11]

However, it is not only the race of the defendant which appears to have a determinative effect on the decision to seek the death penalty. A report published in the Stanford Law Review revealed that patterns of racial disparity based on the race of the victims can also be found. The report cited statistical data relating to the imposition of the death penalty which showed that in Arkansas, Florida, Georgia, Illinois, Mississippi, North Carolina, Oklahoma, and Virginia, the death penalty was sought more often when the defendant was black than when the defendant was white. For example, in Arkansas, findings showed that defendants in cases involving a white victim were three-and-a-half times more likely to be sentenced

---

[8] "Race of Death Row Inmates Executed Since 1976, available at http://www.deathpenaltyinfo.org/article.php?did=105&scid=5 (As of February 17 2005) Death Penalty Information Center, February 17, 2005.

[9] Death Row U.S.A., Winter 2005, Quarterly Report by the Criminal Justice Project of the NAACP Legal Defense and Educational Fund, Inc., January, 2005.

[10] Death Row U.S.A., *Ibid.*

[11] Source U.S. Census Bureau, Data Derived from Population Estimates, 2000 Census of Population and Housing.

to death; in Illinois, four times, in North Carolina, 4.4 times, and in Mississippi, five times more likely to be sentenced to death than defendants convicted of murdering blacks.[12]

In the late 1970's, Professors David Baldus, Charles Pulaski and Georgia Woodworth of the University of Iowa examined over 2,000 murder cases in Georgia. Professor Baldus's study became the basis for the appeal to the United States Supreme Court in the case of *McCleskey v. Kemp*.[13] The defendant in that case, Warren McCleskey, had been convicted and sentenced to death for killing a white police officer during a burglary attempt.[14] Professor Baldus's study was part of an effort to provide statistical data showing that the decision to seek the death penalty was based, in substantial

---

[12] Gross, S. R. and R. Mauro, "Patterns of Death: An Analysis of Racial Disparities in Capital Sentencing and Homicide Victimization," 37 Stanford Law Review 27 (1984).

[13] McCleskey v. Kemp, 481 U.S. 279, 321 (1987); See Justice Brennan's dissent: "Furthermore, even examination of the sentencing system as a whole, factoring in those cases in which the jury exercises little discretion, indicates the influence of race on capital sentencing. For the Georgia system as a whole, race accounts for a six percentage point difference in the rate at which capital punishment is imposed. Since death is imposed in 11% of all white-victim cases, the rate in comparably aggravated black-victim cases is 5%. The rate of capital sentencing in a white-victim case is thus 120% greater than the rate in a black-victim case. But another way, over half - 55% - of defendants in white-victim crimes in Georgia would not have been sentenced to die if their victims had been black. Of the more than 200 variables potentially relevant to a sentencing decision, race of the victim is a powerful explanation for variation in death sentence rates - as powerful as nonracial aggravating factors such as a prior murder conviction or acting as the principal planner of the homicide. These adjusted figures are only the most conservative indication of the risk that race will influence the death sentence of defendants in Georgia. Data unadjusted for the mitigating or aggravating effect of other factors show an even more pronounced disparity by race. The capital sentencing rate for all white-victim cases was almost 11 times greater than the rate for black-victim cases. Furthermore, blacks who kill whites are sentenced to death at nearly 22 times the rate of blacks who kill blacks, and more than 7 times the rate of whites who kill blacks. In addition, the prosecutors seek the death penalty for 70% of black defendants with white victims, but for only 15% of black defendants with black victims, and only 19% of white defendants with black victims."

[14] McCleskey v. Kemp, *Ibid.* at 283-285.

part, on the race of the defendant and the race of the victim. The majority of the Supreme Court refused to overturn Warren McCleskey's death sentence. Justice Powell, writing for the majority of the Court, stated that the data relating to systemic discrimination should be presented to legislative bodies and not to the courts.[15]

However, four dissenting Justices acknowledged the validity of Warren McCleskey's claim that the decision to seek the death penalty had been used in a racially discriminatory manner. Justice Blackmun, writing for him and three other dissenting justices, stated

> *The Baldus study demonstrates that black persons are a distinct group that are singled out for different treatment in the Georgia capital sentencing system. The Court acknowledges, as it must, that the raw statistics included in the Baldus study and presented by petitioner indicate that it is much less likely that a death sentence will result from a murder of a black person than from a murder of a white person. White-victim cases are nearly 11 times more likely to yield a death sentence than are black-victim cases. The raw figures also indicate that even within the group of defendants who are convicted of killing white persons and are thereby more likely to receive a death sentence, black defendants are more likely than white defendants to be sentenced to death.[16]*

Professor Baldus and his associates discovered several distinctive patterns indicating that the death penalty is more likely to be requested by the prosecution and administered by the courts when the victim is white. For example, in Georgia, for the period covered by the study, district attorneys had demanded the death penalty 70 percent of the time when the defendant was black and the victim was white.[17] In contrast, when the defendant was white and the victim was black, the

---

[15] *Ibid.* at 319.
[16] *Ibid.* at 353.
[17] *Ibid.* at 351.

same district attorneys asked for the death penalty only 19 percent of the time. When both defendant and the victim were black, the district attorneys requested the death penalty only 15 percent of the time. The conclusion of the "Baldus Study" showed conclusively that a defendant convicted of killing a white person in the state of Georgia was 4.3 times more likely to receive a death sentence than someone convicted of killing a black person.[18]

A study by the United States General Accounting Office in 1990 confirmed that Professor Baldus's study was accurate. The General Accounting Office report, prepared for the Judiciary Committees of the United States Senate and House, stated that of 28 studies examined, 82% found the influence of race to be a factor in the charging and sentencing of defendants to death, i.e., that blacks who killed whites were more likely to be sentenced to die than those blacks who murdered blacks.[19] The race of the victim was found to be a particularly strong indicator of who would be charged with a capital offense.

The racial bias of the criminal justice system's sentencing decisions is not limited to the death penalty. Even the most ardent supporters of the death penalty have acknowledged that there is a grave disparity in the administration of the criminal laws in the United States.[20] While African Americans comprise 12 per cent of the country's population, they account for 48 per cent of the inmates in state and federal prisons. The Bureau of Justice Statistics has estimated that 28 per cent of black men are sent to jail or prison during their lives.[21] African-Americans are stopped more frequently

---

[18] "Comparative Review of Death Sentences: An Empirical Study of the Georgia Experience," Pulaski, Charles A.Jr. and Woodworth, George, 74 *Journal of Criminal Law & Criminology* 661, (1983).

[19] "Death Penalty Sentencing: Research Indicates Pattern of Racial Disparities," 5, U.S. General Accounting Office, GAO-GCD-90-57 (Feb. 1990). Available at http://161,203.16.4/t2pbat11/140845.pdf.

[20] "Death Penalty Sentencing: Research Indicates Pattern of Racial Disparities," *Ibid.*

[21] Harrison, Paige M., J. Karlberg, "Prison and Jail Inmates at Midyear 2002," Bureau of Justice Statistics Bulletin, April 2003. Available at http://ojp.usdoj.gov/pub/pdf02.pdf.

by police, charged with higher-level offenses, afforded less competent counsel, and punished more severely than whites convicted of the same crimes. A report from the respected Human Rights Watch found that there is a pattern of racial disproportion in arrests and sentencing in drug related cases in Georgia as well as nationally. In 2000, Human Rights Watch also reported that blacks comprise 62.7 percent and whites 36.7 percent of all drug offenders admitted to state prisons. Those same studies show that there are five times more white drug users than black. Yet, relative to population, black men are admitted to state prison on drug charges at a rate that is 13.4 times greater than that of white men. In large part because of the extraordinary racial disparities in incarceration for drug offenses, blacks are incarcerated for all offenses at 8.2 times the rate of whites. One in every 20 black men over the age of 18 in the United States is in state or federal prison, compared to one in 180 white men.[22]

This statistics are even worse in some states, including Georgia. For example, in seven states blacks constitute between 80 and 90 percent of all drug offenders sent to prison. In at least fifteen states, black men are admitted to prison on drug charges at rates that are from 20 to 57 times greater than those of white men. In two states, one in every 13 black men is in prison. In seven states, blacks are incarcerated at more than 13 times the rate of whites.

An Amnesty International report published in April 2003 points out that racial disparities can be found throughout the criminal justice system in the United States.[23] One of the points made by Amnesty International is this:

> *Given the appallingly low standards of many court-appointed lawyers in numerous jurisdictions, there is an ever-present risk that minority defendants may*

---

[22] Fellner, J., "Punishment and Prejudice: Racial Disparities in the War on Drugs," Human Rights Watch Report, Vol 12, No. 2(G), May 2000.

[23] "United States of America: Death by Discrimination - The Continuing Role of Race in Capital Cases," Amnesty International Report, April, 2003.Available at http://web.amnesty.org/library/index.

*be represented by lawyers who are not only
incompetent, but are also openly bigoted . . . [E]ven
when the attorney is not an overt racist, a lack of
cultural sensitivity to other ethnic groups may affect
their ability to prepare adequately for the case   White
attorneys who are unable to relate to the black
community may be unable to properly defend their
black clients.[24]*

This 2003 report also found that the murder rates for black
and whites victims are almost equal.[25] However, eighty per cent of
defendants executed since the death penalty was reinstated have
been executed for murders involving white victims. In addition, this
report showed that all-white juries convicted more than twenty per
cent of black defendants who have been executed.[26]

A central contributing factor making racial prejudice and racial
bias so pervasive with regard to the use of the death penalty is the
fact that much of the discretion given to prosecutors and law
enforcement officials is unchecked. A recent law review article,
quoting a speech given by Professor Charles Ogletree, states

*[T]he criminal justice system is, at all levels of its
operation, highly discretionary.   The police have
discretion to decide whom to stop and frisk.   State
prosecutors have discretion to determine whom to
prosecute, and what charges to bring.   And judges*

---

[24] "United States of America: Death by Discrimination - The Continuing Role of
Race in Capital Cases," *Ibid*.

[25] SUNY Downstate Medical Center: The Social & Health Landscape of Urban &
Suburban America (June 30, 2004), http://www.hsbklyn. edu/urbansoc_healthdata.
"The murder rate is the age-unadjusted homicide rate per 100,000 population.
Homicide includes murder and non-negligent manslaughter, which is defined as the
willful (non-negligent) killing of one human being by another and excludes deaths
by negligence, suicide or accident."

[26] SUNY Downstate Medical Center: The Social & Health Landscape of Urban &
Suburban America, *Ibid*.

> *have a great deal of discretion, before trial, when the jury is selected, through the trial itself, and after the trial during sentencing. The existence of such discretion makes possible the pervasive and cumulative discrimination faced by many African Americans who come into contact with the criminal justice system.*[27]

In Georgia, the decision of whether to seek the death penalty is entirely within the discretion of the county district attorney. An example of this unfettered discretion by a district attorney can be found in the Ocmulgee Judicial Circuit which encompasses eight counties in south central Georgia. Between 1974 and 1991, the district attorney in that circuit sought the death penalty in 28 cases. The defendants were black in 22 of the cases.

There is presently no judicial or legislative oversight of a district attorney's decision to seek the death penalty.[28] There is no legal recourse to the prosecutor's decision to seek the death penalty and there is no way to assure that the decision is not based upon personal and institutional racial prejudices. In recent years, the Georgia General Assembly has insisted on providing mechanisms for the oversight of the fiscal aspects of both the Executive and Judicial Branches of government. The lack of accountability by the district attorneys concerning which cases become death penalty cases should, by itself, lead to a call for at least greater scrutiny of the application of the death penalty statute. The absence of legal checks and balances with regard to this decision has led to international castigation of the United States for ignoring the reality of racial discrimination.

---

[27] Charles Ogletree, Matthew O. Tobriner Memorial Lecture: The Burdens and Benefits of Race in America, 25 Hastings Const. L.Q. 219, 228, (1998).

[28] The Official Code of Georgia Annotated 17-10-32.1 (Unless the district attorney has given notice that the state intends to seek the death penalty pursuant to the Uniform Rules of the Superior Courts, the judge shall sentence the defendant to life imprisonment).

Between July 1973 and July 2003, district attorneys in Georgia sought the death penalty 835 times.[29] A question raised by the United States Supreme Court in Warren McCleskey's case[30] is whether the Georgia General Assembly will take steps to insure that the cases designated as death penalty cases by prosecutors will be free from the taint of racial bias and prejudice from this point forward. Despite the "reservations and declaration" by the United States government that "[T]he US Constitution provides enough protection to citizens with regard to racial discrimination,"[31] the Georgia General Assembly should not ignore the historical data and present facts of the discriminatory application of the death penalty statutes in Georgia.

One attempt at providing some oversight to the decisions of district attorneys came in 1999 when members of the Georgia General Assembly introduced legislation titled the "Georgia Racial Justice Act."[32] The Georgia Racial Justice Act, if enacted, would have prohibited the execution of any person if the sentence were imposed based upon a showing that the race of the victim or the race of the defendant was a factor in the decision to seek the death penalty. The Georgia Racial Justice Act would also have required that local district attorneys keep statistical records so that comparisons of similar cases could be made within each Superior Court jurisdiction. Specifically, the Georgia Racial Justice Act provided that

> a.   *No person shall be put to death under color of state law in the execution of a sentence which was imposed based on race.*

---

[29] Mears, M., "An Analysis of Death Penalty Cases in Georgia by Judicial Circuits, 1973 - 2003," The Multi-County Public Defender Office, Monograph, (2004).

[30] Op. cite. McKleskey v. Kemp, Majority opinion written by Justice Powell.

[31] Op. cite. The International Convention on the Elimination of All Forms of Racial Discrimination, Reservations and Declarations submitted by the United States of American, 1994.

[32] House Bill 137, Georgia Racial Justice Act (1999).

b.   *An inference that race was the basis of a death sentence is established if valid evidence is presented demonstrating that race was a statistically significant factor in decisions to seek or impose the sentence of death in the State of Georgia at the time such death sentence was sought or imposed.*

c.   *Evidence relevant to establish an inference that race was the basis of a death sentence may include evidence that death sentences were sought or imposed significantly more frequently:*

    i.   *Upon persons of one race more than upon persons of another race; or*

    ii.   *As punishment for capital offenses against persons of one race more than as punishment for capital offenses against persons of another race.*

d.   *If statistical evidence is presented to establish an inference that race was the basis of a sentence of death, the court shall determine the validity of the evidence and if it provides a basis for that inference. The evidence shall take into account, to the extent it is compiled and publicly made available, evidence of the statutory aggravating factors and shall include comparisons of similar cases involving persons of different races.*

e.   *If an inference that race was the basis of a death sentence is established, the death sentence shall not be carried out unless the state rebuts the inference by clear and convincing evidence. The state cannot rely on mere assertions that it did not intend to discriminate or that the case fits the statutory criteria for seeking or imposing the death sentence.* [33]

---

[33] *Ibid.* at 1-2.

The original Georgia Racial Justice Act was sponsored by Representatives Bob Holmes (53rd District), Barbara Mobley (69th District), Tyrone Brooks (54th District), and Nan Orrock (56th District). The legislation was assigned to the House Judiciary Committee which held one brief hearing on the legislation but never voted on it. Consequently, The Georgia Racial Justice Act was never passed out of the committee and the full membership of the General Assembly has also never voted on it. Although there is support for the Georgia Racial Justice Act in the Georgia General Assembly, the elected representatives have had little opportunity to consider passing legislation which would address the unfettered discretion given to district attorneys to seek the death penalty. The Georgia Racial Justice Act was not aimed at repealing those laws which provide for the death penalty. The purpose of the legislation was to help ensure that racial discrimination is not a part of the imposition of the death penalty. The Georgia Racial Justice Act would have provided at least a modicum of oversight to the currently unfettered decision of the district attorney to select which cases, and which defendants, are to be subjected to the death penalty.

The Georgia Racial Justice Act should be reintroduced and enacted by the Georgia General Assembly. Currently, there are no safeguards, no protective measures, and no oversight to the use of the death penalty in Georgia. There is a legitimate need for legislation aimed at providing a procedure which will insure that legal avenues are available to any defendant sentenced to death to seek recourse from a decision by a district attorney to seek the death penalty when there is evidence that the district attorney's decision was based upon racial factors, either the race of the defendant or the race of the victim. A prosecutor who is not basing his or her decision upon racial motivations should welcome this legislation.

There is precedent for the passage of this type of legislation. In 1998, the Commonwealth of Kentucky passed a Racial Justice Act as a statement against racism in the use of the death penalty. Before the passage of Kentucky's Racial Justice Act, a Kentucky State Senator said that the Racial Justice Act "was simply a method of insuring racism did not play a role in death sentences." Another

State Senator said, "This is [not] a vote on whether we're soft on crime. . . I'm not soft on crime. I'm strong on justice."[34]

Some members of the Georgia General Assembly have not been eager to support Georgia's version of the Racial Justice Act because many district attorneys seemingly oppose objective scrutiny of their decisions to pick and choose which defendants are subject to the death penalty. Some legislators apparently see The Racial Justice Act as unpopular legislation with no voter constituency, except among those who are opposed to the death penalty itself. The Georgia Racial Justice Act has not been reintroduced. The Georgia Racial Justice Act is one way to correct and avoid the continuation of racial discrimination in our state. Positive protective legislation has seemingly always faced an uphill battle in our nation's history just as regressive legislation and judicial decision have been hard to change once put into place by our courts and legislative bodies.

Throughout our history we have seen pervasively evil laws receive popular public approval. Not only have evil laws allowing racial discrimination received popular support, courts have, in the past, affirmed discrimination as constitutionally sound policy on behalf of individual states. In the 1850's, the United States Supreme Court not only affirmed slavery but also declared unconstitutional a law which would have prevented the spread of slavery to the new western states.[35] In 1892, Louisiana enacted a law that required separate railway cars for blacks and whites. In an 1896 challenge to that law, Homer Adolph Plessy took a seat in a "whites only" car of a Louisiana train and refused to move to the car reserved for

---

[34] The Advocate, Vol. 20, No. 4 (July 1998).

[35] Dred Scott v. Sandford, 19 Howard, 393 (1857). Chief Justice Tanney, writing for the majority of the United States Supreme Court stated: "Upon these considerations it is the opinion of the Court that the act of Congress which prohibited a citizen from holding and owning property of this kind in the territory of the United States north of the line therein mentioned is not warranted by the Constitution and is therefore void; and that neither Dred Scott himself, nor any of his family, were made free by being carried into this territory; even if they had been carried there by the owner with the intention of becoming a permanent resident."

blacks. He was arrested and convicted. The United States Supreme Court upheld the Louisiana law and enunciated the infamous "separate but equal" doctrine that was not overturned until 1954.[36] Unbelievably, we only have to go as far back as the early sixties to find proposed civil rights legislation and proposed voters' rights legislation being condemned by many in the general public. In the mid-sixties, many southern states were still enforcing laws which legalized segregation and prohibited African Americans from exercising the right to vote. Courageous legislators in many southern states and courageous members of the U.S. Congress enacted laws which effectively did away with the vestiges of legal racial discrimination. If those courageous legislators had listened to what was "popular," it is doubtful the Civil Rights Act of 1964 or the Voting Rights Act of 1965 would ever have been introduced, much less passed.

Notwithstanding the United States government's reservation set forth in the International Convention on the Elimination of All Forms of Racial Discrimination, legislation is needed to help end racial discrimination in death penalty cases. The racial discrimination and bias is real and it continues in Georgia and the rest of the states which utilize the death penalty as a punishment option. Justice Harry Blackmun, in 1994, wrote, "Even under the most sophisticated death penalty statutes, race continues to play a major role in determining who shall live and who shall die."[37] The federal government's own General Accounting Office has found credible evidence that the race of the victim influences the likelihood of a defendant being charged with capital murder or receiving the death penalty. In other words, those who murder whites are more likely to be sentenced to death than those who murder blacks.[38]

Selecting which individuals are going to be subjected to the death penalty in Georgia is currently in the hands, and hearts, of forty-nine elected district attorneys. There is no oversight, no control,

---

[36] Plessy v. Ferguson, 163 U.S. 537 (1896).

[37] Callins v. Collins, 114 S. Ct. 1127, 1135 (1994) (Blackmun, J., dissenting from denial of certiorari).

[38] Op. cite. GAO, February 1990.

and no recourse from the decisions made by these district attorneys to seek the death penalty. If Georgia is going to insure "a policy of eliminating racial discrimination in all its forms," as demanded by international treaty obligations and by federal and state constitutions, Georgia legislators must step forward and demand oversight of these decisions determining who will live and who will die within our justice system. The continued racially discriminatory use of the power to seek the death penalty in Georgia and in our nation presents a moral, ethical, and legal crossroad for each member of the Georgia General Assembly, as well as for each citizen in Georgia. The implementation of the Georgia Racial Justice Act would not abolish the death penalty in Georgia, but it would be the first giant step toward erasing the historically proven discrimination which exists in the manner in which death penalty cases are selected in Georgia. The citizens of Georgia should expect nothing less from their elected officials.

Capital Punishment: Helping or Hurting?

Komanduri Murty and Vandana Murty

Capital Punishment is society's self-defense.
—Ronald Reagan

Killing demeans the state, and a society that insists on killing its murderers violates the precepts that make it possible for us to live together.
—John P. Conrad

The above two quotations summarize the typical arguments made for each side of the death penalty debate. The controversy over the death penalty is an age-old social issue and has a long history of dispute between abolitionists and retentionists. Since the implementation of this punishment, there has been a contradicting situation between political leaders, state officials, and professionals including criminal justice practitioners, academicians, psychiatrists, and social workers. Political leaders and state officials try to instill confidence among the American public that capital punishment is the perfect solution to deter violent crime. While, on the other hand, clusters of professionals and concerned citizens question whether capital punishment is a just punishment, whether it serves its intended purpose, whether it is cost-effective, whether it is color-blind, and finally, whether the state has a moral right to execute the death of a human being.

There is a plethora of literature covering the various aspects of this debate and aiding both voices to be heard. (See for example, Shin (1978), van den Haag and Conrad (1983), White (1987), Aguirre and Baker (1993), Murty (1993), and Sarat (2001)) Death penalty advocates maintain that: (1) the death penalty is a social retribution and a proper punishment, (2) unless the criminals are punished by death, the criminals will be paroled, and will repeat the violent crime, (3) the death penalty incapacitates the criminal and thereby deters crime, (4) it is a cost effective correctional measure. However, statistical data and pertinent research provide evidence to the contrary.

Although capital punishment may prove no possibility of recidivism, it is flawed by the irreversibility of possible judgment error. The final verdict is not necessarily correct at all times and judicial error may result in the execution of the innocent. There have been 123 exonerees in twenty-five states since 1973. New technology such as DNA fingerprinting has led to even more supposed convicts made innocent. As Justice William J. Brennan, Jr. said, "perhaps the bleakest fact of all is that the death penalty is imposed not only in a freakish and discriminatory manner, but also in some cases upon defendants who are actually innocent." There are many cases where it has been proved that men held in prison for nearly half their lives were actually innocent and framed by circumstantial evidence. Furthermore, by the time a man is executed, he has already spent twenty to thirty years of his life in jail. The capital punishment is executed at a time where the criminal is at an age where he is unlikely to commit the crime anyway. The average age of a person on death row is 49. The oldest person to be on death row is a sixty-nine year old man. At this age, the man had already spent twenty-four years in jail. In some cases such as Stanley Tookey Williams, the accused criminal may actually be contributing to the community in the time he/she is waiting on death row. A founding member of the Los Angeles gang, Crips, Williams was sentenced to death in 1981 after killing four people. During his fourteen years on death row, Williams became an anti-gang activist. He wrote books and gave speeches advising children from backgrounds like his own not to follow his footsteps. Because of his obvious and effective evolution as a human-being and his passion to help youth that have followed a path of eventual self-destruction, Tookey was nominated by twelve prominent individuals around the world for the 2001 Nobel Peace Prize. Despite all of this, California Governor Schwarzenegger declined clemency for Williams and he was executed March 2005. This shows that the state will never forgive one for one's actions. In this particular case, Williams was one of the only men in that area who was making an effort towards re-educating children from neighborhoods similar to his. He was an effective leader because of his experiences and his ability to relate to youth. Instead of using Williams as a tool in preventing similar murders, by killing their leader, the state most likely spurred the next generation to commit more murders in rebellion.

The capital punishment also falls short in acting as retribution. Foremost, the application of the death penalty is not uniform across the nation. There are twelve states that do not even employ capital punishment and seven states that, while it is left as an available punishment, have not used it since 1976. Even the methods of execution are not uniform. There are five possible methods in the United States: hanging, firing squad, electrocution, gassing, and lethal injection. The most common mode of execution among the states is lethal injection. However, if a judge warranted, any of these five methods could be used. In summary, as of 1976, seventeen states have not utilized the death penalty; a murderer could kill someone in Minnesota and be sentenced to life in prison while another murderer could commit the same type of crime in Texas and be killed by a lethal injection or, if he committed the crime in Georgia, he may be electrocuted. This inconsistency in the method and implementation of the capital punishment makes it an unjust process. Ninety percent of those executed could not afford a defendant lawyer when standing on trial. They were given a court-appointed lawyer. Evidently this causes further incongruity in that richer killers are allowed better representation despite the heinous crime committed while poorer killers are unable to defend themselves properly merely because of their socioeconomic situation. The legal standard should be the same for every type of crime, unless there are extremely special cases of remorse and obvious repentance. By retaining these blatant discrepancies in the system, the state is making allowances for some criminals and overly punishing other criminals of the same kind.

Perhaps the largest retentionist contention is the death penalty is an effective deterrent. The underlying theory to this claim is that a potential criminal is less likely to commit a capital crime due to fear of losing life in a region where capital punishment exists. This theory assumes a person who commits a capital crime has a rational mind and outweighs the risk of losing his life over the perceived fulfillment of his motives. Thus, the deterrence theory does not account for the fact that many capital crimes are committed under the influence of alcohol, drugs, upsurge of passion, gang culture, or mental illness. Even when a man of rationality commits the capital crime, the potential criminal may be prepared to face capital punishment. The potential criminal undervalues his life because of compelling aggravation to take the potential victim's life. In either of these scenarios, the deterrence theory fails. In essence, the purpose of deterrence for which the capital punishment was originally established and promoted is defeated. Several studies over the decades have consistently proven that capital punishment has no deterrent effect on crime; in fact states that have capital punishment experience double the amount of violent crime than states without the capital punishment (Sellin (1955), Gibbs (1968), Ehrlich (1973), Bohm (1991), Collins (2000)). The death penalty only brutalizes human nature and agitates a potential criminal to commit a murder by invoking the idea, "I will not be killed more than once, let me take down as many as I can."

To add to the already lacking fear are the prolonged judicial procedures (appeal after appeal), long waiting on death rows, and painless execution. While on death row, the criminals are living in fairly posh environments. Following the discipline of "humane punishment" the state houses the criminals such that, for most, the living standards are raised when in jail. Assuming the criminal is guilty, the execution is made sure to be painless. The most commonly used method, lethal injection, causes the criminal to fade quickly into unconsciousness before causing his body functions to systematically shut down. There is no suffering to his death. To add insult to injury, before the injection, the criminal is allowed one final wish. Not only did the person against whom this criminal committed the heinous crime not have twenty to thirty years to prepare for his/her death, he/she most likely was not allowed a final wish. The most recent example of this preposterous practice is of Timothy McVeigh, the man responsible for the bombing of the Alfred P. Murrah Federal Building in Oklahoma City. McVeigh admitted to the bombing without any remorse and described the many children's lives lost as "collateral damage" to his anti-government statement. He was given two pints of mint chocolate chip ice cream as a final meal before receiving the injection. This sort of treatment could almost be described as rewarding as opposed to punishing.

The idea of cost-effectiveness among proponents of capital punishment is based on the misconception that the cost of execution is less than the cost of supporting a criminal for life in prison. However, the premise of this theory is far from practicality. It costs approximately sixty-two dollars per day to support a death row inmate as opposed to thirty-nine dollars to support a person in jail. In addition, when all costs relating to the death penalty, such as longer trials, sanity proceedings, automatic and other appeals, prolonged death row waiting, along with associated custodial costs, and other intrinsic costs are considered the cost of execution remains exponentially higher than the cost of life imprisonment. In North Carolina they spend, on average, 2.16 million dollars per death row inmate. Each injection costs nearly one hundred dollars and there are also unnecessary salaries that tax payer's money pay, such as the medical examiners that supervise the execution. On the contrary, if the criminals are subjected to life imprisonment, and are utilized in the prison workforce, the resulting revenues may offset the expenses. Prison inmates could be used for community service projects, intensive labor on behalf of the government and could also be re-socialized to be contributors to society with the same amount of money that is used in the process of their death.

In addition to these grounds, opposition to the death penalty may also be considered because of judicial discrimination. The death penalty is more frequently inflicted on the poor, the black, the male, and the ignorant than on the rich, the white, the female, and the professional killers. There have been several sociological and statistical studies performed as evidence to this fact. Before *Furman v. Georgia* (1972) the most striking ratio pattern in capital sentencing was a disproportionate number of black executions. For example, between 1930 and 1967 approximately forty-nine percent (1630 out of 3334) of those executed for murder were black. Kleck (1981) observed that the death penalty was applied discriminately against blacks in certain southern states, particularly in the early part of the century. Murty (1993) in a study sponsored by the Georgia Supreme Court Commission on Racial and Ethnic Bias in the court system reviews a total of thirty studies conducted within the southeast United States. He concludes all studies, with an exception of one, found discrimination against racial minorities in death penalty cases. Aguirre and Baker (1993) found an extremely close association between white racial prejudice and support for the death penalty. That is, white persons who discriminate against black persons are more likely to support the death penalty. Their study suggests that the majority of white persons support capital punishment because it serves as an outlet for expressing anti-black attitudes. Also, there is a strong correlation between Conservative Protestantism and support for the death penalty. Race, religion, gender, and economic status all contribute to the prejudiced application of the death penalty.

The death penalty is a primitive way of revenge and promotes hatred. The underlying message of capital punishment is that murderers always remain an excludable segment of the population and continue to be hopeless for rehabilitation and reformation of character. Moreover, by killing the killer, the state cannot adequately compensate the victim's family because the lost life will never be restored. In essence, a vicious cycle is set off; promoting the belief that killing is the only answer to killing.

State killing damages us all by weakening rather than strengthening democratic political institutions. It leaves America angrier, less compassionate, more intolerant, and more divided. As a country, we may ask, what is the political meaning of a state killing in a democracy? Does it express or frustrate popular sovereignty? Is capital punishment compatible with democratic values? In addition, we may also ask, who wins this game? When the state kills someone on behalf of the victims, is justice fully served, or has the state only orphaned another family?

References

Aguirre, Adalberto and David Baker. "Racial Prejudice and the Death Penalty" *Social Justice, A Journal of Crime, Conflict and World Order.* Vol 20, Spring-Summer, 1993.

Bohm, R. "American Death Penalty Opinion, 1936-1986: A Critical Examination of the Gallup Polls" *The Death Penalty in America: Current Research.* Cincinnati, OH: Anderson Publishing, 1991. pp. 113-145

Collins, R. "N.H. Senate OK's Death Penalty Ban" *Boston Globe.* May 19, 2000. p.B1.

Ehrlich, I. "Participation in Illegitimate Activities: A Theoretical and Empirical Investigation" *Journal of Political Economy.* May/June, 1973. pp. 521-565.

Gibbs, J.P. "Crime, Punishment, and Deterrence" *Southwestern Social Science Quarterly.* March, 1968. pp. 515-530.

Hart, H.L.A. *Punishment and Responsibility.* Oxford: Clarendon Press, 1968. p.89.

Kleck, G. "Racial Discrimination in Criminal Sentencing: A Critical Examination of Evidence with Additional Evidence on the Death Penalty" *American Sociological Review* 46: 783-805. 1981.

Murty, Komanduri S. "Racial Minorities and Courts in the Southeast United States (A Literature Review)" Atlanta, GA: Georgia Supreme Court Commission on Racial and Ethnic Bias in the Court System. October, 1993.

Sarat, Austin. *When the State Kills, Capital Punishment and the American Condition.* Princeton: Princeton University Press. 2001.

Sellin, T.T. " The Death and Police Safety" 1955, rep. in Bedau, H.A. ed., *The Death Penalty in America*. N.Y.: Doubleday, 1964.

Shin, Kilman. *Death Penalty and Crime: Empirical Studies*. Fairfax, VA: George Mason University. 1978.

van den Haag, Ernest and John Conrad. *The Death Penalty.* New York: Plenon Press. 1983.

White, Welsh. S. *The Death Penalty in the Eighties, An Examination of the Modern System of Capital Punishment.* Ann Arbor: The University of Michigan Press. 1987.

DOMESTIC VIOLENCE

Domestic Violence, Law Enforcement and African Americans

Joanne V. Rhone

Domestic violence is both a national and international crisis. UNICEF projects that twenty to fifty percent of the world will become victims of domestic violence in their violence in their lifetime.[1] Domestic violence in the U.S. was brought to public attention in the 1970's that abuse women were experiencing abuse at the hands of their intimate partners in the family. Spotlight on this issue over time revealed multiple terms to describe the phenomenon and its primary victim – "spouse abuse", "intimate partner violence", and "partner violence". These descriptors have permitted a closer examination of the nature of domestic violence, its victims, their responses and needs; the motivation of the perpetrators, and strategies needed to "stop the violence".

Domestic Violence is a pattern of assaults and controlling behavior including physical and sexual abuse, psychological attacks, and economic control that adults and adolescents (mostly males) use against their intimate partners (mostly females). These behaviors may include threats, manipulation, the using of children, and assertion of male privileges in all major family decisions. Only some of these behaviors are illegal. The most common illegal behaviors are assaults and sexual assaults.

---

[1] Sushma Kapor, Domestic Violence Against Women and Girls. UNICEF: Innocenti Research Center, June 2000.

Legal Justification: Deeply rooted in social thought, supported by law, are the rights of men over women. Historically, Roman law gave husbands' power over their wives including the power to control them by force. Both civil law and religious doctrine gave men control over their wives. Saint Paul writes in Ephesians, "Wives submit, yourselves unto your husbands to the Lord. For the husband is the head of the wife even as Christ is head of the church, and he is the savoir of the body. Therefore as the church is subject to Christ, so let the wives be to their own husbands in everything."[2] English common law, the foundation for American law, gave men the right to beat their wives as long as the weapon they used was "a rod no bigger than a thumb"[3]. The right of husbands was legally sanctioned in America as early as 1864 when a North Carolina court ruled:

> *that the state should not interfere with domestic chastisement unless "some permanent injury is inflicted or there be an excess of violence". Otherwise, the law "will not invade the domestic forum or go beyond the curtain" preferring instead to "leave the parties to themselves, as the best mode of inducing them to make the matter up and live together as man and the wife should.*[4]

The legal rights of men to control their wives by force without any sanctions created narrow gender roles that were reinforced by the structure and function of the political, economic, and educational institutions in America – a nation segregated by race. The administration of laws governing the relationship of husbands and wives reflected the social norms operative in the United States. By

---

[2] Ephesians 5:22-24.

[3] W. Blackston, Commentaries on the Law of England, 444 – 445 (facsimile of the 1st ed. Of 1764 -1769), 1979.

[4] S.E. Eisenbberg and P.L. Micklow. The Assaulted Wife "Catch 22" revised. Women's Rights Law Reporter, 3. 1977, p. 138 – 161.

1870, wife beating was made illegal in most states.[5] Yet the social norms held wives economically dependent, responsible for raising the children, and lacking the political power to change their circumstances.

Modern Trend: In the 1960's, ninety years later, James Brown's R&B tune declared once again the place of men. "This is a man's world." The song popularized the expression that a man is the king of his castle and head of the family. These declarations were challenged in the 1970's as women sought greater freedom for themselves through changes in the existing social order. Both the civil rights and women's movements addressed the racial and sexual oppression, marginalization, disfranchisement and discrimination in America. These movements were met with resistance often expressed in violence. Out of the women's movement, domestic violence emerged as a social problem. Women sought to create safe shelter for battered women, to make abuse of women socially and legally unacceptable, and to make this crime a public rather than a private matter.

The Social Problem: The scope of the problem of Domestic Violence is ever increasing in number of incidents and the breath of its impact. It occurs across all populations, irrespective of race, class, religion or culture. Young women and poor women are disproportionately affected[6]. Every nine (9) seconds a woman is physically abused. Approximately 5.3 million intimate partner violent incidents occur each year among women ages 18 and older. Women compromise fifty-two percent of the population in the United States and nearly one-third (31%) of them report being physically or sexually abused by a husband or boyfriend in their lives. Nearly 25% of women have been raped and/or physically assaulted by an intimate

---

[5] E. Pleck, Domestic Tyranny: The making of social policy against family violence: colonial times to the present. New York: Oxford University, 1987.

[6] Heise, L. & Garcia-Moreno, C. "violence by Intimate Partners. World Report on Violence and Health: Genre: World Organization.

partner and more than 40% of these women who experienced rape and physically assaults sustained a physical injury[7]. Thirty percent of the women killed in the U.S. die at the hands of a husband or boyfriend. Women who kill their abuser do so at an extremely lower rate than men who commit 85% of all homicide[8]. Women who kill abusers have a higher conviction rate than men and receive from 7 to 9 more years in prison than do men who kill their intimate partner. Women who report being raped and/or physically assaulted since the age of 18, three quarters (76%) were victimized by a current or former husband, cohabitating partner, date or boyfriend. Violence by an intimate partner accounts for about 21% of violent crimes experienced by men[9]. In 92% of all domestic violence incidences/ crimes are committed by men against women. Women separated from their spouse had a victimization rate 1 ½ times higher than separated men, divorced men, or divorced women[10].

In addition to domestic violence among adults, increasing numbers of teenage girls are experiencing intimate partner violence. Forty percent of teenage girls, age 14 to 17, report knowing someone their age that has been hit or beaten by a boyfriend[11]. Adolescents with abusive partners report increased levels of depressed moods, substance abuse, antisocial behavior, and in females, suicidal behavior[12]. Sixty-seven percent of all victims of sexual assaults reported to law enforcement agencies were juveniles under the

---

[7] Tjoden, P. & Thoennes, N. Report of the prevalence, incidence and consequences of violence against women: Findings from the National Violence Against Women Survey. Washington, D.C.: U.S. Department of Justice, 2000b. Publication No. NCJ18337.

[8] Violence by Intimates: Analysis of Data of Crime by Current or Former Spouses, Boyfriends and Girlfriends, U.S. Department of Justice, 1994.

[9] Ibid.

[10] Sex Difference in Violent Victimization, 1944 U.S. Department of Justice, 1997.

[11] Now/Kaiser Permanente Poll, December 1995.

[12] Roberts, T.A., Klein, J.D., and Fisher, S. Longitudinal effect of intimate partner abuse on high-risk behavior among adolescents. Archives of Pediatrics & Adolescent Medicine. 2003; 157(9): 875-81.

age of 18, and 34% of all victims were under the age of 12[13] . One in five female high school students report being physically or sexually abused by a dating partner[14] .

The breath of domestic violence has expanded from the home to school and to the work place. Husbands and boyfriends commit 13,000 acts of violence against women in the workplace every year. It is estimated that family violence cost the nation from $5 to $10 billion annually in medical expenses, police and court cost, shelters and foster care, sick leave, absenteeism, and non-productivity. Victims of intimate partner violence, whether in the workplace, home or school, report lasting health problems ranging from chronic pain, STD's, hysterectomies, and mental health problems[15] .

Acts of domestic violence most often occur out of the public's view. It is in the home where children witness these assaults on their mothers by their fathers or male figures in the home. Children's exposure to battering in the home is the strongest risk factor for transmitting violent behavior from one generation to the next[16] . Studies show that child abuse occurs in 30 – 60% of family violence cases that involve families with children[17] .

Impact: Violence between intimate partners has short and long-term psychological effects on women, men, children and the community. Children who witness domestic violence are at great risk of developing psychiatric and developmental problems, school failure, violence against others, low self-esteem, and are at-risk of modeling the batterer's behavior in their adolescence and adulthood[18] .

---

[13] Rennison, C. Intimate Partner Violence, Special Report 1993 – 2000. Washington, D.C.: Bureau of Justice Statistics, U.S. Department of Justice; 2000. Publication no. NCJ 178247.

[14] Massachusetts Youth Risk Behavior Survey (YRBS), August 2001.

[15] Roberts, Klien & Fisher, op, cit.

[16] American Psychological Association. Presidential Task Force on Violence and the Family, APA, 1996.

[17] Edleson, J.L. "The overlap between child maltreatment and women battering". Violence Against Women, February, 1999.

[18] Roberts, Klien & Fisher, Op. cit.

Women who experience intimate partner violence conceal their experience until the need for medical service or act to seek safety. Women's opportunities for personal development, and work experience are blocked by their partners, through physical force, psychological intimidations, and isolation. The solution most offered is for women to leave their abusers; however their lack of resources and sense of self-efficiency are strong barriers to leaving.

Men who batter as a means of maintaining power and control commit the crime of assault and battery. They face arrest, prosecution, fines, and incarceration that interrupt their lives – work, school, and freedom as well as forced separation from the family.

The community and society experience the loss of tranquility in the family and the economic benefits from the human resources of both batterer and victim. The cost of incarceration and injury deprives the community of financial resources for positive development of its members.

Law Enforcement: In recent years, the criminal justice system has intensified its social control role through increased incarceration, probation and parole. Studies show that since 1980, less that 15% of the U.S. prisoners are detained for violent offenses[19]. The increase in prison population (approximately 1.5 million) is due to harsh criminal justice policies rather than rising violent crimes. The criminal justice policies calling for mandatory sentencing for illicit drug sales and use; "three strikes and you are jailed for nearly life"; privatization of prison, victim restitution; and prison labor utilization have placed a heavy burden on the African-American community. These recent policies have increased states level of spending by 30% in the criminal justice system[20]. Georgia's state budget for prisons over the past ten years has grown from 400 million to 1 billion annually while spending on higher education

---

[19] Dominguer, S.R. "The Prison-Industrial Complex: What's really driving the rush to Lock "Em Up". The Washington Post, March 17, 1996.
[20] Justice Policy Institute. Report entitled From Classroom to Cellblocks: A National Perspective, 1995.

has decreased. These policy changes supported by increase funding of the criminal justice system suggests that the U.S. is building a powerful engine for "justice" that narrows the "pursuit of happiness" for those caught in its net.

The current state of relationships between African Americans and the criminal justice system parallels to what W.E.B. Du Bois described in 1904, 100 years ago. Du Bois identified several causes of crime among Negroes (African Americans): prejudice that limit the opportunities of the Negro; less legal protection of Negroes; laws that are drawn to ensnare ignorant, unfortunate an careless Negroes; courts that administer one type of justice for whites and another for Negroes; punishment that does not distinguish the young Negro from the old or the male from the female; and punishment that breeds crime rather than halt it[21].

Du Bois's observation 100 years ago still remains as current reality exemplified by today's policies and practices of the criminal justice system and the effect on African Americans. There is a continual distrust of the police, the most visible agent of the criminal justice system. They do not symbolize "protection" in the African-American community. Recent high profile cases such as O.J. Simpson and Rodney King confirm this perception and have widened the gap between the system and the African-American community.

Domestic Violence law enforcement policies and practices have undergone considerable changes over the last decade. Advocates to "Stop Domestic Violence" focused their attention on police response to domestic calls, and the "male dominated" system's failure to exercise its comprehensive authority. Advocates strategies targeted the development of a national uniform protocol to insure implementation of the law and practices to reduce domestic violence homicides[22]. Arrest, prosecution, and child custody issues were identified as key issues in law enforcement and domestic violence.

---

[21] Dubois, W.E.B. Some Notes on Negro Crime. Proceedings of the Ninth Conference for the Study of the Negro Problem, held in 1904 and sponsored by Atlanta University. Atlanta: Atlanta University Press.

[22] Rennison, C. Op. cit.

Under the existing law, domestic violence is a crime against the state, rather than a personal dispute. Many prosecutors have a "no drop" policy that allows them to proceed even if the victim wishes to drop the charges. Prosecution is usually deferred for first time misdemeanor cases, provided the offender agrees to complete a specialized treatment program. There is evidence that a combination of arrest and treatment are effective in reducing recidivism for domestic violence. The verdict on the effectiveness of treatment is still out[23].

The biases in the culture of law enforcement are reflected in the day-to-day practices of mishandling cases of violence against women; violation of defendant's rights especially defendants of color, and failure to address sexist/racial/ethnic biases within the criminal justice system. Additionally, this system fails to address the problem of battering among its own police officers. Most officers are not arrested, denied use of a gun, suspended or fired. Some are mandated to counseling.

The system addresses the issues of protection of victims of domestic violence through the issuance of restraining orders. Restraining orders have become more streamline over past five years. The failure of the perpetrators to comply with restraining orders is more likely to carry criminal penalties rather than civil penalties. Women who obtain a restraining order must keep it on their person at all times. This order does not provide guaranteed protection for women with a history of severe offenses by an intimate partner. Under such circumstances both women and children are in danger particularly if the female is separated from the batterer.

Law enforcement of domestic violence crimes in the African-American community has shown three patterns: (1) arrest and incarceration; (2) differential treatment according to education and employment status at the time of arrest[24]; and (3) differential

---

[23] Domestic Violence Institute. Community Insights on Domestic Violence Among African-Americans: St. Paul Min.: University of Minnesota, 1998.

[24] Hindelang, M. "Race and Involvement in Common Law Personal crimes: American Sociological Review (43): 93-109, 1978.

treatment of African-American males and females. These differential approaches to law enforcement are explained as individual officer's racial and sexist biases, and the system's lack of options due to the absence of culturally specific services in the African-American community[25].

Funding for law enforcement programs, through the Violence Against Women's Act 2000, targets service for batterer to include mandated counseling from six months to a year along with monitoring of batterers' progress. The focus of counseling emphasizes the batterer's accepting responsibility for the violence and responsibility for stopping it. These programs exclude substance abusers and severe batterers' as they are less likely to benefit. Unfortunately many African-American male batterers are often denied this alternative to incarceration due to substance abuse and prior arrest history.

Legislation on domestic violence crimes, provides for only assault behavior. However, the cultural contexts of violence – patriarchal, capitalism, sexism and racial oppression are virtually ignored.

Historically, the social control of African Americans is embedded in law as demonstrated through slavery and the Jim Crow era. Social controls today are camouflaged in social policies (i.e. mandatory sentencing, welfare reform, no student loans with a felony record) that adversely affect the African-American family and community. The changing constellation of family formation and values have been noted as causes of many of the nations "social problems" – youth violence, premarital births, abortions, school failures, increased single parent households and interpersonal violence[26]. Scientific evidence of the relationship between the social problems and changing family formation has not been presented. Empirical evidence has focused on identifying factors contributing

---

[25] Domestic Violence Institute. Op. cit.
[26] Tucker, M.B., and Mitchell-Kernan, C. (Eds.) (19956). The decline in marriage among African-Americans: Census, Consequences, and Policy implications. NY: Russel Sage Foundation, 19956.

to changes in family formation and consequence within a white male dominated society.

In the U.S., the timing of family formation, types of family formations, and living arrangements have undergone dramatic changes over the last 30 years. American's marry later, get divorced, remarry, cohabitate, and increasingly live as singles. The changes in family formation and living arrangements among African Americans have been substantial between 1970 and 1990. The proportion of early marriages declined by 50% and divorce rate far exceeded that of the overall population, 358 per 1000 among African Americans compared to 166 per 1000 of the general population. After divorce African-American women are less likely to remarry[27].

There is strong evidence that African Americans value marriage as a foundation for family life. They believe, however that adequate income is critical to successful marriage. The declining economic viability of African-American men due to high rates of incarceration are key factors that influence family formation among African Americans[28].

Changes in the African-American family mirror changes in its community and vice versa. The deterioration of sub segments the African-American community through drug sales, high unemployment rates, decrease in educational achievement, unsafe housing conditions, and an increase in the number of children in foster care are powerful negative and regressive forces that erodes a sense of personal and collective power. Intimate personal violence becomes an extension of community violence that robs children of a sense of safety and security – the foundation for positive growth and development. According to McGhee, the most salient characteristic of the black family today is the absence of the black male as a family member[29]. Incarceration, homicide, unemployment

---

[27] U.S. Bureau of the Census. (1991b.) <u>Statistical Abstract of the United States</u>: 1991, (111th ed.). Washington, DC: U.S. Government Printing Office.

[28] Wilson, W.J. <u>The truly disadvantaged</u>. Chicago: The University of Chicago Press, 1987. Darity W., Myers, S.L. "Public Policy trends and the fate of the Black Family". Humboldt Journal of Social Relations, 14, 134-164 (1986/87).

[29] McGhee, James D. Running the Gauntlet: Black men in America. National Urban League Research Department. (Washington, DC) 1984.

and accidents are key factors in male absence from African-American families. In America, a man's worth is determined by his ability earn money. Long term unemployment and underemployment are pervasive in low-income areas of the African-American community. These conditions have devastating effects on the males' opinion of himself and others' opinions of him. The frustration, anger, and stress associated with "failure" and denial of a second, third, fourth, and even a fifth chance creates a sense of hopelessness, a life without purpose, and a lack of love from the community and family.

Domestic violence in the African-American community is one area of violence that has not received the selective attention needed to begin the tasks of healing the wounds of physical, psychological, social, economic and political assaults. Attention, reform, and multiple strategies are needed: (1) to redirect societal thinking about the fundamental causes of domestic violence; (2) to promote enlightened policies and practices in a criminal justice system that do not provide "justice for all", and (3) to launch a national strategy to rebuild the weakened and broken segments of the African-American community and family. These strategies must focus on violence toward the African-American community as well as violence within it. The "Talented 10th" must be the drum majors in this effort. Historically Black Colleges and Universities must lead this effort through research. They must counteract the stereotypical views of African Americans, especially African-American children. African-American males and females must recommit themselves to each other in order to rebuild the foundation of the community-the family. Religious institutions and public organizations serving predominately African Americans must teach dignity and self-respect, self-worth, love of self and others, and gender equality. This task is urgent and conversations about this matter must occur everyday.

COMMUNITY POLICING

Community Policing in the African-American Community: A Perspective by Chief Thetus A. Knox

Chief Thetus A. Knox

Introduction: The concept of *Community Policing* has varied connotations among scholars as well as criminal justice professionals. Friedmann defined this concept as.

"Community Policing is a policy and a strategy aimed at achieving more effective and efficient crime control, reduced fear of crime, improved quality of life, improved police services and police legitimacy, through a proactive reliance on community resources that seeks to change crime causing conditions. This assumes a need for greater accountability of police, greater public share in decision making, and greater concern for civil rights and liberties."[1]

Community Policing is a cornerstone to successful law enforcement in general, and with the African-American community in particular. This segment of our population stands to reap more of the benefits of Community Policing than most other, as African Americans have historically had a very acrimonious relationship with the police.

This paper emphasizes the importance of employing the philosophy of Community Policing, particularly in the African-

---

[1] Friedmann, R.R., "Community Policing: Some Conceptual and Practical Considerations", *Home Affairs Review,* 1996 Volume XXXIV (6) p 115.

American community. Examples of this philosophy in utilization along with their associated successes are explained. The successful implementation of Community Policing in African-American neighborhoods creates a more harmonious relationship between the police and such communities. This increases mutual cooperation and exchanges of information.

Implementation: As all other cultures, African Americans have unique social customs, mores, and traditions. The challenge for the police executives that serve an African-American community is to recognize this fact, and to it to their advantage.

The City of Atlanta's Police Department is a proponent of the Community Policing philosophy. I served as commander of the Atlanta Police Department's Zone Four precinct that covered 80,000 residents (of which 81% are African-American) for a decade. During this period, I realized that officers must be proactive in order for this philosophy to be successful. In other words, officers must engage the community they serve, and in doing so, shall make a conscientious effort to determine the community's needs.

The commander at his/her level should make a concerted effort to identify those officers that have a natural ability to engage the community. The primary thrust of Community Policing, particularly in the African-American community involves this engagement. The late criminologist, Dr. Trojanowicz referred to the police cruiser as "the metal cocoon."[2]

Police officers are usually trained to aggressively patrol the streets. This is a sound deployment tactic, and one that is crucial to the basic operation of any police agency. However, officers cannot fully attain information relative to their respective patrol areas if they do not engage the community by leaving the patrol vehicle.

As commander of the Zone Four precinct, my officers were required to make at least three personal contacts with citizens per day. Emphasis was placed upon visiting merchants and residents.

---

[2] Trojanowicz, R.C., "Community Policing Guidelines for Police Chiefs *Community Policing Pages,* 2005 Edition Volume 10, (1) p 3.

These contacts were invaluable in forging the relationships with the community that prove ever so crucial in combating crime.

I found that a common complaint that many residents initially had was that they hardly ever saw the police. One strategy I employed was to have an officer to devote his time exclusively to citizen contacts. The officer would respond to emergency calls just as the other officers, but his primary function was to cultivate relationships between the police and the citizens of Zone Four. This strategy proved successful, as the officer was lauded for his diligence. We seldom received similar complaints again within this area.

African Americans, in general, have experienced many unpleasant episodes with law enforcement officers, resulting in their negative image of police. Such an image constitutes the challenge as well as the need to adopt this philosophy within the African-American community.

A conscientious attempt to break the barriers that exist between African Americans and police needs to take place before the Community Policing philosophy may become successful. An officer, for instance that drops by a little league baseball game is greeted all too often with, "Officer, is there something wrong?" The wise and perceptive officer would respond to such a question with, "No, I just dropped by to enjoy the game."

Police executives should bear in mind that Community Policing initiatives are limited only by their imagination. African Americans are afflicted with a variety of social ills, as are all races, to include poverty, unemployment, alcoholism, and illicit drug usage. Efforts to assist people cope and solve the problems they face daily can be addressed through Community Policing.

During my term as commander of the Zone Four precinct, my officers presided over several initiatives that proved successful. These efforts were targeted towards African-American youth, elderly, merchants, and residents. The initiatives undertaken contributed to a significant reduction in overall crime rates.

Initiatives: As a commander in Southwest Atlanta, I initiated the Southwest Atlanta Teen Anti-Violence Program. This program was implemented in September of 1994 for the purpose of offering proactive programs to prevent violent behavior through early intervention, education, and parental involvement.

The Apartment Managers' Initiative was developed in 1995. Its purpose was to enhance the relationship between police and apartment managers in and around apartment complexes. Typically, undesirable tenants, criminals, and opportunists continuously move from one complex to another, committing various acts of crime. This open line of communication provided the opportunity to create safer communities for Southwest Atlanta residents.

The Citizen's Advisory Council was formed to address issues related to the delivery of police services. The council was comprised of individuals from various community organizations committed to improving the quality of life for the community at large. The partnership of the department and the council served as a linking mechanism in strengthening the community oriented policing concept.

The West End Strategic Planning Group was formulated in 1998 with the assistance of other city and state agencies, to include the Fulton County District Attorney's Office. Public safety concerns for business owners and citizens of the West End area were addressed.

I was selected as the Chief of Police for the City of Riverdale, Ga. in October of 2004. Riverdale has incorporated the concepts of Community Policing by collaborating with citizens to address specific issues within their communities. Projects are consequently developed and implemented under the auspices of the 'collaborative' to effectively impact the identified issues. The City of Riverdale is over 50 percent African-American. The following projects are currently in operation:

- The Neighborhood Watch is a partnership between the police and residents to proactively address issues on the neighborhood level. Specific emphasis is placed upon the prevention of burglaries, larcenies, and the identification of suspicious persons.

- Officers are required to conduct Park and Walks, requiring the officer to exit the police vehicle and meet with persons within the confines of their assigned areas. This patrol tactic allows residents and business owners to become acquainted with officers when they would not otherwise have.

When I was appointed as Chief of the Riverdale Police Department, residents in the African-American community welcomed my commitment to implement the Community Policing philosophy. I reaffirmed this commitment by selecting proven and capable former Atlanta police executives who incorporated these initiatives into my officers' training.

Traditionally, the effectiveness of an agency was measured in terms of number of arrests made, number of citations issued, and by other technical matters. I strongly disagree with these measures as advocates of proactive policies and strategies.

The criminal justice system is overwhelmed with those who are on parole, probation, or are currently serving prison sentences. The majority of these persons (over 50 percent) are African-American, while they constitute only 12 percent of the American population.

While the Community Policing philosophy and its successful adoption is popular with most police agencies, there are some who resist it. The obvious and most important way to reinforce the commitment to Community Policing includes changing hiring and training practices, performance reviews, and promotion policies to reflect a serious commitment to Community Policing. Many departments have also found it useful to initiate formal and informal recognition and awards programs that reinforce the values of Community Policing. Police chiefs should also remember the benefit of spontaneous letters of commendation as an effective way of getting the message across.[3]

---

[3] Trojanowicz, R.C., *Ibid.*

While serving as commander of Zone Four in Atlanta, I saluted officers on a yearly basis that employed those practices inherent in a successful Community Policing initiative. Members of Zone Four's business community also lauded the efforts of these officers.

Acquiring Support: Community Policing in the African-American community poses unique challenges. Many African Americans are very cynical of the police making any attempt to forge relationships that formerly did not exist. A statement made by the recently apprehended Brian Nichols, the suspect accused of a murderous rampage in downtown Atlanta on March 11, 2005 provided a stark account of what many African Americans feel about the American criminal justice system.

Accordingly, Nichols' interview with local, state, and federal officials revealed that the three persons he initially murdered were symbolic of this system's inequities.[4] While the accused allegedly committed very heinous and reprehensible crimes, there are many within the African-American community that understand his reasoning; though they do not agree with his method of addressing the issue. One of the key ingredients in a successful Community Policing initiative is the cooperation of the community at large. Barriers separating the community from the system must be eradicated in order to accomplishing this task.

Ironically, while the African-American community has resisted contact and association with the police, African Americans suffer greatest from the lack of effective police response. My officers initiated the "One Street Back at a Time" initiative. This initiative was a collaborative effort between officers, citizens, local, and county entities. The premise was that if these entities worked intensely in a small geographic location, the problems afflicting this area could be eliminated. Thus, the "one street at a time" concept proved successful.

Police executives should be mindful that when implementing Community Policing in the African-American community, emphasis

---

[4] Warren, B., "Revenge On System Cited As Motive For Rampage." *Atlanta Journal Constitution,* 15 March 2005, p A-1.

should be placed upon the fact that the effort is collaborative. While the police are an integral part of this philosophy, they should not spearhead all of the efforts involved. As a solution, the Citizen's Advisory Council was created.

The council comprised of the residents of Zone Four. Like many of the other initiatives, the council met on a quarterly basis. By design, the chairperson of the council was always a citizen within the community. The purpose was to involve the community, and in doing so, to force the community to take ownership of the issues they faced.

Police executives should be mindful that the Community Policing effort should include the participation and support of average citizens, and not just community leaders. Unlike community relations programs, Community Policing is a grass-roots effort that allows the police to build bridges of trust with everyone in the community. The input of the mother receiving public assistance should be considered just as seriously as that of the self-appointed community spokesperson. It is also important that the self-appointed community leaders do not block the participation of the average citizens.[5] I made myself available to the council, and served as a facilitator when issues were discussed at the quarterly meetings. The council was assured that the police department would support their initiatives, but was mainly just a cog in the wheel.

Conclusion: The benefits of employing the Community Policing philosophy are immense, particularly in the African-American community. Modern police executives would be wise to embrace this philosophy, as it has demonstrated remarkable success in many agencies across the nation. The successes that the Zone Four officers derived from employing this philosophy should serve as a model for those with inquiries.

The Riverdale Police Department has a three pronged approach to fighting crime. These are as follows: Aggressive Enforcement, Information Sharing, and Community Involvement.

---

[5] Trojanowicz, R.C., *Ibid.*

Aggressive Enforcement is the cornerstone to any successful police operation. Criminals need to actually *fear* the prospect of being apprehended by police, and the justice meted forth in subsequent proceedings.

Information Sharing is crucial. The teamwork and collaborative effort demonstrated by local, state, and federal officials on March 11, 2005 in Metropolitan Atlanta was remarkable. However, this interagency cooperation and information sharing among other agencies should occur on a daily basis for effective police operations.

Community Involvement, though mentioned lastly in the three-pronged approach, is nevertheless just as, if not more important than the others. Community Involvement effectively is the cornerstone for a successful Community Policing program. This is evident in its successful implementation in the African-American community.

Successful Community Policing Strategies within the Atlanta Police Department

Alan J. Dreher

Introduction: As a law enforcement professional for the past twenty-six years I have observed first hand the vital role the community plays in law enforcement. Officers, investigators and police executives through their interaction with citizens, community leaders, and local business owners have helped reduce crime in the city of Atlanta by 23 % over the past three years. To continue this decline it is imperative that we have community support.

"Community Policing" as a philosophy has been around since the mid 90's but having walked a foot beat in Washington, DC in 1980, I like many other law enforcement veterans was Community Policing long before that. Having walked that foot beat, I know how important it is that we train our officers to get to know the citizens and business owners on their beat. Chief Pennington and I hold our commanders accountable for ensuring that officers know how to patrol. They are instructed to drive slowly, windows down, radios off, no cell phones and to pay close attention to what is happening around them. Foot beat officers are instructed not only to patrol but to educate citizens on how not to become victims.

Jean-Paul Brodeur in his book, *How to Recognize Good Policing,* defines communities as "collections of people who are tied to particular places, who share common concerns, and who have available to them common lifestyles" (Brodeur 1998, 133). The city of Atlanta has numerous communities, representative of many ethnic backgrounds, all of which share the same common goal of a safer crime free neighborhood. The term "Community Policing" has many definitions, but appears to be supported by a common set of guiding principles, three of which are; a focus on problem solving and prevention, recognizing that the "community" however defined plays a critical role in solving neighborhood problems, and recognition that police organizations must be restructured and reorganized to be responsive to the demands of this new approach (Brodeur 1998, 7).

Community Policing Principles

Problem Solving: In September 2003 over 120 City of Atlanta residents were interviewed in focus groups. The interviews were conducted by Linder & Associates as a part of the plan of action for rebuilding the police department. The citizens interviewed were from all six police zones and were representative of the race makeup of those neighborhoods. An additional 803-person random sample telephone survey was conducted in November of that same year. The survey approximated the demographics of the City of Atlanta for both race and gender within the margin of error. Three of the major problems perceived by citizens were panhandling 65% drug dealing 70.3% and slow emergency response time (Linder 2004, 88- 90). To respond to these as well as other citizen complaints Chief Pennington and I increased the number of discretionary units working in each zone.

Discretionary units known primarily as Strike, FIT (Field Intelligence Teams) and Impact teams work in groups of 4-6 officers and focus specifically on problems relevant to that zone. In Zones 3 and 4 (Southwest Atlanta) for example, discretionary units concentrate on open-air narcotics sales, pedestrian robberies and auto thefts. Zone 5 (downtown) units are instructed to focus on panhandling, pedestrian robberies, larcenies from auto and auto theft. Because they do not respond to 911 calls discretionary units are also available to respond to emergency situations such as shots fired, burglary in progress, and domestic violence calls.

The department has benefited from the implementation of these teams in that they have played a significant role in our 23% crime reduction. Enforcing quality of life ordinances and targeting open-air narcotics dealers has taken suspects off the street before they could commit more serious offenses. Because of this, Homicides, aggravated assaults and pedestrian robberies have shown a decrease of 14% 24% and 20% respectively.

Community Involvement: Although placing additional personnel in the zones has helped, law enforcement officers alone cannot be expected to resolve the crime problems that communities face. Even the most conscientious beat officer is not as aware of the crimes being committed on his beat, as are the citizens who live there. They know who lives in their community and who does not, what houses are taking in stolen property, and who is responsible for bringing drugs into the neighborhood. To ensure that citizens play an active role in Community Policing, officers and supervisors must advise them of what they can do. Herman Goldstein offers these suggestions in his article, "What Can the Community Do? (Goldsten 1990, 126).

An informed, organized, and involved community can work with police to identify, analyze, and implement solutions to community problems. They can do this by mobilizing their members to share information with police and by partnering with neighborhood-based organizations, such as churches, schools and private businesses to combat crime and recruit volunteers for community-based programs. Two other strategies, denying criminals access to space and monitoring court actions allow citizens to become involved in the criminal justice process. Neighborhood organizations can also encourage prosecutors to develop drug courts, community courts and alternative sentencing programs (Goldstein 1990, 126). Community prosecutors, also play a vital role in tracking and prosecuting violent offenders in Atlanta. They meet regularly with citizens groups and are instrumental in garnering support from citizens at preliminary and sentencing hearings.

Reorganization and Restructuring: The Atlanta Police Department has undergone a major reorganization to bring focus and accountability to crime reduction efforts. Three of the changes, decentralization of the criminal investigation division, consolidation of Narcotics (FOD based and CID based) Units, and centralization of the Crime Prevention Inspectors have lead to a decrease in investigatory response times and a renewed focus on crime prevention.

By decentralizing the Criminal Investigation Division we have enhanced investigative effectiveness and efficiency and made investigators more accessible to citizens. Prior to decentralization, all CID units were housed in police headquarters, and were assigned to specific units. Investigators now work out of zone precincts and are cross-trained to investigate multiple crimes.

Another change made in response to the Linder Survey was the combining of Narcotics, and Red Dog Units. Prior to 2003, The Red Dog Unit, Atlanta's street level narcotics enforcement unit was assigned to the Field Operations Division and narcotics investigators were assigned to the Criminal Investigations Division. By combining the two units as part of the Special Enforcement Section, Red Dog Units can focus primarily on citizen complaints concerning outside narcotics enforcement and investigators can focus on undercover investigations.

Centralization of the Crime Prevention Inspections Unit under one director has lead to a more focused approach citywide and a renewed interest in crime prevention. In addition to organizing community meetings, implementing neighborhood watch programs, and participating in crime prevention seminars, CPI's (Crime Prevention Inspectors) are working with officers and investigators to reduce Part I Crimes. They advise citizens not to leave their car running with the keys in it, provide identity theft victim's information on how to check their credit history, and instruct business owners on the best methods of target hardening.

Conclusion: Dr. Cheurprakobkit, Chief Knox and I all agree that Community Policing strategies are needed to enhance the quality of police services and effectiveness. Dr. Cheurprakobkit, through his research has shown that overall communities support law enforcement, however, discrepancies exist in how different ethnic groups, including African Americans view police. Chief Knox reiterates this point in her paper entitled, "Community Policing in the African-American Community: A Perspective by Chief Thetus A. Knox" (2005).

Chief Knox's paper, based on her 32 years of law enforcement experience, her tenure as commander of Zone 4 and her current position as the first female, African-American Chief of Riverdale have allowed her to observe first hand how African-American citizens view law enforcement and what changes can and should be made to foster a better relationship. She reminds police executives that they "should be mindful that the Community Policing effort should include participation and support of average citizens, and not just Community leaders. The input of the mother receiving public assistance should be considered just as the self-appointed community spokesperson" (Knox 2005, 8).

Dr. Cheurprakobkit, through his research revealed several factors that effect citizens' attitudes towards police. These include but are not limited to neighborhood characteristics and interactions with police, past experience with the police, and race. Data for his study was obtained from citizens living in Marietta Georgia and was based on their interaction with police during traffic stops or in response to incident reports taken by officers (Cheurprakobkit 2005, 1). His data like that taken by Linder & Associates showed a noticeable difference between black and white respondents. The Linder survey, for example showed that 51.5% of African Americans believe that crime has increased over the last several years as opposed to 31.4% of whites (Linder 2004, 88). Dr. Cheurprakobkit's research showed that white respondents 84%, more than black respondents 65%, reported positive experiences with police (Cheurprakobkit 2005, 5).

Although there is still work to be done as it relates to community perception I believe overall community support has increased. The crime reduction the city has experienced over the past three years has been a collaborative effort, future reductions will be also. Crime reduction is only one benefit of Community Policing; the other is community support.

On April 29, 2005, the Atlanta Police Department laid to rest Red Dog Officer Mark Anthony Cross. Officer Cross had been killed on a traffic stop, leaving behind a wife and two small children. He was a well-liked, well-respected officer who did his job well and made a difference. There was as there always is an outpouring of community support. Citizens sitting on their cars watched as the motorcade made its way to the church and children staying at a nearby daycare waved as police cars passed by. The church was filled to capacity, and I am of the opinion that many of those in attendance did not know Officer Cross, they came to show their support to his family and his department. This was evident as I left the church and drove by a group of citizens standing on the corner holding a handwritten sign. It simply read, *"Thanks APD, We appreciate all you do."*

References

Brodeur, J., *How to Recognize Good Policing; Problems and Issues.* California: Sage Publications Incorporated, 1998.

Cheurprakobkit, Sutham, "The Impact of Race, Police Experience, and Feeling of Safety on Attitudes Toward the Police" 2005.

Goldstein, Herman. *Problem-Oriented Policing.* New York: McGraw-Hill, 1990.

Fragile Momentum, *Plan of Action for Rebuilding the Atlanta Police Department to Help Secure Atlanta's Position as Capital of the New South* (Linder & Associates, 2004).

Knox, Thetus, "Community Policing in the African-American Community: A Perspective by Chief Thetus A. Knox," 2005.

IMPACT OF INCARCERATION, IMPRISONMENT, AND POLICE CONTACT

The Effects of Crime and Imprisonment on Family Formation

Obie Clayton[1] and Joan Moore

Introduction: The nearly universal perspective of marriage as an indispensable social institution has been changing significantly in recent decades. Besharov and West present evidence that shows that over the "past fifty years, for all Americans, marriage rates have declined while divorce rates and out-of-wedlock births have climbed. Negative changes have been greatest among African Americans."[2] In 1998, approximately 29% of African-American women aged fifteen and over were married compared to 55% of white women.[3] Between 1998 and 2002, the percentage of married African-American women had increased slightly to 31%. During this period, a higher percentage of African-American men were married than African-American females, but a higher percentage were also never married. Findings indicate that between 1975 and 2002, the proportion of African-American women who were married declined from approximately 55% to about 41%.

---

[1] I would like to thank my research assistant, Brandeis Malbrue for her assistance and the Vera Institute of Justice for allowing us to use parts of Dr. Moore's prior research.
[2] Besharov, D.J. and A. West, "African-American Marriage Patterns," in *Beyond the Color Line: New Perspectives on Race and Ethnicity in America* A. Thernstrom and S. Thernstrom (Eds.). (Stanford, CA: Hoover Institution Press, 2002), p 95.
[3] Besharov, D.J. and A. West, *Ibid.*

When attention is focused on never married women, we see that: "between 1950 and 1998, the percentage of never married white women aged fifteen and over rose from 20% to 22%, a 2% rise. But the percentage of never married African-American women nearly doubled, from 21% to 41%."[4] Recent census figures place the number of never married African-American women at 42%.

When one takes divorce into consideration, the preceding figures are even more startling. In 1990 there were 358 divorces for every 1000 African-American women compared to 166 for white women.[5] African-American women are less likely to remarry after a divorce, meaning that African-American children of divorcees are more likely to spend a substantial portion of their lives in single-parent households. Social science evidence suggests that children who live in female-householder families are much more likely to live in poverty as compared to children in married family households.[6] African-American female-headed families experience higher poverty rates than any other type of family.

The preceding trends seem to suggest that marriage has evolved to be seen less as a way of life meant to guide intimacy and define commitments, especially to children. Instead it is now perceived more as a vehicle for fulfilling the psychological needs of adults.[7] Many societal events have promoted individualism more than obligation to the familial unit. This has led to a change from the norm that once taught men and women a sense of responsibility to the family and their children.[8] There is an increase in women having or adopting children out of wedlock. With the increased availability

---

[4] Besharov, D.J. and A. West, *Ibid.* p 96.

[5] Tucker, B.M. and C. Mitchell-Kernan, eds, *The Decline in Marriage Among African-Americans* (New York: Russell Sage Foundation, 1995).

[6] U.S. Bureau of the Census. *Marriage*, "Divorce and Remarriage in the 1990's," *Current Population Reports*, 180 (1992): 23 Washington, DC: U.S. Government Printing Office.

[7] Popenoe, D, *Life without Father: Compelling New Evidence that Fatherhood and Marriage are Indispensable for the Good of Children and Society.* (New York: The Free Press, 1996).

[8] Gallagher, M, *Abolition of Marriage: How We Destroy Lasting Love.* (Washington DC: Regnery Publication, Inc, 2003).

of birth control and abortion and the decline in the practice of forced ("shotgun") marriages, sexual behavior is no longer inextricably linked to childbearing and marriage.

Nock[9] argues that many of the problems affecting today's marriages are the result of "institutional change rather than moral decline." Nock states that with more and more women entering the paid labor market, the convention of marriage must, by necessity, change. He contends that the male's role as breadwinner has been weakened and, at the same time, there has been more dependency on the female's ability to contribute to the family's income. This pooling of resources and female entry into the labor market has characterized African-American families for hundreds of years. However, it may no longer be a goal among males to become the primary provider. Therefore, when we speak of African-American families, it becomes a central concern to define "family" contextually and to identify those institutional factors, which encourage marriage and shape families.

Marriage and marriage rates are affected by many social, economic and demographic variables; for instance, demographers place a great deal of emphasis on sex ratios and look for imbalances. Sociologists and economists argue that marriage is more than a mathematical model and is affected by factors such as employment, education, earnings, uncertain job prospects, military service, imprisonment, and other related reasons.[10] However, all social scientists will agree that some individuals are more marriageable than others and certain variables have more explanatory power than others. In our opinion, incarceration has not been given nearly enough attention in the literature as a key factor in the decline in

---

[9] Nock, M.K, "Progress Review of the Psychosocial Treatment of Child Conduct Problems." *Clinical Psychology: Science and Practice, 10.* Pgs. 1-28. (2003) p 40.
[10] Reynolds, F and W. H. Frey, "Changes in the Segregation of Whites from Blacks During the 1980s: Small Steps Toward a More Racially Integrated Society." Research Report No. 91-257.(University of Michigan, Ann Arbor: Population Studies Center ,1992).
Tucker B.M. and R. J. Taylor, "Demographic Correlates of Relationship Status Among Black Americans." *Journal of Marriage and the Family,* 51 (1989).

marriage rates for African Americans. What researchers have pointed out with a high degree of accuracy is the number of minority men behind bars or on parole or probation.

Therefore, this paper concentrates on the effects of prison on family formation and community stability. The higher the rate of imprisonment, the greater the number of socially and economically handicapped ex-inmates who strain existing family networks and are handicapped in forming new ones. This choice of incarceration for social control ignores the impact of imprisonment, parole and probation supervision; incarceration, even short-term, versus alternatives to incarceration pose different issues for communities.

African-American Family Disintegration and Imprisonment: Our studies suggest that one of the biggest casualties of this incarceration of African-American men has been the nuclear family. In most cultures, the family represents the foundation that nourishes achievement, provides support, enhances self-esteem, shapes our ideals and goals, and tempers our behavior. Marriage represents the foundation of the family. Without marriage, the concept of family changes. The once cherished two-parent African-American family is vanishing. In 1960, for example, seventy-three percent of black families were married couples.[11] However, in 1993, 46 percent of black families were of this type, representing a decline of 27 percent. The failure of black men and women to marry is understood to be a leading factor in the crisis affecting today's African-American family.[12] We focus here on how incarceration as the societal response to antisocial behavior has become increasingly self-destructive, generating family disintegration, which leads to more criminal activity.

---

[11] United States Government, *1985 Statistical Abstracts of the United States.* (Washington, D.C.: United States Government Printing Office, 1985). p 407.

[12] Billingsley, A, "Black Family Diversity." *The State of Black America 1990.* (New York: The National Urban League 1990).

The Prisonization of Black America: During the past three decades, the number of Americans behind bars has increased tremendously at a rate exceeding 6% per year. In terms of aggregate numbers, approximately 2 million Americans (461 per 100,000) are currently in prison or jail.[13] The United States now has the highest recorded incarceration rate of any nation in the world, having surpassed South Africa and the Soviet Union. However, aggregate numbers paint only a partial picture of incarceration in the United States. Historically, certain ethnic and demographic sub-groups, such as African Americans and males, have been incarcerated at higher rates than either whites or women. African-American men have disproportionately absorbed the recent increases in incarceration rates. To make the preceding point more salient, look at what has occurred between 1978 and 1997: during this 20 year period the total U.S. adult prison population more than tripled, from 246,581 to 1,195,498. Of this increase of 948,917 persons, 426,397 or 45%, was African American. These figures do not include another 800,00 African-American men who were either in local jails, on probation or parole in 1997.[14]

A study by the Soros Foundation reports that African Americans are incarcerated at a rate 6 times greater than their white counterparts. If we were to disaggregate the figures we would find that one-third of African-American men between the ages of 20-29 are either in prison or jail. Applying life-table analyses to incarceration rates we discover that for blacks in the United States resident population, it is likely that 16.2%, regardless of their sex, will be admitted to prison during their lives, nearly twice as likely as Hispanics (9.4%) and 6 times more likely than whites (2.5%).[15] Many legal and extra-legal factors have been given for the high

---

[13] http://russellsage.org/programs/proj_reviews/incarceration.htm.

[14] "Americans Behind Bars: The International use of Incarceration, 1992-93." Available at: *http://www.sproject.com/rep3.htm.*

[15] Bonczar T.P. and A. J. Beck, "Lifetime Likelihood of Going to State or Federal Prison". *Bureau of Justice Statistics Bulletin*, NCJ 160092. (Washington DC: U.S. Department of Justice, 1997).

incarceration rates of African-American men, but racial profiling, mandatory minimum sentences and especially the disparities in drug laws have had a dramatic effect on the young male incarceration rates especially in urban inner-city neighborhoods.

Michael Tonry asserts that the effects of these "recent punishment policies [has been] to destabilize inner-city communities.[16] At low levels of incarceration what happens to felons, both in prison and when they are released, is largely an individual and family matter. Whatever happens to them is not terribly important to their communities; there aren't enough of them to matter. However, at high levels of incarceration, what happens to them is important to their communities. Anti-drug laws have resulted in a dramatic increase in the imprisonment rates in inner-city communities. There are more men and women from such communities in prison, more ex-offenders on their streets-not just isolated individuals, and more of their families are affected. In turn, people who have not been directly involved with the criminal justice system begin to be affected. Existing strains within the community are exacerbated.

The Effects of Illegal Drugs on Incarceration Rates: The intent of this paper is not to argue that violent or sociopathic offenders should not be locked up, but rather, that too many African-Americans are being taken out of their families and communities for nonviolent and other property crimes, weakening both family and community. As Marc Mauer (1991), Assistant Director of the Sentencing Project, has stated, "...the impact of the war on drugs has been responsible for much of the increase in the prison population, with 46 percent of new court commitments since 1980 being due to drug offenses." To make the preceding point more salient, *USA Today* (1989), in a special edition on drugs and race, presented the startling statistic that even though African Americans constitute less than 16 percent of cocaine users they accounted for approximately 44 percent of all drug arrests.[17] This study was supported by research from the

---

[16] Tonry, M, *Malign Neglect—Race, Crime, and Punishment in America* (New York: Oxford. 1995.)

[17] "Special Report: Drugs and Race," *USA Today*, December 30, 1989.

National Institute of Drug Abuse in which it is estimated that 80% of all cocaine abusers in the United States are white and 14% black.

The irony of the war against drugs is, while more young men are being apprehended and convicted, drug use is increasing.[18] Conservative estimates on the costs associated with this war on drugs are at $100 billion for the period 1970-1996. Even more startling than the costs is how these funds have been allocated. For example, only 3 percent of these monies were spent on rehabilitation and education programs. These statistics illustrate the need for us to reevaluate our national drug policies. We as a nation must realize that 90 percent of prisoners reenter society and many of them lack either education or job skills, forcing many to commit further crimes in an effort to survive. The Russell Sage Foundation Working Group on Mass Incarceration supports the preceding assertion and shows that for low-skilled men, a ten percent decrease in real wages in the formal labor market results in a 10-20% increase in criminal activity. A lack of formal education and unemployment is highly correlated with criminal offending.

The increased rate of imprisonment in the past three decades has coincided with a number of deleterious changes in the inner city. Economic restructuring, in particular, has ravaged job opportunities for poorly educated men and women of color. Many are unemployed or have dropped out of the labor market altogether. Bruce Western argues that incarceration severely limits the employment opportunities of African-American men.[19] Western further states that the nation's unemployment figures fail to take the incarcerated population into account when discussing unemployment in the labor market. Western shows that when the incarcerated population is taken into account, the employment figures for young black males steadily declined between 1982 and 1996. The lack of opportunity in the labor market has forced many young African-American males into an informal economy that features illicit as well as legal jobs.

---

[18] www.olywa.net/when/part02.html.

[19] Western, B. and B. Pettit, "Incarceration and Racial Inequality in Men's Employment". *Industrial and Labor Relations Review*, 54, 1, (2000)

One important new aspect of inner city communities is that criminalized activities, particularly drug marketing, have become a significant segment of their economy.[20] In this economic climate, the risk of imprisonment is almost "a form of business license tax."[21] At the same time, many of their communities have been hard hit by drug abuse and the violence that is often associated with drug dealing. Again, increased imprisonment of local dealers has rarely helped. Confounding the problem is that drug related crimes are not the sole domain of males. Since crack cocaine hit the street in the 1980s, women have been increasingly represented among users and dealers.

African-American Women and the Criminal Justice System: What has gone virtually unnoticed in the literature is that the incarceration rate for African-American females has increased at a rate higher than for black males since the mid-1980s. According to 1996 Uniform Crime Report data, the incarceration rate for African-American women was 456 per 100,000. White and Latina women experienced an incarceration rate of 68 per 100,000. The female incarceration rate has been increasing at a dramatic pace; between 1986 and 1995 the number of women in prison increased by 250 percent. This is ironic because the female crime rate increased by only 38 percent during this time period. The prevailing explanation for this high imprisonment rate is that judges are giving harsher sentences regardless of gender.[22] About 55% of admissions to prisons are for crimes that used to carry probation as a penalty.[23] Convictions related to violent crime are more prevalent among imprisoned women, as they are less likely than men to be sent there for non-violent offenses. However, African-American women

---

[20] Hagedorn, J, "Neighborhood, Markets, and Gang Drug Organizations." *Journal of Research in Crime and Delinquency* 31. Pgs. 264-294. (1994).

[21] Bullock, P., *Aspiration Vs Opportunity.* (Ann Arbor MI: Institute of Industrial and Labor Relations, 1973). p 113.

[22] Bonczar T.P. and A. J. Beck, *Ibid.*

[23] Bureau of Justice Statistics, "Recidivism of Prisoners Released in 1983," (Washington DC: U.S. Department of Justice 1989).

appear to be receiving the brunt of the "get tough" policy. For example, with all things being equal, if a pregnant black woman is convicted of a drug offense, she is 10 times more likely than a white woman to spend time in prison.

The increase in the number of African-American women in prison has deleterious effects on the families of those involved. Imprisoned women who give birth are separated from their children usually within a few days after they are born thus severely weakening the mother-child bond. Moreover, a significant number of these women have young children at home and it is the child who suffers most from these forced separations.

The increasing number of female inmates poses different problems for inner city communities. As previously stated, contemporary drug laws have sent large numbers of women to prison. Most of them are mothers and, unlike male inmates, most were the primary care givers prior to imprisonment.[24] In one of the few studies of the families of jailed mothers (who were predominantly Chicana and African American), paints a picture of severe disruption during the mother's jail term.[25] In addition, the usual problems faced by an inmate upon release-finding money, a job, and a place to live—are exacerbated for women with children.[26] A recurring theme is who will take care of the children? Children of inmate mothers suffer severe displacement and this affects them throughout their lives.

With regard to childcare, in recent years many more grandmothers have been recruited as care givers for the children of imprisoned parents. Grandparent caregivers face special problems, both personal and with bureaucratic regulations.[27] Though grandparental foster care is traditional in African-American and

---

[24] Krisberg, B. and M.A. Jones, "Images and Reality: Juvenile Crime, Youth Violence and Public Policy." *National Council on Crime and Delinquency*, (San Francisco, CA, 1994). p 27.

[25] Hagedorn, J, *Ibid.*

[26] Nock, M.K., *Ibid.*

[27] Minkler, M. and K. Roe, *Grandmothers as Caregivers,* (Newbury Park, CA: Sage1993).

Latino communities, an element of coercion has been added to what is historically an economic and social expedient. What happens when grandparents cannot care for the children of prisoners may become increasingly important in the future.

There is a body of literature which suggests that children who have a parent in prison are much more likely to become involved with drugs, experience difficulty in school, engage in delinquent acts and suffer from other emotional problems.[28] If it is the mother who is imprisoned these problems are dramatically increased.[29] In addition to the social and behavioral problems experienced by children who have an incarcerated parent, communities also suffer.

Growing Up in a Criminal Environment: Juveniles and Crime: The statistics clearly indicate that the youth of our country are committing a disproportionate amount of the crime and especially the violent crime. African-American youth in this regard are caught up in a larger national trend across race. Fox (1996) points out: "From 1985 to 1994, the rate of murder committed by teens, ages 14-17, increased 172 percent. The rate of killing rose sharply for both black and white male teenagers, but not for females."[30] Between 1978 and 1993 the homicide rate for juveniles rose about 177 percent while the adult rate for this same period dropped 7 percent. For the crimes of aggravated assault, rape and robbery, the juvenile crime rate rose by 79 percent during the period 1985 to 1994. In 1994 juvenile courts handled 336,100 person offenses or 22 percent of the docket. In 1985 person offenses committed by juveniles accounted for only 16 percent of the case load. An examination of violent crimes committed by juveniles between 1983 and 1993 reveals that they committed 128,000 crimes against the person or 19 percent of all violent crime.[31]   Overall, arrests for

---

[28] Butterfield, F., *Ibid.*

[29] Bonczar T.P. and A. J. Beck, *Ibid.*

[30] Fox, J.A., *Methods in Quantitative Criminology,* (New York: Academic Press. 1996).

[31] Blumstein, A and A. Beck, "Focus Contributing to the Growth in U.S. Prison Populations," *Crime and Justice.* (Washington D.C: The National Academies Press, 1999).

violent crimes rose 46% for teenagers while only 12 percent for adults. Further, homicide and other violent acts against persons have been increasing most rapidly among younger segments of the youthful population: between 1989 and 1994, the arrest rate for youth (children) aged 14-17 has come to surpass that of young adults ages 18-24.[32]

The juvenile homicide figures are especially unnerving. The following findings from a study conducted by James Alan Fox (1996) indicate violent crime among our youth is rampant:

- *Remaining just above one percent of the population, black males ages 14-24 now constitute 17 percent of the victims of homicide and over 30 percent of the perpetrators. Their white counterparts remained about 10 percent of the victims, about 18 percent of the perpetrators, yet declined in proportionate size of the population.*
- *Guns, and especially handguns, have played a major role in the surge of juvenile murder. Since 1984, the number of juveniles killing with a gun has quadrupled, while the number killing with all other weapons combined has remained virtually constant.*
- *The largest increase in juvenile homicide involves offenders who are friends and acquaintances of their victims.*
- *By the year 2005, the number of teens, ages 14-17, will increase by 20%, with a larger increase among blacks in this age group (26%).*
- *Even if the per-capita rate of teen homicide remains the same, the number of 14-17 year-olds who will commit murder should increase to nearly 5,000 annually because of changing demographics. However, if offending rates continue to rise because*

---

[32] Fox, J.A., *Ibid.*

> *of worsening conditions for our nation's youth, the*
> *number of teen killings could increase even more.[33]*

The juvenile crime rate is extremely disturbing because it increases the likelihood that these youth will engage in subsequent adult criminality, thus leading to a life characterized by lower levels of education, marginal jobs and lower life-time earnings. All of these factors affect the structure of the family.

Why are youth turning to crime? The correctional literature suggests that it is the shock effect of prison that deters individuals from becoming recidivists. However, in contrast, it has been found that the earlier a person is exposed to the prison environment, *"the more they get used to it, and prison loses its stigma."*[34] If this is true then we have a serious problem in this country. To make this point more salient, approximately 1.96 million children have a parent or immediate relative in prison on a given day with another 1.96 million having had a parent or relative serve time. As Larry Sherman states, "… if you increase the number of people arrested and sent to prison, you may actually be creating another problem. There is a multiplier effect".

As we have shown in the previous pages, the number and proportion of African Americans who are in prison is an extremely grave problem in American society. As many scholars have pointed out, there are more African-American men under correctional supervision than there are in colleges and universities.[35] Given these startling statistics, it is highly unlikely that one would be able to find an inner city child who does not know someone who is either in prison or has been. As Larry Sherman suggests, this phenomenon

---

[33] Fox, J.A., *Ibid.*

[34] Butterfield, F., *All God's Children: The Bosket Family and the American Tradition of Violence*, Avon Books

Clear, T.R.and D.R. Karp, The Community Justice Ideal: Preventing Crime and Achieving Justice, (Boulder, CO: Westview Press 1999).

[35] Snell, T.L, *Correctional Populations in the United States, 1993*. NCJ-156241. U.S. Department of Justice, Office of Justice Programs, Bureau of Justice Statistics. (1995).

has serious implications for the youth in these communities who often times view "doing time" as an initiation rite. Spencer and Markstrom-Adams suggest that these negative role models prevent many youth from actively planning and organizing their lives according to prescribed standards.[36] Further, this criminal involvement and other forms of aberrant behavior binds this population together and ensures that they will not be involved in mainstream America.[37]

The explanations offered by Spencer and Markstrom-Adams borrow heavily from the work of Sutherland (1939) who advanced the theory of differential association as the major cause of crime.[38] For Sutherland, criminal behavior is learned in a social environment that rewards, directly or indirectly, criminal behavior. Psychologists and social psychologists also argue that children learn by imitating, identifying and internalizing the actions of their parents or guardians. The children of inmates have seen their parents arrested, they have visited prisons and quite often they have seen them engage in criminal activities. The people in their neighborhoods are very similar to their parents and in time they identify with the criminal way of life. They view the economics of crime such as drug dealing and fencing as the way of life and much better than working in a minimal wage job.

These youth often have a difficult time entering the labor force to begin with in the absence of family, friends and neighbors who are in a position to hire them or serve as intermediaries. The criminal record that many carry with them places them at a further distinct disadvantage in the labor market, creating what are called the "left behinds." Western found that incarceration functioned as a key life event that triggered a cumulative spiral of disadvantage lowering wages and wage growth over a man's life span. Incarceration was

---

[36] Spencer, M.B and C. Markstrom-Adams, "Identity processes among Racial and Ethnic Minority Children in America." *Child Development, 61*. Pgs. 290-310. (1990).

[37] Snell, T.L, *Ibid.*

[38] Edwin H. Sutherland, *On Analyzing Crime.* (Chicago: University of Chicago Press, 1973).

estimated to reduce earnings by 10-20 percent, and the rate of wage growth was reduced by 30 percent.[39] It is essential that the factors responsible for the worsening labor market position of African Americans be understood as a prerequisite to developing effective policies and training programs designed to ameliorate their plight. Prison, for youthful offenders, is not an effective solution to the problems confronting the nation. As we will attempt to illustrate, incarceration for this population may actually increase criminal offending.

Prisonization and the Strengthening of Gang and Neighborhood Peer Groups: It is important to discuss prisonization at this juncture because the literature on prisonization is concerned with the "negative effects of institutionalization on prisoners' commitment to pro-social norms, values, and beliefs," in other words, what the inmate carries out of the prison.[40] These sub cultural effects are more serious for younger inmates and are exacerbated by longer sentences. And, in recent years, sentences have been lengthening.[41]

For younger inmates, prison serves to strengthen and reinforce neighborhood criminal ties. One researcher remarked that concentrated neighborhood based law enforcement strategies (like New York's Tactical Narcotics Teams) have turned Rikers Island, a New York City jail, "into a [neighborhood] block party!"[42] All of the drug dealers in the neighborhood, gang and non-gang alike, are swept into jail at the same time. Prisons and jails are ideal institutions for strengthening peer- group relationships that have later repercussions on the streets.

However, not all inmates come to prison with strong ties to the outside world. State-raised youth whose adolescence involves

---

[39] Western, B., "The Impact of incarceration on Wage Mobility and Inequality." (Unpublished paper) 2001. p 28.

[40] Bowker, L., *Prisoner Subcultures,* (Lexington, MA: Lexington Books, 1977).

[41] Tonry, *Ibid.*

[42] Curtis, R. and S.R. Freidman, et al, *Street-level Drug Markets: Network Structure and HIV Risk,* (New York: National Development and Research Institutes, 1994).

frequent probation supervision and trips to juvenile detention facilities and whose young adult years are spent in and out of prison have only the most fragile ties to family and friends in the community. These youth are the most fully prisonized. In California, they have been held responsible for the development of the more violent prison gangs, such as the *Mexican Mafia* and *Nuestra Familia*.[43] Although these gangs developed in prison, they were exported to the streets and by now are established criminal organizations. In several states, law enforcement and media allege that prison inmates control criminal street gangs. Increased imprisonment, at younger ages, and increases in the imprisonment of women, enlarges the numbers of state raised young men.

While the export of prison criminality is a severe problem, it is not simply the number of ex-offenders on the streets but the way in which their experience comes to pervade the social networks in which they participate. It is the widely shared life experience of brutalization that pervades the prisons and impacts the culture of released inmates involved in street networks. Prisons are single sex, very racist, and often very violent. Researchers and practitioners speculate that the increased violence in street networks may be affected by the export of violent prison interpersonal styles. A similar speculation may be pertaining to racism. There is some evidence that ex-inmates hang around with younger men, who are impressed by these "veteranos." These are "dinosaurs, roaming the streets long after their time is gone," according to one former gang member.[44] Often these younger street groups are the only people from whom ex-inmates can command deference.

Such street networks may be relatively impervious to sanctions—formal or informal. Their members become inured to criminal justice sanctions, and their friends do not stigmatize them if they do wind up in prison. The prisoner subculture is intensely hostile to established authority, and these attitudes, too, are exported to the

---

[43] Moore, J. and R. Garcia, et al, *Homeboys: Gangs, Drugs, and Prison in the Barrios of Los Angeles.* (Philadelphia: Temple University Press, 1978).
[44] Moore, M. and R. Garcia, *Ibid.*

streets. In the early 1980's, surveys attempting to measure criminal employment were conducted among inner-city African-American youth in several cities. Among those who admitted committing a crime, approximately three-quarters felt that they faced very little chance of going to prison, and even if they did, the vast majority – 92% – felt that they would not lose friends.[45]

For many families, the criminal justice system, including prison, is a painfully familiar bureaucracy, bordering on the routine. For others, there may be an omnipresent threat of imprisonment, since many inner-city families that are basically conventional are also involved in petty hustling.[46] The pervasiveness of prison in these communities means that parents and spouses of inmates can expect to receive support from extended kin, neighbors, members of their churches, and friends. Does this fact relate to the much discussed— but also little studied – issue of whether inner-city communities are more tolerant of deviance? It is doubtful; although the answer probably involves variation both in inner-city community composition and also in what is meant by deviance.

Routinization of prison may have a particularly negative effect on inner-city youth: they may become already socialized to prison. Every additional inmate released to the community increases the chances that community youth will learn directly about prison and become yet more persuaded that prison lies in their own futures. For inner-city youth, anticipatory socialization to prison is exacerbated by the fact that prison permeates the national youth culture, well beyond the ghettoes and barrios.[47] Prison oriented ghetto items, for example, prison-style clothing, celebrity "gangsta rappers," and images of prison on MTV, pervade middle class white youth culture. For at-risk youth, this commodification of prison glamorizes the prison experience. What is trendy play for the children of the middle class

---

[45] Viscusi, W., "The Risks and Rewards of Criminal Activity: A Comprehensive Test of Criminal Deterrence." *Journal of Labor Economics*. Pgs 317-340 (July, 1986).

[46] Valentine, B., *Hustling and Other Hard Work*, (New York: Free Press, 1978).

[47] Krisberg, B. and M.A. Jones, *Ibid.*

is all too real for those in the inner city. Regardless of how these youth feel, what really happens to them once they are incarcerated and released?

Post-Prison Marginalization and Recidivism: After reuniting with their families, getting work is the most pressing concern for men and women released from prison and they are rarely successful.[48] There is almost no assistance provided to make this extremely difficult transition successful. Annually, over 500,000 parolees are leaving prison and re-settling in mostly low-income resource strapped communities. In 1998, a mere 7,200 of the approximately 142,000 inmates released from prison in California had completed a reentry program prior to release.[49] In 1991, only 21% of California's parolees were working full time. The prison experience is profoundly destructive of work habits. Most time in prison is idle, and most of the relatively rare prison work is characterized by a slowdown that represents resistance to authority.[50] Inmates rarely come out of prison with enhanced job skills, and they often acquire very dysfunctional work habits and attitudes. The ordinary strains of a civilian workplace are difficult for them. In general, the earlier the prison experience, the more dysfunctional the work habits.[51]

A prison record presents an obstacle to finding a job, and so does the intense post release parole surveillance, which often interferes with work. Parolees return to prison more often for

---

[48] Petersilia, J, "Challenges of Prisoner Reentry and Parole in California." (*The California Policy Research Brief Series*. 2000).

[49] Petersilia, J, *Ibid.*

[50] Correctional Association of New York; and J.D. Vigil, "Street Socialization, Locura Behavior, and Violence among Chicago Gang Members" in J. Kraus, S. Sorenson, and P. Juraez (eds.), *Proceedings: Research Conference on Violence and Homicide in Hispanic Communities.* Los Angeles: UCLA and Vigil, J.D. 1989.

[51] Fagan, J,. "Separating the Men from the Boys: The Comparative Advantage of Juvenile Vs. Criminal Court Sanctions on Recidivism among Adolescent Felony Offenders," in *Serious, Violent, and Chronic Juvenile Offenders,* J.C. Howell et al. (Thousand Oaks, CA: Sage Publishers, 1995) pgs. 238-260.

technical violations than for new crimes.[52] Immediate post release difficulties in obtaining work lead many former prisoners to adopt lifestyles, and both peers and mates, based on idle time and pre-prison associations. They "hang out" and their wives continue to bear the burden of supporting the family financially and emotionally.[53] These lifestyles impede adaptation to work, even under the most supportive working conditions.[54]

Marginalized men and women become more marginalized. Ex-inmates' joblessness may have the most significant effect on their communities. Prison erodes inmates' sexual, social, and coping skills. In particular, prison erodes marriages, and newly released inmates have difficulty in reestablishing old relationships or forming new ones that extend beyond casual sex. Men often lack money, a car, and other resources necessary for dating. Once in a domestic setting, the former inmates may be prone to greater domestic violence. It is particularly difficult for women to form relationships after prison.[55] Increased rates of imprisonment mean there will be greater numbers of such economically and socially impaired men and women on the streets leading to greater familial and community disruptions.

For a significant fraction of ex-offenders, the obstacles to obtaining jobs and establishing stable families become insuperable. Anecdotal data from several field researchers supply substantial

---

[52] Irwin, J. and J. Austin, *It's About Time: America's Imprisonment Binge*, (Belmont, CA: Wadsworth, 1994.)

[53] Anderson, E., "Sex Codes and Family Life Among Poor Inner-City Youths," in *Annals of the American Academy of Political and Social Science*, William Julius Wilson (ed.) 1989.

Fishman, L. *Women at the Wall*. (Albany: SUNY Press 1990).

[54] Majors, R. and J. Billson, *Cool Pose*, (New York: Simon and Schuster, 1992).

Mauer, M., "The Problems of Africa-American Males and the Criminal Justice System." Paper presented to the Senate Committee on Banking, Housing, and Urban Affairs. (March 19,1991.)

Padfield, H. and R. Williams., *Stay Where You Are: A Study of Unemployables In Industry*. (Philadelphia, 1973).

[55] Moore, J. and A. Mata., *Women and Heroin in Chicano Communities*, (Los Angeles: Chicano Pinto Research Project 1981).

evidence of what is called dereliction.[56] After they exhaust family resources, many ex-offenders wind up on the streets, homeless.

Gender Role Modeling: There is a large body of literature on poor African-American males that argues that the street subculture plays a major role in their lives. Its importance is inversely proportional to the men's weakened job chances, and perhaps, to their vulnerability to arrest and imprisonment, although the latter is rarely mentioned.[57] Street subcultures are substantially influenced by the presence of ex-offenders, and by the expectation of many members that they, too, will wind up doing time.

Street subcultures have many aspects, but this chapter is concerned with what Majors and Billson call the cool pose, a stance adopted by many inner-city men to cope with the many threats to their self-respect. This façade of aloofness and control, according to the authors, "Counters the... damaged pride, [and] shattered confidence... that come from living on the edge of society." The cool pose is particularly well suited to the inmate role - the prison norm that one should "hold one's mud" – and in this respect the pose transcends racial subcultures. The prison experience and the post-prison adaptations of inner-city men contribute to the all male street orientation and reinforce the cool pose—with all of its ramifications.[58]

The cool pose also inhibits the formation of nurturing relationships, according to the authors. Young black fathers who cannot find jobs experience severe strains.[59] They lose power in relationships with their children and girlfriends and, as a result, depreciate the institution of marriage altogether. Their scorn for marriage is part of the cool pose.[60]

---

[56] Irwin, J. and J. Austin, *Ibid.*

[57] Majors, R. and J. Billson, *Ibid.*

[58] Majors, R. and J. Billson, *Ibid.* p 8.

[59] Majors, R. and J. Billson, *Ibid.*

[60] Laseter, R., "Black Men: Work and Family Life," (Unpublished paper), University of Chicago, Chicago Urban Poverty and Family Life Conference (1991).

Impact on Marriage: Depletion and Prison Record Apartheid: It has been argued that the mere fact of taking a community's men away to prison has strong negative consequences for family formation. Perhaps the most widely discussed impact of the so-called depletion effect is that it contributes to the shortage of "marriageable males." Wilson (1987) framed this discussion by noting the sharp decline among African Americans in the ratio of men with jobs to every 100 women of the same age.[61] As the proportion of young black men who are imprisoned or on parole has grown to 20-29 percent and the numbers of young Black women imprisoned multiply rapidly, clearly roughly one quarter of young African Americans are directly impacted in their efforts to form and maintain families. Rates of imprisonment for black men have been increasing more than 6% a year.[62] Thus, whatever the depletion effect is now, it may well become even more significant in the future.

Bowser (1995) argues that if one is concerned with the effect of the criminal justice system on marriageability, the depletion effect—that is, the absence of men—is less important than the fact that having a prison or jail record lowers employment chances and thus lowers marriageability.[63] This broadens the concern: Instead of focusing only on those who are in prison, we must look at men living in the community who have criminal records of any sort and at the ways in which short term incarceration affects work. Though data are not firm, conservative estimates suggest that as many as a quarter to a third of young African-American males have records. Field studies of low-income communities leave no doubt that in some neighborhoods and in some networks there are even higher percentages.[64] Given what we know about multiplier effects of

---

[61] Wilson, W.J., *The Truly Disadvantaged,* (Chicago: University of Chicago Press, 1987).

[62] Irwin, J. and J. Austin., *Ibid.*

[63] Sampson, R. J. and J. H. Laub., "Crime and Deviance over the Life Course: The Salience of Adult Social Bonds." *American Sociological Review* 55 (1995). Pgs 609-27.

[64] Bowser, B. P., *Racism and Anti-Racism in World Perspective*, (Thousand Oaks, CA: Sage Publications, 1995).

prisonization on the socialization of youth, the normative order of social life, political efficacy, it is clear that the sector of African-American families affected is much larger than the approximately 25 percent of potential heads-of-family in the status of incarcerated or ex-offender.

Where do we Go From Here: We have tried to illustrate in this paper that the effects of incarceration have dramatically affected both the African-American family and community. Our central findings are:

- Almost one in three potential African-American family formations for the age group 20-29 is severely impacted or destroyed by the prevention of marriageable status for the men through the criminal justice system – they are either in prison or jail, on probation or parole.

- Directly related to the fact that more African-American men are under the control of the prison system than are involved in higher education, the imprisonment of African-American men leads to low educational attainment and low earnings capacity, preventing their attainment of a lifestyle above the poverty line to their children and communities

- The stress on the African-American family and community is rapidly becoming compounded by the removal of mothers, often the only subsistence providers, from their children: the fastest growing segment of the prison population is African-American females.

The grim statistics presented here provide evidence of how African Americans are over-represented in our prison system. A sizeable number of African Americans have simply given up hope and have removed themselves from the mainstream of society. Many of our African-American youth have adopted a counterculture lifestyle that has made them unattractive to potential employers. These youth are truly America's disadvantaged, often without family or community support. This disadvantaged youth of today becomes tomorrow's unemployed, undereducated, stigmatized and criminalized father within the struggling black community. The black community must be allowed to rehabilitate this crucial sector of young black men by shifting social control to methods much less disruptive and negative. For instance:

1. Increase opportunities for educational attainment for imprisoned young men and women so that their chances of acquiring adequate earnings upon release and for reintegration into society will be improved.

2. Extending the Enterprise Zone idea to include the funding of Community Reintegration Enterprise benefits. This would provide priority support for businesses that employ ex-offenders, encouraging all those with the economic resources to make a difference in the lives of young ex-offenders to participate in helping them to rebuild their lives and communities.

3. Financial support of a paralegal component capacity for voters' registration organizations so they can effectively and in a timely manner restores voting rights to former parolees.

4. Expanding the dialogue on development of alternatives for nurturing youth, opening new possibilities beyond the nuclear family (particularly in light of the tendency for prison culture to be reproduced). For instance, attention should be paid to overcoming sole reliance on parents, who themselves are often struggling to over-come effects of the prisonization culture of American society, to provide supervision and help with homework and school projects through making better use of school library facilities (which are usually closed) for after-school educational enhancement and homework programs.

5. Development of a bonding system and distinction between crime types such that risk can be assessed, covered and not spread as stigma across every released

prisoner. Perhaps many parolees could be covered by a bonding system or insurance, deductible from their wages, which would cover any liability caused by the insured parolee while employed, thus indemnifying the employer and securing the parolee's worthiness.

6. Mounting of a public service ad campaign directed at educating young people about the dangers of prisonization and the criminal justice system, to themselves and to their loved ones and families, urging them not to make particularly mistakes which are well-known to land them in its clutches, and advertising resources to help them to be know, and protect and defend themselves against incarceration.

Better collective socialization of children must become a focus of planning and strategy rather than simply capitulating to the situation of community resource depletion due to middle-class flight, so well described by analysts such as.[65] In this period of privatization critical thought must be given to the idea that relegating access to social and cultural capital to determination by what private family units can provide condemns the children and young adults of the existing poor to attempting to compete while controlling extremely unequal resources. Renewed focus on increasing resources collectively is critical.

Efforts must be directed at preventing the hegemony of prison, ex-offender and illicit cultural icons. While it has been argued that a large proportion of African Americans have prison culture as a part of their lives, it is not the case that they are receiving knowledge of the experience that will help them avoid it. Rather, the media and veterans of the prison system may systematically distort the experience by glamorizing it or presenting behavior strategies reflecting accommodation to its realities rather than struggle against it. The campaign to present fully the nature of the problem could

---

[65] Wilson, J.W, *The Truly Disadvantaged,* (Chicago: University of Chicago Press, 1987) Moore, J. and R. Garcia, *Ibid.*

begin with public service, but should spread and be waged in all forms of communications. The initial intense desire of ex-offenders to re-enter society and change must be supported and nourished. It is unbelievable that given what we know about the likelihood that an imprisoned youth had a thoroughly "bum" deal throughout his young life, the system should be set up such that his or her immediate experience after prison is immediate and strident disadvantage, pervasive and thorough. Therefore, policies, which offer help, such as increased educational opportunities in prison and opportunities for employment in jobs with futures after prison, are critical. Finally, to help stop what in too many cases becomes a inter-generational cycle of involvement with the criminal justice system, special efforts must be made to prevent the imprisonment of African-American men and women as the primary solution to anti-social behavior, because this solution appears to be a large cause.

We suggest that increased research be focused on exposing the connection between prisonization and family and community destruction. Full understanding of the impact of this trend may lead not only to the creation of alternative socialization support mechanisms, but also to the reinvigoration of the nuclear family itself among African Americans. We are at a point in our nation's history where we cannot simply lock them up and throw away the key.

The Impact of Race, Police Experience, and Feeling of Safety on Attitudes Toward the Police

Sutham Cheurprakobkit

In recently years, the practice of community-oriented policing (COP) has brought the police and citizens closer together than ever before. Evidence can be seen in many police programs like neighborhood watch, crime stoppers, police storefront, citizen patrol, and citizen police academy, to name just a few. The police-citizen relationship and interaction under the COP umbrella to help solve and prevent crime as well as neighborhood disorder has no doubt increased the number of contacts between the police and the citizens and exposed the police to more public view and scrutiny.[1] In order to enhance the quality of police service and effectiveness, many law enforcement agencies have started to seek input from citizens. In general, citizen surveys on public satisfaction with police performance produce favorable perceptions of the police .[2] Closer examination of the analyses, however, reveals several factors influencing citizens' attitudes.

---

[1] Cheurprakobkit, S., "Police-Citizen Contact and Police Performance Attitudinal Differences between Hispanics and Non-Hispanics," *Journal of Criminal Justice* 28 (2000). p 325.

[2] Cheurprakobkit, S. and R. Bartstch, "Police Performance: A Model for Assessing Citizens' Satisfaction and the Importance of Police Attributes," *Police Quarterly* 4 (2001). p 449; Madison Police Department, "*1998 district survey results* [online]," Available at: http//:www.ci.madison.wi.us/police/distsurvey98html.

Previous studies showed that key factors significantly affecting people's attitudes of the police include neighborhood characteristics and interactions with the police [3] and language spoken, experience with the police, and race. [4] For example, people who live in a high crime area are less likely to approve of police performance. Blacks are more likely than whites to rate the police unfavorably. The ratings of the police by Spanish-speaking Hispanics tend to be in between those of whites and blacks. Police experience is also found to determine attitudes. That is, citizens who have positive contact with the police will rate the police more favorably than those with negative experiences with the police.

The current study examines the impact of three major factors (i.e., race, police experience, and feeling of safety) on attitudes by surveying people who have contact with the Marietta, Georgia Police Department (MPD). This study examines their attitudes toward police demeanor and police performance. All of the samples were in contact with the MPD either as a complainant or victim on a call or as a suspect on a call. The purposes of the study are two-fold: (1) to find out the level of satisfaction of those the police serve in order to address any deficiencies that appear; and (2) to satisfy a Commission on Accreditation for Law Enforcement Agencies (CALEA) standard required to maintain the Department's accredited status. In particular, the study addresses two key questions: (1) Are African American's attitudes toward the Marietta Police Department different from others'? (2) Will police experience (i.e., positive or negative experience) and feeling of safety have any impact on people's attitudes toward the police?

---

[3] Maxson, C. and K. Hennigan, eds. *Factors That Influence Public Opinion of the Police.* U.S. Department of Justice, Office of Justice Programs, National Institute of Justice, 2003). p 5.

[4] Cheurprakobkit, S. and R. Bartstch, "The Effects of Amount of Contact, Contact Expectation, and Contact Experience with Police on Attitudes Toward Police,"*Journal of Police and Criminal Psychology* 19 (2004). p 58;Sutham Cheurprakobkit, "Police-Citizen Contact and Police Performance Attitudinal Differences between Hispanics and Non-Hispanics," *Journal of Criminal Justice* 28 (2000):325.

Methodology:

Samples: The data for this study were obtained from a 2004 survey on citizens' attitudes about the police in Marietta, Georgia. The study samples were citizens the MPD served in a police capacity, which resulted from a traffic accident or one of the seven types of incident reports being completed (theft, burglary, auto theft, domestic violence, simple and aggravated battery, strong arm and armed robbery, and aggravated assault). Most of the samples are Marietta residents; some are not. They were either victims/complainants or suspects.

Surveys were mailed to 125 citizens (whose names and addresses were randomly taken from official police records by a designated police records clerk) every Friday beginning in April 2004 through September 2004. Since some of the incidents occur less frequently than others (i.e., robbery and aggravated assault), surveys were mailed to each one of those incidents. A cover page explaining the purpose, benefits, and confidentiality of the study, and the sample's right not to participate in the survey, along with the prepaid envelope, was attached with the survey. Of the 3,000 surveys mailed out, 393 complete and usable surveys were returned, which was a response rate of 13.1%. Due to the increased personnel and postage costs, there was no follow-up survey to increase the response rate.

The Spanish version of the survey instrument was also developed through the help of linguistic expert because there were Hispanic samples who could not understand English. Both versions of the instrument were sent to the samples so that respondents could choose to complete the version they felt most comfortable with.

Survey Instrument: The survey instrument was constructed to serve the purpose of this project. Independent variables consisted of seven demographic variables (i.e., gender, language spoken, race, age, annual income, educational level, and length of time living in the neighborhood), experience with the police (positive or negative experience or both), and feeling of safety in neighborhood (safe versus unsafe). Table 1 describes the respondents' demographic characteristics.

The survey was designed to examine citizens' attitudes toward the police in two aspects. First, the survey asked about people's attitudes toward police demeanor (politeness, fairness, helpfulness, and concern). The answer category for the police demeanor questions ranged from 1 to 5, with 5 indicating "very satisfied" and 1 indicating "very unsatisfied." Second, eight aspects of police performance (crime prevention, crime protection, crime fighting, helping victims, solving problems, professional conduct, professional knowledge, and quality of services) were also measured using a 1 to 5 scale, with 5 meaning "very good" and 1 meaning "very poor."

Findings: The data in Table 2 show that white respondents (84 percent) more than black respondents (65 percent) reported positive experiences with the police. However, about 23 percent of both groups expressed that they had negative police experiences. The overwhelming majority of white and black participants (91 percent and 85 percent, respectively) also believed their neighborhood was safe.

The respondents were also allowed to comment on their experience with the police. The analysis of the comments revealed that both positive and negative police encounters fell under the police demeanor category (or the service aspect) more than the police performance category. The most stated positive comments given by the respondents included police being pleasant, cordial, caring, polite, nice, kind, friendly, helpful, and concerned, respectively. For the negative comments, the most frequently mentioned were that the officer did not care, was rude, had a bad attitude, and that the police did not return calls and follow through on their cases.

As might be expected, respondents as a whole expressed their satisfaction with the way the police acted during their encounter (Table 3). The majority of respondents (72 percent to 86 percent) thought the officer handling their case was polite, fair, helpful, and concerned. Police demeanor that received the highest score was politeness (mean = 4.35), whereas police being concerned was the least satisfactory aspect (mean = 3.95).

Due to the skewed nature of the distribution among the demographics, police experiences, and feeling of safety, a Spearman correlation was employed to calculate the relationship between these variables and attitude as shown in Table 4. Gender, race, police experiences, type of respondent, and feeling of safety were coded as dummy variables. The results revealed that four demographic variables (gender, income, educational level, and length of stay in neighborhood) were not correlated with any of the four dependent variables. Type of respondent was significantly and positively correlated with attitude toward fairness. That is, a victim/complainant was more likely than a suspect to think the police were fair.

Compared to blacks, non-blacks rated all four police demeanors more favorably. This finding supports that of Cheurprakobkit's [5] study, which found that blacks believed the police were fairer, more concerned, and more polite toward whites and Hispanics (both English and Spanish speaking) than toward them. Although this result comes as no surprise because of the historically fragile police-minority relations, one might question the effectiveness of the implementation of the police outreach programs under today's community policing philosophy.

Older people seemed to rate police demeanor more favorably than younger people. As mentioned in Cheurprakobkit[6] his study's finding and the finding of this study are inconsistent with those of Arcuri,[7] Morello [8] and Schack and Frank ,[9] which were conducted in the 1970s and 1980s when the practice of COP was still immature, resulting in the less favorable view of the police by older people.

---

[5] Cheurprakobkit, S. and R. Bartstch, *Ibid.* p 333.

[6] *Ibid.*p 330.

[7] Arcuri, A., "The Police and the Elderly," in *The Elderly Victim of Crime,* ed. D. Lester (Springfield, IL: Charles C. Thomas Publishers, 1981). p 106.

[8] Morello, F., *Juvenile Crimes Against the Elderly* (Springfield, IL: Charles C. Thomas Publishers, 1982).

[9] S. Schack and R. Frank, "Police Service Delivery to the Elderly," *Annual American Academy Police Science* 438 (1978):81.

The present study, however, was conducted after police officers, including the Marietta police officers, had absorbed the gist of COP that emphasized the human aspect and the quality of life, as well as crime prevention.

Table 4 also shows significant correlations between police experience and the dependent variables. People with positive police encounters tended to view the police as being polite, fair, helpful, and more concerned than those who had no positive police contact. In contrast, people who have had negative experiences with the police seemed to feel less satisfied with all four police demeanors. These findings confirm previous studies [10] regarding the impact of police experience on attitude. If citizens view their encounter with police officers as positive, they almost always rate the police more favorably.

Table 5 reveals what respondents thought about police job approval. Again, overall, people rated police performance favorably, with about 74 percent and 84 percent of respondents rated the police as either "good" or "very good" in doing their job. The two highest ratings of police performance were professional conduct (mean = 4.23) and professional knowledge (mean = 4.22), in that order. Police ability to solve problems (mean = 3.85) and ability to prevent crime (mean = 3.94) were rated the lowest.

Table 6 reveals the similar correlation results presented in Table 4. Only respondents' age, race, police experience, and feeling of safety were found to significantly relate to the dependent variables. Age was positively correlated with all the police performance aspects, except crime protection. That is, compared to younger people, older people would better approve of police performance.

Race was negatively related to attitudes toward police performance. Blacks were more likely than non-blacks to disapprove of police performance. People who had positive police experience and who felt safe in their neighborhood also thought the police performed their job better than those who did not have positive

---

[10] Cheurprakobkit, S. and R. Bartstch, *Ibid.*

police interaction, who encountered negative police experience, and who were fearful of crime in their neighborhood. Again, these findings support previous studies' findings, which consider race, experience with the police, and crime safety issues as key factors determining people's attitudes.

In Table 7, the mean scores were calculated and compared for 11 groups of respondents: 1) people with positive police experience, 2) people with negative police experience, 3) people with both positive and negative police experience, 4) whites, 5) blacks, 6) people who feel safe in their neighborhood, 7) people who feel unsafe in their neighborhood, 8) whites who feel their neighborhood is safe, 9) whites who feel unsafe in their neighborhood, 10) blacks who feel their neighborhood is safe, and 11) blacks who feel unsafe in their neighborhood.

Regarding the types of respondents' experiences with the police, the means between these three groups were different. The overall means for those who only had positive police experiences were found to be the highest among the three groups (means ranging from 4.07 to 4.65). The overall means for those with only negative police experiences were the lowest and were marginally above the midpoint of 2.5, except for a few police attributes), whereas the means for those who experienced both positive and negative police encounters were in between the two groups. These findings are consistent with Cheurprakobkit's [11] who pointed out in his study that a certain police experience, either positive or negative, can predict how people evaluate police performance; that when citizens have both positive and negative contacts with the police, the positive experience can both neutralize the negative police experience and has a relatively greater impact on attitudes; and that how police interact with citizens during the course of their encounter appears to greatly affect citizens' attitudes.

As might be expected, race and feeling of safety significantly affected attitudes. Whites rated both police demeanor and police performance more favorably than blacks, with the overall police

---

[11] Cheurprakobkit, S. and R. Bartstch, *Ibid.* p 333.

demeanor mean scores of 4.28 for whites and 3.74 for blacks and the police performance mean scores of 4.14 for whites and 3.75 for blacks. Citizens also rated the police more positively if they felt their neighborhood was safe. The overall police demeanor and the police performance mean scores were 4.13 and 4.23 for those who felt safe and were 3.46 and 3.63 for those who did not, respectively. Once the impact of race was further analyzed by the level of perceived safety in the neighborhood, respondents' attitudes toward the police were even more clearly distinguishable. Respondents, either whites or blacks, who thought their neighborhood was safe tended to rate the police more favorably. The overall attitudes of whites toward police demeanor and police performance were more positive than those of whites who believed their neighborhood was unsafe, but were less positive when compared to whites, who perceived more crime in their neighborhood. Similarly, among blacks, those who felt their neighborhood was safe rated the police the highest (mean = 3.90 for police demeanor and mean = 3.93 for police performance), followed by blacks (mean = 3.74 for police demeanor and mean = 3.75 for police performance) and blacks who felt unsafe in their neighborhood (mean = 2.72 for police demeanor and 2.79 for police performance), in that order.

Discussions and Conclusions: The findings of this study clearly reveal the impact of police experience, race, and feeling of safety, which confirm those of previous studies that view these three factors as critical determinants of citizens' attitudes toward the police. However, several interesting points are worth mentioning here. First, based on this study, when each of these three factors is analyzed individually, police experience appears to be more influential on attitudes than either race or feeling of safety. Those who perceive their encounter with the police as positive have the highest ratings of the police (mean = 4.51 for police demeanor and mean = 4.25 for police performance), whereas negative encounters with the police produce the lowest rating (mean = 2.82 for police demeanor and mean = 3.08 for police performance).

Second, feeling unsafe in the neighborhood seems to have a greater impact on blacks than whites. Blacks who perceive more crime in the neighborhood have a less favorable view toward the police than whites who feel unsafe. In fact, blacks in the perceived high crime area rate the police the lowest in both their demeanor (mean = 2.72) and their job performance (mean = 2.79).

Third, people's experiences with the police tend to be service-oriented and humanistic in nature; therefore, their attitudes appear to be affected more by police demeanor (police being polite, fair, helpful, and concerned) than by police performance (e.g., crime prevention, crime fighting, professional conduct, professional knowledge, etc.). This finding is not surprising given the magnitude of police-citizen interactions under the community policing philosophy and the nature of police work in that police spend more time maintaining order and providing services to citizens than fighting and dealing with crime. Overall, the study's results show that the police demeanor category is rated higher than the police performance category. However, when the respondents are blacks, the overall mean scores for police demeanor and police performance are relatively the same.

In closing, if the police are to gain real favorable job evaluation, they should not consider the general public attitudes as a whole as a single measuring indicator of their performance. There is a need to further assess the impact that several factors have on attitudes, especially police experience, race, and feelings of safety. The current study indicates that positive police-citizen interaction and feeling safe in the neighborhood produce positive ratings of police performance; therefore, more efforts and resources must be spent to create a safe and friendly neighborhood in the community. However, even more serious efforts are needed toward the black community. As Cheurprakobkit stated, blacks' negative attitudes toward the police have remained unchanged for many years, and "it may be time for law enforcement agencies to develop and implement some other proactive and innovative policing programs that are more conducive to bringing the police and blacks together."[12]

---

[12] Cheurprakobkit, S. and R. Bartstch, *Ibid.* p 334.

References

Arcuri, A. "The Police and the Elderly." In *The Elderly Victim of Crime,* ed. D. Lester, 106-128. Springfield, IL: Charles C. Thomas Publishers,1981.

Bartsch, Robert, and Sutham Cheurprakobkit. "The Effects of Amount of Contact, Contact Expectation, and Contact Experience with Police on Attitudes Toward Police," *Journal of Police and Criminal Psychology* 19 (2004):58-70.

Cheurprakobkit, Sutham. "Police-Citizen Contact and Police Performance Attitudinal Differences Between Hispanics and Non-Hispanics," *Journal of Criminal Justice* 28 (2000):325-336.

Cheurprakobkit, Sutham, and Robert Bartstch. "Police Performance: A Model for Assessing Citizens' Satisfaction and the Importance of Police Attributes," *Police Quarterly* 4 (2001):449-468.

Madison Police Department. *1998 District Survey Results* [online], 1999, Accessed 3 March 2005; available from http://www.ci.madison.wi.us/police/distsurvey98.

Maxson, Cheryl, and Karen Hennigan, eds. Factors That Influence Public Opinion of the Police. U.S. Department of Justice, Office of Justice Programs, National Institute of Justice, 2003.

Morello, F. *Juvenile Crimes Against the Elderly.* Springfield, IL: Charles C.Thomas Publishers, 1982.

Schack, S. and R. Frank. "Police Service Delivery to the Elderly," *Annual American Academy Police Science* 438 (1978): 81-95.

Table 1: Characteristics of Participants

Characteristic	Frequency	Percentage
Gender		
Male	199	52.5
Female	180	47.5
Language Spoken		
English	340	87.9
Spanish	23	5.9
Both	24	6.2
Race/Ethnicity		
White/Caucasian	269	70.8
African American	64	16.8
Hispanic/Latino	27	7.1
Asian	11	2.9
Other	9	2.4
Age		
25 or younger	49	12.5
26–35	69	17.6
36–45	77	19.6
46–55	82	20.9
56–65	57	14.5
66 or older	59	15.0
2003 Household Income		
Under $13,000	32	8.8
$13,001-$20,000	32	8.8
$20,001-$30,000	43	11.8
$30,001-$40,000	31	8.5
$40,001-$50,000	33	9.1
$50,001-$60,000	31	8.5
$60,001 or more	161	44.4

Characteristic	Frequency	Percentage
Education Level		
Less Than High School Degree	24	6.3
High-School Degree/GED	89	23.2
Vocational/Technical School	53	13.8
Associate Degree	47	12.3
Bachelor's Degree	117	30.5
Master's Degree or Above	53	13.8
Length of Time Living in Current Neighborhood		
Less Than 1 Year	53	14.1
Between 1 and 3 Years	84	22.4
Between 4 and 6 Years	59	15.7
Between 7 and 9 Years	48	12.8
Between 10 and 12 Years	24	6.4
More Than 13 Years	107	28.5

Table 2: Frequency and Percentages of Participants' Responses on Police Experience and Feeling of Safety, by Race

Question Item	blacks (N=64)		whites (N=269)	
	yes	no	yes	no
Have you had any *positive* experience with the police who handled your case?	37 (64.9%)	20 (35.1%)	190 (84.1%)	36 (15.9%)
Have you had any *negative* experience with the police who handled your case?	13 (22.8%)	44 (77.2%)	52 (23.2%)	172 (76.8%)
Do you think you live in a safe neighborhood?	52 (85.2)	9 (14.8)	230 (91.2)	22 (8.8)

Table 3:
Descriptive Results Regarding Attitudes About Police Demeanor

	Very Satisfied/ Satisfied	Neutral	Unsatisfied/Very Unsatisfied	Mean Score
Politeness	330 (86%)	29 (7.6%)	25 (6.5%)	4.35
Fairness	302 (80.3)	34 (9.0)	40 (10.7)	4.17
Helpfulness	298 (79.3)	36 (9.6)	42 (11.2)	4.14
Concern	269 (72.0)	54 (14.4)	51 (13.6)	3.95

Note: The scale ranged from 1 to 5, with a high number indicating more satisfaction.

Table 4: Correlation Results Between Independent Variables and Attitudes toward Police Demeanor

	Gender	Race	Age	Income	Education	Time Living in Neighborhood	Positive Experience	Negative Experience	Type of Respondent	Feeling safe
Politeness	-.04	-.15**	.22**	.06	-.03	.05	.54**	-.54**	.06	.17**
Fairness	-.05	-.18**	.21**	.10	-.02	.08	.56**	-.64**	.11*	.16**
Helpfulness	-.01	-.17**	.19**	.08	-.02	.04	.66**	-.61**	.07	.20**
Concern	.02	-.15**	.23**	.03	-.05	.06	.58**	-.64**	.03	.16**

Note: Gender (1=male, 0=female); Race (1=black, 0=non-black); Positive Experience with Police (1=yes, 0=no); Negative Experience with Police (1=yes, 0=no); Type of Respondent (1=Victim/Complainant, 0=Suspect); Feeling Safe (1=yes, 0=no)

Table 5:
Descriptive Results Regarding Attitudes About Police Performance

	Very Good/ Good	Fair	Very Poor/ Poor	Mean Score
Preventing Crime	246 (73.6%)	60 (18.0%)	28 (8.4%)	3.94
Protecting One From Crime	252 (75.0%)	58 (17.3%)	26 (7.8%)	3.96
Fighting Crime	254 (77.5%)	54 (16.5%)	20 (6.1%)	3.99
Helping Victims	254 (76.6%)	45 (13.6%)	33(9.9%)	4.00
Solving Problems	357 (69.1%)	66 (19.8%)	37(11.1%)	3.85
Professional Conduct	289 (84.0%)	35 (10.2%)	20(5.8%)	4.23
Professional Knowledge	286 (84.4%)	38 (11.2%)	15(4.5%)	4.22
Quality of Service	278 (80.6%)	47 (13.6%)	20(5.8%)	4.10

Note: The scale ranged from 1 to 5, with a high number indicating better performance

Table 6: Correlation Results Between Independent Variables and Attitudes toward Police Performance

	Gender	Race	Age	Income	Education	Length of Time Living in the Neighborhood	Positive Experience	Negative Experience	Type of Respondent	Feeling Safe
Preventing Crime	.05	-.13*	.18**	.08	.01	.02	.40**	-.45**	-.02	.30**
Protecting You From Crime	.08	-.07	.12*	.07	-.02	.01	.43**	-.47**	-.03	.31**
Fighting Crime	.04	-.16**	.17**	.13*	.03	.01	.41**	-.43**	-.05	.24**
Helping Victims	.02	-.13*	.15**	.06	-.01	.03	.47**	-.56**	-.01	.21**
Solving Problems	.02	-.18**	.12*	.08	-.01	.02	.43**	-.52**	-.04	.25**
Professional Conduct	.02	-.16**	.17**	.09	.01	.03	.52**	-.52**	.02	.16**
Professional Knowledge	.05	-.15**	.13*	.09	-.01	.05	.50**	-.45**	-.02	.15**
Quality of Service	.07	-.13*	.18**	.09	-.03	.04	.51**	-.50**	-.02	.16**

Note: Gender (1=male, 0=female); Race (1=black, 0=non-black); Positive Experience with Police (1=yes, 0=no); Negative Experience with Police (1=yes, 0=no); Type of Respondent (1=Victim/ Complainant, 0=Suspect); Feeling Safe (1=yes, 0=no)

Table 7: Means of Thirteen Dependent Measures by Type of Police Experience, Race, and Feeling of Safety

Dependent Variable	Type of Experience			Race		Feeling of Safety		Race and Feeling of Safety			
	Positive (n=256)	Negative (n=73)	Both (n=31)	whites (n=210)	blacks (n=63)	Feel Safe (n=319)	Feel Unsafe (n=44)	Whites Safe (n=226)	Whites Unsafe (n=22)	Blacks Safe (n=51)	Blacks Unsafe (n=9)
Police Demeanor											
Politeness	4.65	3.32	4.00	4.47	4.02	4.40	3.89	4.50	4.09	4.14	3.22
Fairness	4.52	2.74	3.42	4.29	3.71	4.25	3.70	4.37	3.82	3.84	2.78
Helpfulness	4.54	2.81	3.81	4.29	3.69	4.22	3.52	4.35	3.95	3.90	2.44
Concern	4.33	2.41	3.23	4.07	3.54	4.03	3.42	4.15	3.60	3.70	2.44
Overall Mean	**4.51**	**2.82**	**3.62**	**4.28**	**3.74**	**4.23**	**3.63**	**4.34**	**3.87**	**3.90**	**2.72**
Police Performance											
Preventing Crime	4.10	3.00	3.43	4.05	3.66	4.06	3.13	4.13	3.45	3.88	2.56
Protecting One from Crime	4.14	3.00	3.50	4.03	3.81	4.08	3.15	4.12	3.30	4.08	2.44
Fighting Crime	4.16	3.19	3.61	4.11	3.69	4.08	3.39	4.18	3.50	3.86	2.75
Helping Victims	4.24	2.87	3.36	4.11	3.71	4.10	3.43	4.20	3.48	3.88	2.89
Solving Problems	4.07	2.75	3.16	3.95	3.44	3.97	3.13	4.05	3.22	3.67	2.22
Professional Conduct	4.48	3.27	3.88	4.34	3.91	4.29	3.83	4.38	4.05	4.02	3.25
Professional Knowledge	4.44	3.43	4.08	4.32	3.93	4.29	3.90	4.37	4.14	4.08	3.22
Quality of Services	4.34	3.13	3.85	4.21	3.83	4.17	3.71	4.26	3.40	3.96	3.00
Overall Mean	**4.25**	**3.08**	**3.61**	**4.14**	**3.75**	**4.13**	**3.46**	**4.21**	**3.57**	**3.93**	**2.79**

Note: The scale ranged from 1 to 5, with a high number indicating more satisfaction.

The Impact of Massive Incarceration on the African-American Woman, Her Family, and the Community

Gale "Sky" Edeawo

In 1819 the male managers of the New York Society For The Prevention Of Pauperism described the women's quarters at Bellevue Penitentiary as "one great school of vice and desperation" replete with "prostitutes, vagrants, lunatics, thieves and those of less heinous character." What shocked them was the lack of attention paid to these women, not only by the male society, but the lack of attention paid to them by the more fortunate of their gender."[1] In 1819 it was often questioned why incarcerated females received such little assistance or attention. Where were all the female "Angels of Mercy" to speak out on behalf of these women? Pleas asking for caring advocates to work for the rights of incarcerated women were brought forth, even in these early days when the number of incarcerated women was small. It was not until the 1840's that a few middle class American women became motivated to work for the rights and needs of women prisoners.[2] Even then these Angels were few and as women, were extremely limited to what they were allowed to do. Unfortunately, 200 years later we are still suffering from severe inattentiveness of female inmates.

---

[1] Freedman, E.B., *Their Sister's Keepers: Women's Prison reform in America from 1830 - 1930* (The University of Michigan, Ann Arbor, MI.) (1981). p 7.
[2] Freedman, E.B., *Ibid.*

There are many organizations and benevolent societies in existence today that donate much time and money to the charities of their choice. There is also a growing movement for the rights of prisoners; however, the bulk of these efforts is directed towards male inmates, not female inmates. The rate of women entering prison has increased nearly 400% since 1980, with African-American women constituting the largest percentage of this population. Even though the United States incarcerates more women than any other country, and the female prison population is now the fastest growing group in our prison system, female inmates are still dangerously overlooked.[3] Women who have male loved ones in prison will deliberately move to be closer to the incarceration site. Very few men make this effort in the reverse situation. To further emphasize the inattentiveness, it has been documented that on visiting day, male prisons are overcrowded with supportive families, while on visiting days in female prisons, there is not even a 1:1 ratio of visitors to inmate.[4] Some argue this inequality is because female inmates have alienated themselves severed ties with family, however this fact is also prevalent with male inmates. It seems as though a male inmate's offense may be forgive, while a female in jail is not given the benefit of the doubt.

Home For Some: As lonely, frustrating, and regimented as it can become inside the prison walls, there are still women who prefer prison to the outside world. Some women say that at least in prison they are fed, sheltered, have running water, and even a few friends. Others admit to feeling safer in prison; they don't have to worry about being sexually assaulted or abused, or scrounging for food.

There are very few programs to assist women once they return home from incarceration and even fewer helping hands. Regardless of possession of skills, their criminal record disallows them from obtaining desired jobs and living conditions. Within three to six months

---

[3] Johnson, C.P., "Voices of African-American Women In Prison," *Inner Lives.* (2003). p 5.

[4] Johnson, C.P., *Ibid.*

many women find themselves back in an institution, thus continuing the cycle. For most, this is just returning home.

For some families it is relieving when they learn a loved one has been re-incarcerated. The general feeling is that at least their concerns of the whereabouts and safety of the individual are alleviated. Unfortunately, imprisonment has become the only haven for some women. The following quotation is that of a forty-five year old woman, incarcerated for the first time:

> *You do have people who are not trying to go home. They act like they don't care if they go home. They don't have anything to go home to. Prison is a vacation from the streets to them—they feel like they are glad to be here. The streets is too rough if you don't own the street. Prison is better if you don't know what it is like to have a bed; to have clean clothes. Some girls don't have a place to go home to when they get out. You know a person is coming back here when they don't have family, like if they have burnt all their bridges with the family. General assistance takes long time, and it's not enough to find a place. How do you support yourself? It's back into drugs and wild life.* [5]

The "Olden Days" Are Not So Old: As a society, we are in the same situation in regards to the attention given the incarcerated and post incarcerated woman as we were one hundred eighty four years ago. For many female inmates, physical and sexual abuse is a defining feature of their lives. This abuse often begins in childhood and continues into their adult life. [6] There has not been a significant effort towards the improvement of this crucial issue regarding female offenders. As a result, these matters that existed in 1819 also exist in 2005.

---

[5] Owens, B., *In The Mix: Struggle and Survival In A Women's Prison,* (Albany, New York: State University Of New York Press, 1998). p 40.
[6] Owens, B., *Ibid.* p 42.

Over the past two centuries, the number of women entering jail and prison has escalated to a frightening height, especially after the introduction of crack cocaine into our communities in the late 1970's. Most female jails and prisons across the nation are filled to capacity or overcrowded. Roughly 85% of incarcerated women have children less than 18 years of age. Numerous women give birth while incarcerated. Second and third generations of incarcerated women, from the same families, are ending up in the same institutions. This is becoming commonplace. Even when some of the women are serious about wanting to change their ways and become good parents, they have limited faculties, reentry programs and rehabilitation programs at their disposal. The same questions asked in 1819 has still not been answered, "Where is the aid that female inmates so desperately need?"

Crack Cocaine: The United States currently imprisons more people of color, per capita, than any other nation. It costs more to send a person to prison for a year than to Harvard University for a year. The majority of women that have been sent to prison over the last two decades were convicted of drug charges and non-violent crimes. Healthcare for prisoners, both men and women, is practically non-existent.[7] Drug abuse by women in the U.S. has been rapidly increasing. Crack cocaine use has reached dangerous levels; illegal crack houses are open at all hours across this nation. More than 40% of crack house regulars are young women, most of them African-American and Latina. Some are in their adolescence and considered the "cities lost girls."[8] Unfortunately some of these women are already mothers, and are compelled by their addiction to even take their children to these perverted houses with them, exposing them to unmentionable danger. Afterwards, when the women are in a more reasonable state of mind, they feel extremely guilty for endangering the lives of their children. To escape this guilt

---

[7] The Committee On Unjust Sentencing, "The Tallahassee Project" (San Francisco, CA: Last Gasp Of San Francisco, 2001).

[8] Williams, T., *Crackhouse: Notes From The End of The Line*, (New York: Penguin Books, 1992). p 12.

they use even more cocaine and get higher. Soon, most women come to the conclusion that staying in a perpetual high is the only way to cope with the miserable life they are leading.

There are few rehabilitation facilities for women who sincerely want to change their lives. In the meantime, the younger generation is carrying this burden on its back. Children are becoming victims of this war, caught in the cross fire of a do or die situation. Some of these youth die, some grow to be very hard and cold, and others just disappear. Former drug users and active drug users have admitted that crack cocaine is a demonic drug and the worst form of addiction. This drug has saturated many large cities and rural towns throughout America, turning so many of children into orphans, drug dealers, and eventually convicts. Many of them are reaching for the American dream; others are just trying to stay alive.

The War On Drugs: Since the morning Governor Nelson A. Rockefeller proposed life sentence for drug pushers, females in State and Federal prisons has increased by three-fold. The new drug law went into effect at the beginning of September 1973. During the decade after New York's law went into effect, forty-eight other States passed their own Rockefeller-style drug laws.[9] In 1980 there were approximately 10,000 women incarcerated in prisons and jails across the nation, this number escalated to 150,000 by the year 2001. Although these numbers vary in scope, one fact remains common in all the statistical counts: the number of women incarcerated since the passing of the Rockefeller-law and Mandatory Minimum Sentencing law, which grew out of the Rockefeller law, has reached epidemic proportions.

"America's War On Drugs is inflicting deep and disproportionate harm on women, most of them mothers - who are filling prisons in ever-rising numbers, despite their typically minor roles in drug rings."[10] Some reports recommend expansion of

---

[9] Gonnerman, J., *Life on the Outside: The Prison Odyssey of Elaine Barlett.* (New York: Farrar, Strass, and Giroux, 2004). p 49.

[10] The Associated Press, "Drug War Harming Women" Thursday, March 17, 2005.

treatment program geared toward women, they claim prison should be the last resort and urge more vigorous efforts to maintain ties between imprisoned mothers and their children. This ongoing war on drugs has ended up becoming a war on minorities, women and children.

Battered Women: Many battered women prefer life in prison to a life of fear, agony and pain endured as a "free" person in an abusive relationship. Some women end up killing their batterer and are incarcerated as a result. However, they say that after broken bones, repeated rapes, threats placed on them and their children, in and out of courts and emergency rooms, with no one being able to protect them from their abuser "it was either them or jail." They feel that they were forced to take matters into their own hands. Although some of these women are serving long and life term sentences, a few have stated that they have never felt this free in all of their life.

Women Inmates and Mental Depression: Studies show that there is a high incident of depression among women prisoners. Unlike most men, women suffer their depression silently. Women also have a deep commitment to mothering; so being separated from their children can cause deep depression.[11] Incarcerated teenage girls have reported that the stress on their bodies when first incarcerated to a larger and different institution can cause their menstrual cycle to shut down for months. Many women are administered psychotropic drugs such as Zanex, Thorazine, and Librium regularly while incarcerated, to help with their depression.

Due to government cutbacks and the closing of so many mental health facilities more men and women with serious mental disorders are put in prisons instead of hospitals. Severely disturbed prisoners

---

[11] Kupers, T., Prison Madness: *The Mental Health Crisis Behind Bars And What We Must Do About It.* (San Francisco: Jossey-Bass Publishers, 1999). p 114
[12] Watterson, K., *Inside The Concrete Womb.* (Boston: Northern University Press, 1999). p 204

are often kept in solitary confinement because proper, or effective treatment is not available.[12] Once their time is served they are tossed back into the community. Those who are more stable seek help and shelter for themselves, those who are not of sound mind and have no family contacts, are left to roam the streets.

The Children Left Behind: A woman who is locked up faces an immediate and constant anxiety about her children - where they are, whether they are safe and are they being fed? Will they be placed in a children's shelter or a foster home? Children often share the same anxiety as their parents. Children as young as three and four begin to adopt the worries of an adult. Some youth actually begin to feel they are responsible for the absence of their parent. When younger siblings are involved, the older siblings take it upon themselves provide for the younger children. They learn to hide the situation from neighbors and the authorities so shelters won't separate them. Some of these older siblings have not even reached their twelfth birthday. It is no wonder so many of them began to display anger and strange problematic behavior. Society labels them "bad kids." Seldom taking time to deal with the problem of these young ones who have broken hearts due to the absence of a parent, authorities place these children into alternative education programs, boot camps or detention centers. In some instances the children are placed with relatives, this is not always the upside of the situation; as for many relatives keeping these children proves stressful. The children often feel abandoned and unloved, and are known to run away from any shelter they are placed. Grandmothers are usually the nearest loving relative that can be found to assist in the care of the children. Many are over the age of 55, have little income, and not in good health. Life often becomes very difficult for these elderly women who are trying to keep their grandchildren, and sometimes great-grandchildren, under one roof.

Fathers assume responsibility for less than 22 percent of the children in their mothers' absence, in contrast to the 80% of children

---

[13] Watterson, K., *Ibid.* p 209

kept by the mothers in the fathers' absence.[13] Unfortunately, children of inmates are more likely to become inmates themselves, often beginning at an early age. Children who feel neglected by the absence of their parent and youth who are constantly shuffled from shelter to shelter, foster home to foster home, or relative to relative often take to the street. They tend to find refuge in gangs and other at-risk-youth.

The Older Female Inmate: Being older, being female, or being an offender can all have negative implications in our society. Both older offenders and female offenders are often referred to as "forgotten." Older women in prison are almost totally overlooked whether they are black or white. There is very little training given to counselors, medical staff, or correctional officers on the needs of older female inmates.[14]

Conclusion: Jail and prison is the harsh decision chosen over rehabilitation, education and community incarceration. In most cities, such as my own, community incarceration rarely exist. We, the public, must be educated on how this "Lock Them Up And Throw Away The Key" mentality is a danger to us all. The majority of inmates will return to society one day. Most of their children will grow into adulthood one day. What type of adult will these children grow up to be, raised without a mother? What type of inmate, male and female, will return to our community? Will they be angry and disoriented from their long unproductive time served, or will they be weary and docile? They are our friends, our siblings, our parents, children, friends and neighbors, returning to our community. What part will we play in welcoming them home?

---

[14] Federal Bureau of Prisons, "Female Offenders: Meeting Needs of a Neglected Population," *Federal Prisons Journal*. Pgs 1-2. (Spring 1992).

CRIMINAL JUSTICE REFORMS

Sentencing Reform and the African-American Community

Michael Blain

In 1903, W.E.B. Du Bois—the famed visionary, scholar, writer and activist- wrote, "the problem of the 20ᵗʰ century is the problem of the color line." Du Bois was both prophetic and pragmatic in his analysis. Over 100 years have passed since the publication of his seminal book, *The Souls of Black Folk,* in which he made this proclamation, and despite the progress some African Americans have achieved, indeed the "color line" threatens to become the problem of the 21ˢᵗ century as well.

In his use of the term "color line," Du Bois was referring to *systemic* racism and white supremacy. It is vital that we see how those detrimental customs continue to pose a problem for African Americans, who continue to rank at the bottom of almost every indicator of social progress. And, of those indicators, there is perhaps no more egregious example of systemic racism than the experience of African Americans with the U.S. criminal justice system particularly since the inception of the "war on drugs."

In New York State, for example, almost everybody is aware of the state's harsh and draconian mandatory minimum drug laws. Dubbed the "Rockefeller Drug Laws" after then-Governor Nelson Rockefeller signed them into law in 1973 and 1974, the laws have been the subject of enormous public debate since they were passed. The Rockefeller Drug Laws were supposedly intended to target large-scale drug dealers known as "kingpins." However, these laws have instead worked to disproportionately affect low-level nonviolent offenders. Today, there are almost 16,000 people, or 38% of the prison population, incarcerated in New York under the Rockefeller Drug Laws. Moreover, *fully 92 percent* of this population is comprised of people of color, mostly African Americans from New York City. This fact remains despite the fact that African Americans are only approximately 25% of the population of New York City[1] and only 15.9% of New York State's population[2]. This disturbing reality is, unfortunately, not distinct to just this state. Around the country, the war on drugs is waged primarily against African Americans residing in the inner city.

It is interesting to consider what Du Bois might have to say about the war on drugs and the criminal justice system that incarcerates more than 2.2 million people in prisons and jails, nearly half of whom are African American. Although African Americans are approximately 13% of the U.S. population, alarmingly, they are 29% of those arrested for criminal behavior, 44% of those convicted, and almost 60% of all those sent to prison. Conversely, white people are 81% of the U.S. population, 54% of those convicted, and are only 39% of those sent to prison. These statistics forcefully expose the precise "color line" that so seriously concerned Du Bois. The reality today is that one in three African-American men will be sent to prison in their lifetime, and African-American women are sent to prison and jails at almost six times the rate of white women.[3] Furthermore, a sizable portion of the African Americans under correctional supervision for drug offenses are nonviolent offenders. Almost a third of the individuals incarcerated in this country are imprisoned for nonviolent drug charges. These troubling numbers are largely a consequence of the inherent racism codified in the U.S. war on drugs.

---

[1] New York City Department of City Planning; Population Division 2000 Census summary - http://www.ci.nyc.ny.us/html/dcp/html/census/pop2000.html.

[2] U.S. Census Bureau, New York Quick Facts - http://quickfacts.census.gov/qfd/states/36000.html

[3] Austin, J., *Assessment of the Alabama Prison System*. The JFA Institute. Washington, D.C. (2005).

The aforementioned figures are based on national data. Upon further analysis of state data, the racial disparities become even more apparent. In Alabama, for example, African Americans make up only 26% of the population, but are nearly 62% of the prison population.[4]

Racial Disparity Between U.S. and Incarcerated Populations

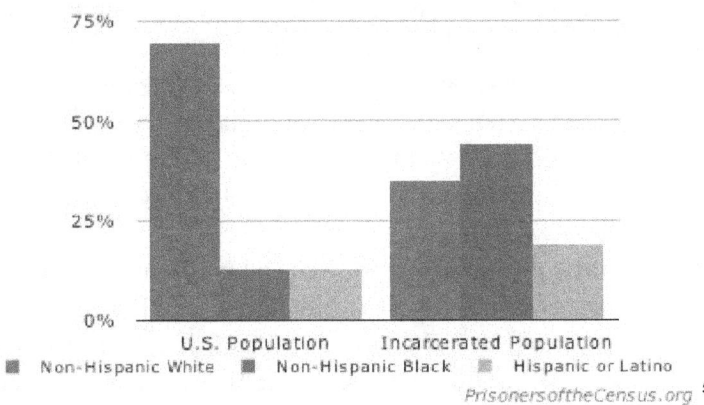

PrisonersoftheCensus.org [5]

For every white person in an Alabama jail there are about four African-American people.[6] In Maryland, eight out of ten people incarcerated for drug offenses are African-American.[7] Wisconsin and Connecticut incarcerate African Americans at a greater rate than did South Africa during apartheid. In each of these states, African Americans are disproportionately represented in the criminal justice system despite the abundance of empirical data demonstrating that the prevalence of drug use is identical between whites and

---

[4] Prison Policy Initiative, *Blacks Are Overrepresented in Alabama's Prisons and Jails.* (May 2004.)

[5] Source: U.S. Census and Bureau of Justice Statistics (Peter Wagner, 2004). Found at the Prison Policy Initiative Website: http://www.prisonpolicy.org/graphs/raceusandincarcerated.shtml

[6] The Sentencing Project, *State Rates of Incarceration by Race*, (2004), p. 3.

[7] Greene, J. and T. Roche, *Cutting Correctly in Maryland.* Justice Policy Institute, Washington D.C. (2003)

African Americans. The National Institute on Drug Abuse of the U.S. Department of Health and Human Services found that "prevalence . . . [of] recent illegal drug use [is] roughly equivalent for non-Hispanic African Americans and whites."[8] This trend of disproportionate incarceration, however, goes beyond those states mentioned. In fact, it is typical in virtually every state in this country.

When considering why this troubling reality exists, one cannot extirpate African Americans from their particular history in this country. One cannot and should not ignore the legacy of slavery and its aftermath when analyzing current social dilemmas as they relate to the black community. In reviewing this paper and information contained herein, it is worthwhile to bear in mind that the 13th Amendment to the U.S. Constitution abolished chattel slavery *"except for people convicted of crimes..."* Post-slavery American history instructs that laws were erected and norms institutionalized to ensure that African Americans remained in slave-like conditions. In the wake of the Civil War and Reconstruction, there were the Black Codes and Jim Crow laws that existed to perpetuate economic and social segregation and criminalization. Today, the war on drugs ensures the continuation of Jim Crow-type conditions. Indeed, when examined, the war on drugs represents such a blatant distortion of "justice" that it cannot be seen as anything less than a modern day incarnation of the Black Codes. While the "color line" that Du Bois intimated in 1903 referred to Jim Crow, in the 21st century it refers to the series of criminal and sentencing legislation that disproportionately relegate African Americans into the throes of the American criminal justice system.

What exactly is the war on drugs? How did we get into this mess? How is it that we have a "war on drugs" in which hundreds of thousands of African Americans are incarcerated for drug-related charges, yet drugs are cheaper, more readily available, and more potent than ever? When President Nixon declared a war on drugs

---

[8] National Institute on Drug Abuse (2003) Drug Use Among Racial/Ethnic Minorities, pp. 22 - http://www.drugabuse.gov/pdf/minorities03.pdf.

in the early 1970s, the prison population in the U.S. was less than 400,000. While writing this paper, that figure has swelled to over 2.2 million. Indeed, the U.S. incarcerates more people than any other nation in the history of the world. Many African-American communities are essentially occupied by the police—often at our very request. What, exactly, is going on then?

First, we allowed our policy makers to pass tough sentencing laws that criminalized drug use and addiction instead of treating it as a public health issue. We allowed our communities to become militarized zones, occupied by the police who claim that they are engaged in a battle in the never-ending war on drugs. We have reached out to the government to help us figure out the problems of drug use and abuse with the goal of revitalizing our communities, yet the government has responded by building prisons and filling them with African Americans.

Undoubtedly, drug use and abuse is a complicated and, for many people, painful issue. We live in a society that is constantly conflicted when it comes to the subject of drugs. Alcohol and tobacco are *legal* drugs which are taxed and regulated. While both have been empirically proven to be dangerous and addictive there are millions of Americans who use these drugs without serious condemnation. However, marijuana, a drug which in all of known history has never caused a single recorded death, remains illegal despite its proven medical utility. Caffeine, largely regarded as one of the most addictive drugs known to humankind, is legal and is readily available to the smallest child who can buy a soda pop. Opium is illegal, but morphine, an opiate derivative, is prescribed regularly by doctors for pain. Methamphetamine—speed—can be concocted with supplies found at any local drug, hardware, and farming supply stores, and is illegal. But pharmaceutical-grade speed (such as Ritalin and Adderal) is prescribed to American children at alarming rates and is still distributed by the military to fighter pilots. The seemingly arbitrary distinction created between these drugs has a direct impact on who is deemed the target of the war on drugs.

This nation's policies governing drugs vary depending on a host of factors and conditions which often have little to do with reason or compassion and everything to do with morality and politics. The Office of National Drug Control Policy continues to promote a "Just Say No" agenda, yet alcohol and cigarette advertisements are virtually ubiquitous and are protected from this message. We are supposed to tell our kids to keep away from drugs, yet multinational pharmaceutical companies are utilizing increasingly aggressive marketing strategies for drugs to cure every possible ailment. Janet Jackson's exposure in the 2004 Super Bowl developed into a near national crisis because the Super Bowl is a "family" event, yet nobody raises any objections to the endless beer commercials that interrupt the viewing and that are clearly targeted towards young people. These contradictions underscore the questionable goals of the war on drugs.

In light of the utter incoherence and contradictions of our society's approach to drugs, it is no surprise that our drug policies are reminiscent of a train wreck. U.S. law recognizes alcoholism as a disease—a *health* issue. An alcoholic does not get arrested for having alcohol in their home, for going to the bar, or for buying booze at the corner market. However, if someone *drives* while intoxicated they are breaking the law. By the same token, cocaine, heroin, marijuana, and crack are all *illegal* drugs, and U.S. law categorizes their possession and use as a *criminal* issue subject to often horrific penalties. Why does the person with a drinking problem warrant our compassion while the person with a crack problem gets our scorn and disdain?

The aforementioned example of crack cocaine is especially pertinent because perhaps no other drug, either licit or illicit, is more associated with African Americans. One only has to recall the crack "epidemic" in the U.S. in the mid-1980s and early 1990s. "Crack addict" became synonymous with "black person." Although crack was a major problem in low-income African-American neighborhoods at that time, it was never solely a "black problem." In 1991, at the height of the "epidemic," 52% of those reporting crack use were white, but 92.6% of those arrested for crack-related possession charges at the federal level were African American. In 1993 88% of those convicted of federal crack distribution were African American and only 4.1% were white. Research shows that illicit drug use nationwide is equally proportionate amongst racial groups. In fact, many studies show that white people actually dominate both drug use and sales in the U. S. today. Nonetheless, the "war on drugs" continues to be waged in and on communities of color, particularly African-American communities. Therefore, it seems counterintuitive that staging the war on drugs in low-income communities was accidental.

The proliferation of the drug war in African-American urban communities is in part attributable to the social disorganization of the ghetto. This author concurs that in poor, black and urban areas "more of the routine activities of life, including retail drug dealing, occur on the streets and alleys in poor neighborhoods. [While in] working and middle-class (white) neighborhoods, many activities, including drug deals, are likelier to occur indoors."[9] Although drugs are used and sold in all types of neighborhoods, undercover police operations are much more successful in poor neighborhoods, and therefore much more common. In middle and upper class communities police infiltration takes longer, costs more, and is less successful. As Michael Tonry summarizes, "no matter why it happens, the police emphasis on disorganized minority neighborhoods produces racial proportions in arrests that do not mirror racial proportion in drug use."[10] And here one must make note that high arrest numbers create a sense of achievement in the war, and provide a cache of available statistics for any incumbent politician to boast about being "tough on crime." It is typical for politicians to volunteer how many criminals they have gotten "off the street" as proof of their efficacy in crime control. Focusing on arrest numbers has become the measuring stick for success in the war on drugs, and the impact has been felt predominately in African-American communities.

---

[9] Tonry, M., *Malign Neglect*, p. 105.
[10] Tonry, M., *Ibid.* p 107.

Yet as bad as the policing policies have been, they are only the front end of a long line of abuses. The other area of outrageous inequity lies in the manner in which sentences are disseminated. Once arrested, African Americans are more likely to receive longer sentences for offenses strikingly similar to those of their white counterparts because of the U.S. court system's increasing reliance on mandatory minimum sentencing schemes. One of the best examples of the inherent flaws of mandatory minimum sentencing is the crack vs. powder cocaine disparity.

The Anti-Drug Abuse Act of 1986 instituted a 100:1 ratio of punishment for crack and powder cocaine. Public Law 99-570 Statue 3207 stipulates that a person convicted of possession with intent to distribute fifty grams or more of crack cocaine will receive the same mandatory minimum ten-year sentence as someone convicted of possession with intent to distribute 5000 grams of powder cocaine.[11] This disparity was amplified under the Federal Anti-Drug Abuse Act of 1988, which mandates a minimum sentence of five years in prison for possession of one to five grams of crack cocaine.[12] Thus, crack cocaine has become the "only drug for which there exists a mandatory minimum penalty for simple possession."[13]

Federal mandatory minimum cocaine sentences (for first offenders)

Type of drug	5-year sentence*	10 year sentence*
Powder cocaine	500 grams**	5 kilos***
Crack cocaine	5 grams**	50 grams***

* There is no parole in the federal system
** A gram equals a single packet of sweetener.
*** A kilo equals 2.2 lbs.

---

[11] Kennedy, R. *Race, Crime, and the Law*, pp. 364.

[12] Kennedy, R., *Ibid.* p. 364.

[13] Kennedy, R., *Ibid* p. 364.

This 100 to 1 punishment ratio is even more alarming when one considers that crack cocaine is derived from powder cocaine—which raises the argument that trafficking in one drug is virtually the same as trafficking in the other. This quandary was addressed in a report published by the *Journal of the American Medical Association* that found similar physiological and psychoactive effects for crack and powder cocaine and challenged the basis for disparate sentencing.[14] One might wonder why those convicted of crack possession are punished so much more harshly. The U.S. Department of Justice confirms that even after "controlling for like amounts of cocaine, in 2000, crack defendants convicted of trafficking in less than 25 grams of cocaine received an average sentence that was 4.8 times longer than the sentence received by equivalent powder defendant."[15] In their research into the impact of mandatory minimum drug sentencing and the crack vs. powder cocaine disparity, Douglas McDonald and Kenneth Carlson found that sentencing crack and powder cocaine traffickers the same for identical amounts of the drug would result in an inversion of the prison population. "Instead of African Americans receiving sentences that averaged 30% longer than that of whites," they wrote, "the average sentence for African American cocaine traffickers would have been 10% shorter than that of their white counterparts."[16] Indeed, the Bureau of Prisons estimates that "70% of the growth in the Federal Prison population can be attributed to longer sentences given to drug offenders."[17] These figures reinforce the "color line" that rigorously separates whites from African Americans in the war on drugs and the concomitant prison industrial complex today.

---

[14] Hatsukami, K. and M. Fischman, (1996) "Crack Cocaine and Cocaine Hydrochloride: Are the Differences Myth or Reality?" *Journal of the American Medical Association* (November 20, 1996)

[15] U.S. Department of Justice Federal Cocaine Offenses, "An Analysis of Crack and Powder Penalties," p. 3 (2002). http://www.usdoj.gov/olp/cocaine.pdf

[16] U.S. Department of Justice Federal Cocaine Offenses, *Ibid.* p. 277.

[17] U.S. Department of Justice Federal Cocaine Offenses, *Ibid.* p. 269.

Collateral consequences of the war on drugs: The term "collateral consequences" is often used to discuss issues that come about in relation to, or are caused by, the war on drugs. It has its origins in the military, where it is employed to justify and sanitize the horrors of war. If a bomb drops on a target and murders hundreds of civilians in the process, those civilian deaths are called "collateral consequences." Their deaths were not "planned," so they must be glossed over and forgotten about. "Collateral consequences" is, at its core, a concept designed to obscure, because it posits that something as horrific as murder can be justified for a "larger" goal.

The devastation inflicted upon African-American communities by the war on drugs is widespread and often obscured by drug war rhetoric. What are the collateral consequences in the war on drugs? Several books have been written discussing this very subject. Several recurring themes illustrate the profoundly negative effects that this war has had on African Americans.

First, criminalizing drug addiction has increased the police presence in African-American communities, which has led to higher arrest rates for African Americans. Subsequent to arrest, disproportionate mandatory sentencing schemes keep nonviolent people in prison for extraordinarily long periods of time. These two forces work in tandem to disproportionately incarcerate African Americans and people of color more than their white counterparts, even though it has been proven that drug use across these communities is the same.

The second collateral consequence, the de-population of African-American communities, is a direct result of the increased policing and mandatory minimum sentences. With so many African-American men in jail and prison, there are more single-parent headed households.

There is an abundance of empirical research demonstrating the deleterious effects of the proliferation of this trend[19]. Furthermore, any effort to revitalize impoverished African-American communities is hindered due to this reduction in capacity. In order for community development to succeed there must be a sustained effort to incorporate as many residents as possible. As increasing

Jail Incarceration Rates By Race and Ethnicity 1990-2003
(Number of jail inmates per 100,000 U.S. residents)

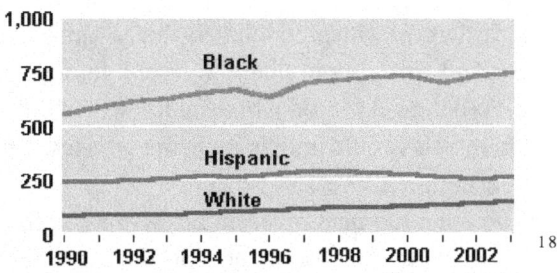

numbers of African-American men and women are taken from these neighborhoods, it becomes more difficult to mobilize for social change.

An additional collateral consequence of the war on drugs with especially grave ramifications is felony disfranchisement. Those lucky enough to get out of prison do so with a felony conviction on their record, which is difficult if not impossible to keep from impacting one's future. Currently, 14 states permanently disenfranchise those convicted of a felony. More than over 1.5 million African Americans have permanently lost the right to vote, even though they have completed their sentences and paid their debt to society.[20] Another 3 million people are disfranchised for varying periods of time depending on individual state policy. Here too, race must be highlighted. Felony convictions—as opposed to a misdemeanor

---

[18] Source: Bureau of justice Statistics Correctional Surveys (The National Probation Data Survey, National Prisoner Statistics, Survey of Jails, and The National Parole Data Survey) as presented in *Correctional Populations in the United States, 1997, Prison and Jail Inmates at Midyear* and Census of Jails 1999.

[19] For more information see Norland Christina (2001) "Father Involvement, Maternal Health Behavior, and Infant Health," *Fragile Families Research Brief*, No. 5, Bendheim-ThormanCenter for Research on Child Well-Being, Princeton University, Princeton, NJ

[20] Mauer, M. and K. Tushar, *Barred For Life: Voting Restoration in Permanent Disfranchisement States* The Sentencing Project, (2005). http://www.sentencingproject.org/pdfs/barredforlife.pdf

conviction for example—are what will result in a person being disenfranchised. Minorities are far more likely than whites to be convicted of a felony offense. Research on arrest statistics from the country's 56 largest cities concluded that, "a nonwhite male was three and a half times more likely to have a felony arrest than a white male. Whereas 14% of white males would be arrested, 51% of nonwhite males could anticipate being arrested for a felony at some time during their lives."[21]

Perhaps no other moment in recent history has highlighted the racism behind voter disfranchisement than the 2000 presidential election in states across the country, especially Florida and Ohio, where tens of thousands of African Americans were systematically prevented from voting, either by questionable laws, police misconduct, or intimidation. To realize the magnitude of this dilemma, one must simply consider that "if only eight tenths of one percent of adult male felons in Florida participated in the [2000] election with 60% of whites supporting Republican candidate Governor George W. Bush and a modest 80% of blacks supporting [former] Vice President Gore, Gore would have gained more than the 538 votes necessary to with the state and thus the presidency."[22] The preponderance of race in the probability of felony arrest makes felon disfranchisement laws a critical issue facing not just individuals, but the collective African-American community.

By prioritizing incarceration over education, federal and state budget allocations to fight the war on drugs illustrate yet another collateral consequence. As the number of incarcerated individuals continues to rise, states must increase the amount of funds allocated to correctional departments. This is usually at the expense of much-needed social service programs aimed at the same vulnerable populations on which the drug war is waged. South Carolina, for example, currently spends $7,751 per pupil on education which is dwarfed by the $13,590 per year that it spends on incarcerating a nonviolent offender. This fact is striking considering that South

---

[21] Miller, J., *Search and Destroy*, pp. 6
[22] Preuhs, R., *State Disfranchisement Policy*, pp. 733

Carolina is among the worst performing states in the country with regard to the number of teens not attending school and not working.[23]

In most discussions of the war on drugs, one of the least discussed consequences is the resulting lower living standards in the communities where the war is waged. Almost a quarter of all African Americans live below the poverty line.[24] In New York City, for example, barely 50% of all African-American men are employed.[25] This is the same city that supplies over 60% of the black and brown bodies incarcerated under the state's harsh drug laws. Valuable resources are utilized to police these communities, yet in times of fiscal crisis, social programs are the first to be cut. social investments such as youth programs and adult job training would have a positive effect on these communities. What remains un-discussed in all of the "lock 'em up" and "just say no" rhetoric is that the policies which they give birth to are quickly decimating the African-American community.

Direct Expenditure by Criminal Justice Function, 1982-2001

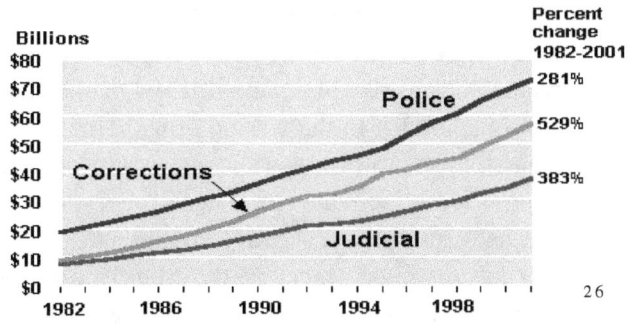

---

[23] Annie E. Casey Foundation, State Profiles of Child Well-Being (2004) p. 59

[24] JFA Institute Powerpoint, Key Social Economic Indicators in Black and White

[25] Levitan, Mark (2003) *A Crisis of Black Male Employment: Unemployment and Joblessness in New York City, 2003*, Community Service Society Annual Report. p. 2

[26] U.S. Department of Justice, Bureau of Justice Statistics, (March 25, 2005) http://www.ojp.usdoj.gov/bjs/glance/exptyp.htm

Substantive drug policy reform: treatment not incarceration: One of the most relevant opportunities to reform U.S. drug policies is to promote substance abuse treatment instead of incarceration for low-level nonviolent offenders. This type of response to drug addiction is not only more humane and cost effective; it has also been proven to reduce recidivism. Increasing the availability and accessibility of substance abuse treatment for indigent low-level nonviolent offenders is the most viable first step toward drug policy reform.

The groundbreaking treatment-instead-of-incarceration referendum that was passed by California voters in November of 2000 has become a model for other states. Proposition 36, also known as the Substance Abuse and Crime Prevention Act of 2000, diverts low-level, non violent drug offenders convicted solely of possession for personal use into community-based treatment programs instead of prison. Within the first six months, Proposition 36 diverted more than 12,000 individuals into treatment instead of prison. The decline in incarceration of female non violent drug offenders has been so significant that many lawmakers are considering closing one or two of the state's four women's prisons to help shrink California's budget deficit.[27]

In Maryland, the passage of Senate Bill 194 marked a pivotal shift in the state's approach to the war on drugs. This bill diverts non violent drug offenders from prison and into treatment. A number of secondary provisions facilitate the successful reintegration of these offenders back into their respective communities.

The most advantageous facet of the Maryland treatment-instead-of-prison legislation is that it addresses the inherent flaws with mandatory minimum sentences by codifying a prosecutor's discretion to forego prosecution in exchange for successful completion of a drug treatment program. Furthermore, it highlights sentencing options for judges and makes explicit their discretion to sentence a convicted drug offender to treatment rather than prison

---

[27] Drug Policy Alliance, Reform in California, http://www.drugpolicy.org/statebystate/california/

or simple probation. In order to further reduce the prison population and thereby reduce state corrections expenditures, SB 194 also modified the procedure for parole and probation revocations to incorporate feedback from treatment providers. Finally, this legislation also provided $3 million in new funding for this innovative program and dedicated a funding stream for drug and alcohol treatment services in the state of Maryland.[28]

A noteworthy facet of both of the preceding legislative reforms is the sizable amount of community support that each initiative enjoyed. In Maryland, a survey of registered voters revealed that "a large majority of voters believe that it is more effective to deal with crime at its roots through counseling and treatment rather than dealing with crime through stricter sentencing."[29] Similarly, the fact that California's policy reform was passed through referendum demonstrates the significant level of public support. An overwhelming 61% of voters supported this measure on November 7, 2000.[30] Both instances reinforce the fact that informing voters of potential alternatives and the concomitant cost savings is a necessary first step in drug policy reform. Too, they underscore the belief that sustainable change cannot occur without community mobilization.

The recent policy shifts in California and Maryland are exemplary of the evolving responses to substance addiction in this country. As the preceding paragraphs detail, the United States currently relies on an overly punitive response to drug use that does nothing to address the underlying problems that foster addiction. This type of approach that has characterized the war on drugs since its inception has resulted only in increasing the availability of more potent drugs; diverting state funds away from education and proactive social programs; and simply warehousing thousands and thousands of people at the taxpayer's expense. By simply expanding public conceptions of possible alternatives to incarceration, state

---

[28] The Campaign for Treatment Not Incarceration 2004 (March 28, 2005) http://www.treatnotjail.org/2004Wrapup.asp

[29] Justice Policy Institute, Maryland Voter Survey Executive Summary (2003), pp. 1 - http://www.treatnotjail.org/facts_md_poll_summary.pdf

[30] California Proposition 36 (March 28, 2005): http://www.prop36.org/about.html

legislatures can make significant advances in not only ameliorating the color line, but in making all Americans safer and healthier.

Conclusion: There is a profound need to think critically when interrogating U.S. policy, and in that thinking, never fail to view policy through the lens of race. This fact becomes quite salient in a discussion of contemporary drug control guidelines. In his text, *Prisons and the New American Racism*, author Paul Street aptly states that,

> *The 'war on drugs' that contributes so strongly to minority incarceration also inflates the price of underground substances, combining with ex-offenders shortage of marketable skills in the legal economy to create irresistible incentives for the sort of income generating conduct that leads back to prison. The dazed and embittered graduates of the prison industrial complex are released back into a small number of predominantly black and high-poverty zip codes and census tracts, deepening the concentration of poverty, crime, and despair, that is the hallmark of modern American 'hyper-segregation' by race and class.*[31]

There must be a more rigorous discussion of the disproportionate impact of drug laws in this country. The ultimate question raised by this paper is: has the war on drugs been effective? In order to answer that we must remind ourselves that the original goal of the war was to slow or prevent drug use. The fact that drug use continues to abound within the borders of this country highlights its failure. Our current approach is overly punitive and fails miserably at achieving its purported goal of reducing drug use and abuse. Furthermore, it callously disregards the underlying factors that perpetuate drug use in the first place, in particular unemployment

---

[31] Herivel, T. and P. Wright (eds.), *Prison Nation*, p. 35

and unaddressed substance addiction. While some groups have benefited materially from the war on drugs— politicians and those businesses involved in prison industries—illicit substances are still as readily available today as they were 20 years ago. The war has failed to stop drug addiction, and failed at stopping the crime associated with the drug economy. The only thing it has thus far accomplished is the further marginalization of African-American communities. A more humane and holistic response to drug use would incorporate both treatment for substance abusers and enhancing the capacity of distressed communities. These seemingly innovative ideas have already proven successful when implemented in states such as Maryland and California, where the availability of drug treatment has led to reductions in the overall prison population as well as the number of non violent offenders returning to prison. If this nation is to continue defining itself as the leader among nations, it must, finally, look deep within its neighborhoods and homes and prisons, face the complex realities of the lives which are too regularly struggling within these places, and heed the call to reform drug policy with all deliberate speed.

Training Pre-service Teachers to work with Juvenile Delinquents: From Theoretical Implications to Practical Applications

Helen Brantley, Lucinda Barron and Gbeorge E. Hicks

Research shows violent crimes perpetrated against youth ages of 12 and 17 have risen sharply. The impact of gun violence is significantly high among young African-American males.[1] Homicides involving guns has been the leading cause of death for African-American males for the past thirty years. The firearm homicide rate for the 15-24 year old age group increased 158 percent during the 10-year period.

Some experts estimate that as little as 1% of the general population will exhibit regular violent behavior. Meanwhile, many children who become violent are not safe in their own homes, schools, and communities. Psychologists state that the impact of post-traumatic stress that children experience as either victim or witness to violence "results in intrusive imagery, emotional constriction or avoidance, fears of recurrence, sleep difficulties, disinterested in significant activities and attention difficulties." All of these interfere with normal development with learning in school and living happy and safe in the community. With an increase of violence and

---

[1] Office of Research, *U.S. Department of Education, Education Reforms and Student At-Risk,* (Washington, D.C., U.S. Government Printing Office 1994).

vandalism in the schools, there is a need to help students and teachers learn effective ways to deal with conflict.

Research suggests that sociological and organizational variables contribute to many violent acts.[2] In addition, research is concerned with the adverse impact of violent acts on the home, school, and community. Startling statistics indicate that violent crime is common among juveniles and that serious juvenile offenders are very.[3] Teen crime is a major focus for TV news shows throughout the United States, and the high youth crime rate is evident in the schools, homes, community.[4]

In many homes, multiple factors such as lack of family bonding, child abuse, poor parental supervision, and parental involvement permeate the social environment. Inconsistent discipline or harsh discipline, exposure to and reinforcement of violence in the home and community of violent behavior contribute to growing concern that it may provide escalation of violence in youth.

Violence contributes to the discussion of the conditions besieging education today as school personnel relate to the current debate on the quality of American education.[5] School officials are inundated by the increase in national concern and reports that demand higher academic standards and heightened academic expectations.[6] As some students attend school to be successfully involved in the learning process, inappropriate actions of a few students deride successful educational programs and services. Overall, about 1,000 crimes per 100,000 students were reported in

---

[2] Chaiken, M.R., *Tailoring Established After-School Programs to meet Urban Realities, Violence in American Schools (New York, 1998).*

[3] DeCecco, J. P. and G. A. Schaeffer, *Using Negotiation to Resolve Teacher-student Conflicts. Journal of Research and Development in Education,* 11 (4), 1978, 64-67.

[4] Roger, M., *Resolving Conflict through Peer Mediation. A Series of Solutions and Strategies 9, 1-13.*

[5] Barron, L., *The Impact of Peer Mediation Training on Adolescent's Problem-solving Skills, Perception of School Climate, and Attitudes Toward Conflict Management.* (Undissertation) University of South Carolina (2000).

[6] Lunenberg, F. C. and A. C. Ornstein., *Educational Administration* (2nd ed.), (Belmont, 1996).

our nation's public schools.[7] Schools are reporting violent acts occurring in classes, hallways, and playgrounds by the 12-17 year old population. Factors such as truancy, frequent absent, peer rejection, poor class performances, early dropout, are predictors of youth violence.

It is difficult for learning to occur in the presence of fear or intimidation. With the rise of violence in our schools, communities are demanding a safe and secure environment for children.[8] Reducing the number of violent acts and the severity of violent acts can aid in providing an educational environment conducive to learning. As many school reform efforts work toward maximizing students' academic learning, teaching students how to get along and resolve conflicts contributes to a positive learning environment.[9]

On the other hand, recent calls to reform and restructure education have led to changes in the preparation of pre-service teachers of today's classrooms. This includes diverse settings servicing those at-risk for violence and Juveniles in other settings. It is becoming more difficult to provide students with a safe and productive learning environment in schools.[10]

As society enters the twenty-first century, reducing violence in schools is becoming more complex. Colleges and universities must prepare pre-service teachers as "highly qualified" to teach in diverse class settings and to provide higher quality and more equitable and accountable classes for poor, minority students, Juveniles, and Youths At-Risks for violence. For example, the No Child Left Behind ACT (NCLB) is designed to *"ensure that all children* have a fair, equal, and significant opportunity to attain a high-quality education and reach, at minimum, proficiency on challenging state academic achievement standards and state academic assessments," which was to be accomplished by shifting

---

[7] Statistical Abstract of the United States, *The National Data Book* 118, (1998) 237-250.

[8] DeCecco, J. P. and G. A. Schaeffer, *Ibid.*

[9] Barron, L., *Ibid.*

[10] Carlin, T. S. and D. Carlin, Philadelphia Peer Mediation Program: Report for 1992-1994 period, ERIC Document Reproduction Service No. ED 384 089, 1994.

funding formulas and sending more federal resources to high-poverty and struggling schools such as those in high crime areas.[11]   Further, three aspects of the NCLB are particularly relevant to teacher education-stipulations regarding "highly qualified teachers" (HQT) and "adequate yearly progress (AYP) and the bill's emerging consequences for low achieving students attending poorly performing schools, those at-risk for violence and those in juvenile diverse settings.   Additionally, NCBL requires that all students have teachers with at least a bachelor's degree, full state certification or a passing score on a state licensing exam, and demonstrated competencies in the subjects they teach.

In alignment with the NCLB Act, recent calls by accreditation bodies have led to policies to restructure education have led to changes in the preparation of pre-service teachers of today's classrooms of those at-risk for violence and those in juvenile diverse settings. If this bill does not live up to its expectations, and as a result of the neglect sited above, these students will continue to be placed in poorly designed programs, taught by teachers who have not been trained to work with their unique needs. Those teachers will continue to instruct them with materials and methods that are designed for use with either regular students or students who are in special education. Juveniles and other diverse students need teachers who can build on the personal, cultural, social, and physical strengths students bring to the school, home and community settings.

Research has documented that effective classes can improve self-esteem, transform attitudes toward teachers and school, and salvage young lives from drug, alcohol addiction, abuse and crime.[12] To overcome such a cycle, teachers must value diversity, promote collaborative learning, modeling, and blending personal and affective needs in the total program. The question of how best to accommodate juveniles in the learning settings hinges on the

---

[11] U.S. Congress. No Child Left Behind Act of 2001: Conference report to Accompany H.R. 1, report 107-334. (Washington, DC: Government Printing Office (2001).

[12] Barr, R. D. and W.H. Parrett, *Hope Fulfilled for At-Risk and Violent Youth k-12 Programs that Work.* (Boston: Northern University Press, 2002).

effectiveness and motivation of the teacher. Teachers must accept the fact that they must work more effectively with struggling students. This perspective is based on an ethical and philosophical foundation aligned to the NCLB Act. Educators are required to apply basic principles of an appropriate curriculum to the developmental needs, abilities and interest of students. Research has shown that a caring classroom and school community can become responsive to families, provide a meaningful curriculum, a stable and safe environment, and opportunities for optimal growth of its students.

Despite the conventional wisdom about youth rebelliousness, young adolescents approaching independence are still intimately tied to their families, teachers and other persons who care about them. Youth at-risk for violence require and desire adult supervision and guidance in making educational and career decisions, in forming a set of values, and in assuming adult roles. The poignant answer of young people to question about why they join gangs is that these groups become the families that they never had. This is a compelling testimony to youth's fundamental need for close, reliable relationships with a supportive, protective group that confers respect and identity and recognizes competence. How can we reshape our program, change relationship, and adjust the instructional strategies based on the unique cultures of juvenile delinquents.

After a survey from pre-service teachers during the spring, 2004 soliciting their responses of their perception on the preparedness to teach juveniles delinquents, a model was put in place. A cluster of several important seminar strands were developed on "best practices" and research in the areas delineated in the survey. (See Table 1.)[13] The pre-service teachers' perception regarding the strengths and weaknesses of their characteristics and teaching performances of knowledge, skills, and disposition in teaching juveniles delinquents in diverse classroom before and after training indicate an increase in the mean scores on all 10 of the survey items. The pre-service teachers felt that they were qualified after

---

[13] Itemized mean Responses on a Self-Assessment of Curricular Modification by Before and After Training of Pre-service Teachers.

training, and reported that they were quite comfortable teaching the model to the juvenile delinquents.

Caring Collaborative and Cultural Training Model with Pre-service Teachers: With the current focus on multicultural counseling, sensitivity to the similarities and differences between cultures require consideration. The model emphasizes conflict resolution and peer mediation activities on a consistent and ongoing basis for juvenile delinquents. Additionally, pre-service teachers may find McFadden's basic premises for transcultural counseling useful for planning conflict resolution programs with juveniles, peer mediation projects, and other interventions that are designed to facilitate peace in schools, home and community.[14] Understanding the students' culture enables pre-service teachers to serve their developmental needs, abilities, interests and career goals.

The Model includes four strands, and each strand has a common thread of family involvement, community partnership, and cultural building throughout. The strands include: Collaboration and Partnership Building; Students and Environmental Management; Assessment and Analytical Strategies and Resiliency Modeling.

Collaboration and Partnerships: It is important to create linkages among social services, law enforcement and criminal justice agencies, housing authorities, community action groups, and other key community groups to establish realistic, defined, and measurable community goals that will be responsive to the needs of the community. To produce positive outcomes, effective behavioral change requires a long-term commitment, accessibility and a community-wide effort. The collaboration and partnership model identifies process measures and short-term outcomes, such as increased levels of community involvement in school activities and county accessibility to enhance levels of parental involvement in class activities. Additionally, activities will also increase among the pre-service teachers and in-service teachers from a positive perspective. This philosophy guides the activities in this strand.

---

[14] McFadden, J., *Transcultural Counseling* (Alexandria, 1993).

The premise of the strands is that classroom pre-service teachers cannot meet the needs and demands of juvenile delinquents on their own. The various roles of educators, community and family must be examined to gain a greater understanding of the human resources within the setting that can be used to forge partnerships to meet the needs of a diverse population. Activities including collaborative problem solving, teacher assistance teams, collaborative consultation, and team teaching are included as essential part of a cluster of several topics during a 12-week field seminar. Each seminar strand is designed to examine, discuss and employ strategies within the context of collaboration with student, class and the community.

Table I: Itemized mean Responses on a Self-Assessment for Curricular Modification by before and After Training of Pre-service Teachers

	Items N=15	*Mean*	*Train*
1	I can define, discuss and apply the collaborative models during my teaching.	2.51 3.50	Before After
2	I can discuss the similarities and differences between strategies of critical thinking, problem solving and creative thinking.	2.52 3.00	Before After
3	I can define, discuss and apply specific skills in the area of interpersonal communication and conflict management.	2.79 3.09	Before After
4	I can define, discuss and apply the interrelationship of environmental management strategies.	2.55 3.51	Before After
5	I can apply the ethical and caring practices of teaching.	2.53 2.93	Before After
6	I can discuss the relative importance of including assessment and analytical methods in my teaching.	2.56 3.25	Before After
7	I can apply responsive cultural thinking to develop skills and concepts across all program areas.	2.63 3.22	Before After
8	I can explain the importance of involving students in evaluation of their own behavior.	2.86 3.33	Before After
9	I can evaluate and select higher thinking materials.	2.79 3.09	Before After
10	I can utilize appropriate assessment techniques in my conflict resolution activities.	2.56 3.01	Before After

Environmental Management Methods: A variety of theoretically based models for managing students and classrooms will be presented in this strand. Pre-service teachers will examine the ethics, policies, and procedures regarding the management of challenging juvenile behaviors. The strand area will include skills in managing ecological factors within various settings, home and community. The discussion considers a variety of strategies, including conflict resolution, for teaching and applying social competencies through modeling to juvenile delinquent.

Assessment and Analytical Method: The strand covers two parts: research and practice. The research portion of the strand area provides a theoretical perspective of various at-risk for violence assessment procedures to help pre-service teachers become informed consumers of assessment procedures. A variety of at-risk approaches include action research of theory, curriculum instruction that works and proven vocational -based assessment, authentic assessment (Portfolio), reflection, outcome-based assessment/criterion-referenced, and norm-referenced assessment are used.

This strand will identify juveniles who are good models. Those students who see the relationship between their school behavior and later opportunities for vocational or college training will serve as mentors along with pre-service teachers who will model the appropriate behavior. For example, often students do not know the required courses they need to take to qualify for college admission in an area of interest. Such absences of knowledge enhance un-motivation in students and prevent juveniles from connecting current relevance of school to the real world of employment possibilities. Students will engage in activities of research and gain practice in application of concepts and skills. Pre-service teachers will role model journaling and self-assessment.

Resiliency Modeling Method: This strand uses the behavior modification process that includes four attributes. They are based on the premise that behavior can be systematically modified in a desired direction. The most important attribute is that behavior can be precisely defined and measured. Another attribute stipulates that behavior forms the basis for developing effective interventions. Behavior is based on effective "best practice" research, and intervention techniques derived from the basic principles of behavior can be used to rearrange settings, environment and conditions to promote developmentally appropriate social, cognitive, physical and emotional behaviors as they interact with juveniles in home, school and community settings.

Implementation: A number of activities are associated with each strand and each strand is categorized according to stages. The first time the group is brought together, each member is provided a copy of the stages. Review each stage separately. Remind each group member that he/she will naturally form, storm, and norm and ultimately perform. Youths appreciate knowing in advanced that they will naturally go through these stages. After going through each stage, each youth should be allowed to indicate where he or she views the collaborative group in terms of its development. Plot the responses using the computer. Continue with collaborative group activities based on the majority response, recognizing that several of the group members may view themselves individually in different places and that the group should attend to these issues as well.

Each of the four stages of collaborative community development is concerned with one or more major issues. In addition, a number of tasks are required at each stage. These issues and tasks are identified below, along with suggested strategies for accomplishing the tasks. These issues and tasks should be reviewed with the group. It is important before the group begins any work that these tasks be accomplished according to the stages delineated under activities.

Activities:

Stage I: Creating community in classrooms: A fact of life in contemporary setting is fact that it demands diversity. Youth in the 21st century do not hide their differences in culture, background, style, sexual preferences or the problematical influences of their family situation. Pre-service teachers engage in ongoing professional activities to improve the social and academic opportunities of juvenile delinquents.

Stage II: Conflict Resolution: Few models exist for the positive handling of conflict, for patience and acceptance, for respectful relations among different individuals and groups of youths. Economic and psychological stress on families, eroding trust in social institutions, run-away media sensationalizing destructive behavior, and an epidemic of violence mitigate against the kind of community and conflict resolution that permeate the classroom culture.

Stage III: Building Community Resilience: The pre-service teacher and the students engage in co-assessment and co-planning to increase roles and responsibilities. The pre-service teacher involves the juveniles in shaping their school program growth and need. Collaboratively, they shift the focus from the problem to success; an essential motivational strategy for Juveniles is established constantly throughout their interaction. As a unit, pre-service teacher and student share responsibility for their own improvement as they collaborate to plan, monitor, and evaluate progress. Potential benefits to juveniles increased self-awareness, active involvement, positive motivation, and goal directed community and career activities.

Conclusion: Professional development and training programs of pre-service teachers are beginning to recognize and rectify the incongruence and inconsistencies of serving a diverse student population including those at-risk for violence and Juveniles in other settings. These programs have begun to acknowledge that all does not mean some. In preparing pre-service teachers for the appropriate education of all students, irrespective of the diversity, professional development activities must begin to acknowledge the interrelated roles of professionals, communities and families in broader perspectives of diversity that includes those at-risk for violence and

Juveniles in other settings. If policy makers mean "No Child is Left Behind," all professionals, including pre-service teachers, must reexamine how they prepare themselves with appropriate strategies to meet an array of challenges in diverse classrooms. Clearly, neither one field nor discipline has all the answers or resources. It will take time, effort and a willingness to take risks, try innovative approaches, and think creatively to explore techniques to acknowledge and serve a much-neglected diversity, those at-risk for violence and Juveniles in other settings.

Trying Children and Adults in Georgia: Can the Seven Deadly Sins be Forgiven?

Amy Howell

Prior to 1899 most state criminal law contained provisions for trying juveniles accused in the same system and in the same manner as adults accused. In 1899 a shift in ideology and cultural changes led to creation of the first juvenile courts. A juvenile court reform movement led to a general consensus that child offenders should be treated differently than adult offenders, and the creation of the juvenile court was meant to provide juveniles with individual treatment.[1] The shift in ideology was provoked by the idea that the community bears a responsibility to raise children to act lawfully, and when a child does not conform to lawful standards, the community has a responsibility to care for that child and help correct the child's behavior. Thus, the state, acting as *parens patrie*, could intervene where the parents failed to properly care for or control their children. Having assumed control, the state had the responsibility to act in the child's best interest. In order to prevent recidivism in youth leading to a life of crime, the state had a duty to intervene in the best interests of the child.[2]

---

[1] Slaten, M., "Juvenile Transfers to Criminal Court: Whose Right is it Anyway?," *Rutgers Law Review* 55 (2003) 821-853.

[2] Slaten, M., *Ibid.*

The juvenile court focused on rehabilitation rather than punishment, and thus eschewed procedural due process safeguards like the right to a jury trial and the right to an attorney. In this era the courts focused on treatment, supervision, and control, rather than punishment. Great emphasis on treating the "whole child" led to a very broad judicial discretion and a high level of informality in the proceedings.[3] Because all juvenile proceedings were labeled as "civil" proceedings, the due process safeguards were inapplicable, even where rehabilitation resulted in a loss of liberty. A primary impetus of the movement toward a juvenile rehabilitation system was specific training in social science and child psychology for juvenile court judges. Though that goal was never fully realized, the juvenile court did thrive as a rehabilitative body up until the early 1960's. The 1964 meeting of the National Council of Juvenile Court Judges, however, forecast a change in the Supreme Court's attitude toward juvenile justice: Chief Justice Earl Warren announced that juvenile courts would be expected to work within the framework of adult courts and to provide due process protections for children.[4] With this announcement, the Chief Justice planted the juvenile court "seeds of change."[5]

In re Gault and Ramifications: Bring Back the "Kangaroo Court!": Under our Constitution, the condition of being a [child] does not justify a kangaroo court."[6] With this proposition and its decision in *In re Gault* in 1967, the United States Supreme Court initiated a watershed in the juvenile justice system. The Court held that children in delinquency proceedings are constitutionally entitled to substantially the same due process protections as adults

---

[3] Some have argued this discretion allowed for discrimination in sentencing and the entire juvenile court system should be abolished. See Barry C. Feld, "Abolish the Juvenile Court: Youthfulness, Criminal Responsibility, and Sentencing Policy," J. *Crim. L. & Criminology* 88 (1997). Pgs 68-136.

[4] Berkheiser, M., "The Fiction of Juvenile Right to Counsel; Waiver in the Juvenile Courts," *Florida L. Rev.* 54 (2002). p 588.

[5] Berkheiser, M., *Ibid.*

[6] *In re Gault,* 387 U.S. 1, 28 (1967).

in adult criminal proceedings.[7] The effect of this decision was a more formalized delinquency proceeding. Juvenile delinquency hearings soon began to mirror adult criminal trials, and this mirroring effect of *Gault* was eventually extended to almost all juvenile cases, including cases of child abuse and neglect.[8]

The *Gault* decision marks a retreat from the high water point of the juvenile court reform movement. Since that time the tide has steadily receded from the informal best interest model toward a more formal punitive model. Although the Court did not intend to cause a retreat from the informal therapeutic work, the effect of *Gault* has been increased formality and an erosion of the distinctions between adult criminal courts and juvenile courts with subsequent cases.[9] In *In re Winship*, the Court found the adult criminal must prove that juvenile delinquency standard of proof "beyond a reasonable doubt." And in *Breed v. Jones*, in applying a ban on double jeopardy to juvenile cases, the Court further obfuscated distinctions between criminal trails and delinquency proceedings.

"*Gault* and *Winship* unintentionally, but inevitably, transformed the juvenile court system from its original Progressive conception as a social welfare agency into a wholly-owned subsidiary of the criminal justice system."[10] While juvenile courts now operate under many added procedural safeguards, they are not required to provide *all* of the procedural safeguards available in the criminal justice system. For example, in *McKeiver v. Pennsylvania*,[11] the Court found that the accused in juvenile proceedings are not entitled to a federal right to a jury trial.

Georgia as a Case Study for Trying Children as Adults: Like many states, Georgia has moved to a system of harsher punishment for juvenile offenders. Many states deal with juvenile

---

[7] *In re Gault, Ibid.*

[8] Meyers, J.E.B., Session 3: Children's Rights in the Context of Welfare Dependency," *U.C. Davis Journal of Juvenile Law & Policy*, Summer (2004).

[9] Feld, "Abolish the Juvenile Court," 73.

[10] Feld, "Abolish the Juvenile Court," 73.

[11] 403 U.S. 528, 541 (1971).

crime by treating juveniles as adult defendants, and Georgia is no exception. There are two main mechanisms in Georgia by which a juvenile's case is processed in superior court: (1) transfer after a hearing in juvenile court, and (2) automatic transfer by operation of SB440.

Transfer Hearings: Discretionary and Mandatory Transfer: Georgia law provides some opportunity for judicial discretion for transfer from juvenile court to superior court and also sets out those situations in which transfer is mandatory. A juvenile court judge *may* transfer a case after a hearing and upon a determination that the child was at least 15 years old at the time of a delinquent offense or was at least 13 years old and committed 1) a delinquent offense punishable by death or 2) a delinquent offense punishable by confinement for life or 3) an aggravated battery that resulted in serious bodily injury to a the victim[12].

Transfer is appropriate where the interests of both the youth and the community require the transfer.[13] A juvenile court *may* order a transfer to superior court when the community's interest in treating the juvenile as an adult outweighs the juvenile's interest in being treated in the juvenile justice system.[14] In *Kent v. U.S.*, the Supreme Court outlined eight factors courts should consider when determining whether to transfer a case out of juvenile court: (1) the seriousness of the alleged offense to the community and whether the protection of the community requires waiver; (2) whether the alleged offense was committed in an aggressive, violent, premeditated, or willful manner; (3) whether the alleged offense was against persons or against property, greater weight being given to offenses against persons, especially if personal injury resulted; (4) the prosecutive merit of the complaint; (5) the desirability of trial and disposition of the entire offense in one court when the juvenile's associates in the alleged offense are adults who will be charged with a crime; (6) the sophistication and maturity of the juvenile; (7) the record and previous history of the juvenile; (8) the

---

[12] O.C.G.A. 15-11-30.2 (a)(4)(A-B).

[13] O.C.G.A. 15-11-30.2 (a)(3)(C)

[14] *In the Interest of J.H.*, 260 Ga. 447, 449, 396 S.E.2d 885 (1990).

prospects for adequate protection of the public and the likelihood of the reasonable rehabilitation of the juveniles.[15] These factors serve as guidelines for juvenile court judges.

Georgia law requires a juvenile be transferred to superior court if specific findings are made after a transfer hearing. Where the juvenile court judge finds reasonable grounds for believing the juvenile committed certain offenses, the judge *must* transfer the case to superior court. First, where a youth was committed in a youth detention center and after a transfer hearing the judge has reasonable grounds to believe the youth committed murder, voluntary manslaughter, aggravated assault or aggravated burglary, the judge *must* transfer the case to superior court. Second, where a youth has been found to have committed burglary on three separate prior occasions, and after a transfer hearing the judge has reasonable grounds to believe that the youth has committed the felony act of burglary, the judge *must* transfer the case to superior court.

Therefore, under the transfer hearing method, there are two ways to waive a case to superior court: mandatory and discretionary. The next section focuses on Georgia's automatic transfer statute enacted by the legislature in 1994. Though heavily contested, the statute remains the law in Georgia.

Intent and Impact of SB440: Automatic Transfers: In 1994, Georgia enacted SB440, commonly referred to as the "Seven Deadly Sins" law, which gives the Superior Courts in Georgia exclusive jurisdiction when any youth age 13 or older is alleged to have committed: (1) murder; (2) voluntary manslaughter; (3) rape; (4) aggravated sodomy; (5) aggravated child molestation; (6) aggravated sexual battery; or (7) armed robbery if committed with a firearm.[16]

Controversial from its inception, SB440 was immediately challenged in the courts. However, in the 1995 term in *Bishop v. State*,[17] the Georgia Supreme Court rejected several constitutional

---

[15] *Kent v. United States*, 383 U.S. 541 (1966).

[16] O.C.G.A. § 15-11-28(b)(C).

[17] 265 Ga. 821, 824, 462 S.E.2d 716, 719 (1995).

challenges to Georgia's procedures for determining when juveniles may be tried as adults. In *Bishop*, the court held that that the statutory scheme does not violate the separation of powers doctrine, the due process rights of juveniles, or the equal protection provisions of the state and federal constitutions. However, Justice Benham, concurring, encouraged the state legislature to create better guidelines to regulate prosecutorial discretion in such cases:

> *As we cope with the reality that society has begotten some children who boastfully, remorselessly stride across the line which separates right from wrong, we must not forget that there are young people who only stray onto the wrong side of the law. We, as a society, must remember that some children are only strayers and we must actively work to rescue, rehabilitate, and nurture them. Our laws must give direction to those responsible for the enforcement of the laws who determine which child shall be set on a course of rehabilitation in the juvenile court system, and which child shall be sent to superior court for punishment.*[18]

Justice Benham's concurrence seeks better guidelines, rather than bright line rules for determining when a child should be tried in the adult criminal system and when that child should remain in juvenile court in the hopes of rehabilitation.

While some scholars have argued that waiver from juvenile courts is inappropriate in all circumstances,[19] a more reasoned approach allows for judicial waiver discretion where a juvenile court judge can render unbiased decisions based on all the facts. The Honorable Arthur L. Burnett, Sr. advocates such an approach and argues that the original goals of the juvenile courts—rehabilitation and representation of the whole child—can still be achieved by (1) offering better guidelines for determining when offenders should

---

[18] *Ibid.* at 824, 462 S.E.2d at 719.
[19] Slaten, M., *Ibid.*

be tried in adult courts, (2) restoring juvenile court discretion, and (3) properly funding the courts.[20]

Increasing Number of Children Tried in Adult System and the Effects: Like many criminal jurisdictions, Georgia is faced with a perception that juveniles are increasingly engaged in violent crime. Georgia has moved in the direction of dealing harshly with juvenile offenders and away from the traditional model of maintaining a wholly separate juvenile justice system aimed at rehabilitation. In Georgia and throughout the nation, an increasing number of children are being tried in the adult criminal system. Georgia Supreme Court precedent reveals an unwillingness to act outside of direct legislative command. Most recently, on February 7, 2005, the court declined to interpret the juvenile criminal code, specifically under O.C.G.A. § 15-11-28(b)(2)(B), to require a competency hearing before a juvenile is transferred to adult criminal court. The court stated: "As a cautionary matter, it may be prudent for trial courts to hold competency evaluations for such juveniles. However, while the majority of states require comprehensive hearings to determine the suitability of transferring a youthful offender out of juvenile court, we are aware of only two states that require competency determinations before such a transfer is allowed. Both those states have statutory schemes that are markedly different from that of Georgia."[21] The court continued, "Any changes to Georgia's current statutory provisions for trying certain juvenile offenders as adults must come from the General Assembly, as this Court is not authorized to rewrite or revise provisions of the Code."[22]

In addition, Georgia's children accused under SB440 often await trial in adult facilities. If convicted at trial, SB441 applies, which requires a mandatory minimum of ten years imprisonment without parole for SB440 offenses. While this is a minimum standard, SB 440 actually allows punishment of life in prison without parole

---

[20] Honorable Burnett, A.L, Sr., "What of the Future? Envisioning an Effective Juvenile Court," *Criminal Justice Magazine,* 15 (2000).

[21] *Lewis v. State*, 2005 WL 276873 at *2.

[22] *Lewis v. State, Ibid.*

for juvenile offenders. Children convicted under the statute generally serve their time in adult prisons where they interact with adult criminals on a daily basis. The "one-two" punch of SB440 and SB441 give children who "stray" onto the wrong side of the law little hope for the future and no chance for rehabilitation.

Compounding the problem, SB440 is disproportionately applied to African-American children. Research reveals that 90% of those convicted under SB440 are African Americans. African American and Latino youth are 45% of Georgia's youth population, but comprise 74.8% of the youth arrested under SB440.[23] White youth were 84% more likely than African-American youth charged under SB440 to have their case transferred back to juvenile court (46% of white Youth were transferred back, versus 25% of African-American youth).[24]

The most extensive and comprehensive research on transfer of youth to the adult criminal justice system has shown conclusively that children are more likely to re-offend when they are tried and incarcerated in the adult criminal justice system.[25] Research funded by the U.S. Justice Department has shown that in Florida, youth tried as adults were a third more likely to re-offend than those retained in the adult system. Transferred youth also re-offended twice as quickly and were twice as likely to be arrested for serious offenses. According to studies by the U.S. Justice Department, youth incarcerated with adults are five times more likely to report being sexually assaulted, and eight times more likely to commit suicide than youth held in juvenile justice facilities.[26]

---

[23] Juveniles Arrested As Adults Under SB440: Fiscal Year 2004-Final Report (2004).

[24] Juveniles Arrested As Adults Under SB440, *Ibid.*

[25] Bishop, D.M., et. al., "The Transfer of Juveniles to Criminal Court: Does it make a difference?" Crime & Delinquency, 42 (April 1996); Florida Department of Juvenile Justice, "Juvenile Transfer to Criminal Court Study: Final Report," January 8, 2002.

[26] Flaherty, M.G., *An Assessment of the National Incidences of Juvenile Suicides in Adult Jails, Lockups and Juvenile Detention Centers* (Urbana-Champaign: The University of Illinois, 1980).

While the juvenile court's goals center on treatment and rehabilitation, the adult system's focus is on retribution and punishment. Recent studies have shown that children have diminished competence for trials in adult court, and therefore these children have diminished levels of culpability. A study released by researchers from the MacArthur Foundation's Research Network on Adolescent Development and Juvenile Justice found that a third of children aged 11 through 13, and a fifth of those aged 14 or 15, understood legal matters at a level akin to mentally ill adults who have been found incompetent to stand trial.[27] Significantly, nearly 50% of the youth arrested under SB 440 were age 15 or younger.[28] This report also showed that the transfer of children into the adult criminal justice system almost surely leads to the prosecution in adult court of children who are not competent to stand trial[29]

The inability of adolescents to make reasoned decisions and to communicate effectively greatly inhibits their capacity to participate in the criminal justice process; fundamental barriers, such as an inability to communicate with their attorney or a lack of understanding in regard to legal concepts such as their Miranda rights, significantly affects meaningful interaction with the system[30].

Back to the Future: *Roper's* Insights for a Return to The Best Interests Standard in Juvenile Courts: In Roper v. Simmons,[31] on March 1, 2005, the United States Supreme Court in a 5-4 decision held unconstitutional the execution of juveniles under the age of eighteen.[32] In ruling, the Court identified "three general

---

[27] MacArthur Juvenile Adjudicative Competency Study (March, 2003), posted at http://www.macfound.org

[28] Georgia Indigent Defense Council, "Juveniles Arrested As Adults Under SB440" *Fiscal Year 2004-Final Report*, (Georgia Indigent Defense Council, Atlanta, GA, 2004).

[29] Georgia Indigent Defense Council, *Ibid*. See also Berkheise, M, "The Fiction of Juvenile Right to Counsel," pgs. 626-630.

[30] Adolescent Brain Development and Legal Culpability, ABA. Juvenile Justice Centers (Winter, 2003).

[31] 125 S. Ct. 1183 (2005).

[32] *Ibid*. at 1200.

differences" between juveniles and adults. [33]   First, the Court found juveniles exhibit a scientifically and sociologically documented "lack of maturity" and "an underdeveloped sense of responsibility."[34] Juveniles are reckless as a result of this lack of maturity, and as a result, the rights of juveniles (voting, serving on juries, marrying) are limited until the juveniles reach the age of maturity. [35]   Because juveniles are prone to recklessness as a result of immaturity, "their irresponsible conduct is not as morally reprehensible as that of an adult."[36] Second, "juveniles are more vulnerable and susceptible to negative influences and outside pressures, including peer pressure."[37] Because juveniles are rarely fully in control of their environment, they are unlikely to possess the experience or freedom to remove them from an uncomfortable or compromising position.[38] "Youth is more than a chronological fact. It is a time and condition of life when a person may be most susceptible to influence and to psychological damage."[39] Thus, because of this lack of control, "juveniles have a greater claim than adults to be forgiven for failing to escape negative influences in their whole environment."[40] And finally, the Court noted that the "character of a juvenile is not as well formed as that of an adult. The personality traits of juveniles are more transitory, less fixed."[41] Because a juvenile is in a state of transition and change, the juvenile's character deficiencies are more receptive to rehabilitation. Thus, "[f]rom a moral standpoint, it would be misguided to equate the failings of a minor with those of an adult, for a greater possibility exists that a minor's character deficiencies will be reformed."[42]

---

[33] *Ibid*. at 1195.

[34] *Ibid*. at 1195 (quoting *Johnson v. Texas*, 509 U.S. 350, 367 (1993)).

[35] *Ibid*. at 1195.

[36] *Ibid*. at 1195 (quoting *Thompson v. Oklahoma*, 487 U.S. 815, 835 (1988)).

[37] *Ibid*. Georgia Indigent Defense Council

[38] *Ibid*.

[39] *Ibid*. at 1195 (quoting *Eddings v. Oklahoma*, 455 U.S. 104, 115 (1978)).

[40] *Ibid*. at 1195.

[41] *Ibid*.

[42] *Ibid*. at 1195-96.

This decision is an important victory for juvenile justice advocates. In a period when the purpose and need for juvenile courts has come into question, this decision provides strong support for the jurisdiction and expertise of the juvenile court. The decision confirms what child advocates have long believed, that the developmental state of adolescence provides a unique opportunity for treatment and rehabilitation. This principle led to the creation of the first juvenile court in 1899 and the distinction between adult criminals and adolescent offenders.

Conclusion: For over ten years, Georgia has subjected its children to the unfair and harsh effects of SB440. Clearly, it is not the intent of this paper to support the contention that no juvenile should ever be tried in the adult system. However, the purpose of this paper is to reveal that the competence of the juvenile court judge to determine whether to waive the case into the superior court should be trusted over the bright line rule of SB440 which pushes cases into the adult system automatically. Recently, the Supreme Court of the United States has vindicated three of the main rationales for not trying children as adults: (1) children lack maturity and sound decision-making skills, (2) youth lack control of their environment and are susceptible to outside influence, and (3) youth character is in the midst of development and therefore inclined toward rehabilitation. *Roper* provides support for the movement to reinstate juvenile court discretion to transfer the appropriate juvenile cases to adult courts for prosecution. Because juvenile courts have the expertise in adolescent development to determine when transfer is appropriate, the children who are most inclined toward rehabilitation will be given that opportunity through juvenile court adjudication.

In light of *Roper*, it is time for Georgians and Georgia's legislators to take heed of the unfair and detrimental impact of SB440 upon Georgia's children. While *Roper* certainly does not dictate all juvenile cases be tried in juvenile courts, *Roper* does reveal that the differences between children and adults "render suspect any conclusion that a juvenile falls among the worst offenders."[43] Applying this to SB440, we may find the "Seven Deadly Sins Law" suspicious in that it classifies juveniles among the worst offenders without taking proper account of the differences between children and adults. We might consider, as the *Roper* Court did, that "juveniles have a greater claim than adults to be forgiven" for transgressions.[44] To put this claim in a religious voice, we might ask whether children of God who violate the "Seven Deadly Sins Law" are deserving of forgiveness.

---

[43] *Ibid.* at 1195.
[44] *Ibid.*

The Criminal Justice System in Georgia: Issues in the African-American Community

Judge M. Yvette Miller

The criminal justice system at both the federal and state levels has three basic parts: law enforcement, which occupies the front line in society's ongoing struggle against crime; the judicial branch, which renders judgment on people accused of criminal acts; and corrections, which incarcerates and rehabilitates those convicted of crimes, and ultimately returns these people back to the community. Together, all of these professionals are charged with insuring the public's safety by enforcing the laws and by taking people who commit crimes off our streets.

According to the Department of Justice, crime, including nonviolent offenses such as burglary and theft, has declined nationwide since 1994. However, the number of adults in the national correctional population has been increasing over this same period. The reason for this increase is that violent crime is up, and a greater number of violent offenders are re-entering the prison system.

So if the crime rate is going down while the incarceration rate is going up, this means that law enforcement officials are relatively successful in identifying the people who commit crimes and who are most likely to be repeat offenders, or *recidivists*. But these trends have some disturbing long-term implications as well. They suggest that our prisons have become places where repeat offenders are kept in close contact with each other for longer and longer; in other words, we are becoming two societies rather than one. If our jails are filled with more and more violent criminals, and if jails themselves beget criminals, then we are in for some serious trouble – if not now, then in our children's lifetimes.

Of course, we see violent crime take the stage right before our very eyes each day on national television and in the news each day in the form of courthouse shootings, school killing sprees, and workplace murders. A recent example is the Brian Nichols case; we often get advance warning that a criminal is about to go over the edge. Both his mother and the judge presiding at his retrial learned that Nichols was dangerous and likely to pose a continuing threat to others, and pointed this out to the Sheriff and other, but to no avail.

Under the Department of Homeland Security, as created by the Homeland Security Act of 2002, more than 87,000 governmental jurisdictions at the federal, state, and local level have some homeland security responsibilities. Efforts to secure our safety from terrorism have become a financial drain on law enforcement activities here at home, in our states and cities.

Georgia's Criminal Justice System: According to the Georgia Bureau of Investigation, there were 380,333 crimes reported in the State of Georgia in 2003. Of this total, nearly 37,000 were violent crimes, such as murder, rape, and armed robbery, with the remainder including such serious property crimes as burglary, larceny, and auto theft. This means that in a state with at least 8.5 million citizens, one's chances of becoming a victim are a little less than one in twenty. This is an alarming rate, and one that runs much higher in populations at risk, which includes women, minorities, and the economically disadvantaged. Our states have always held the front line on the war on crime. They spend more on criminal justice than cities, counties, or even the Federal government. In Georgia the state budget totals more than $16 billion. The criminal justice system costs the state around $1.5 billion a year – about one-tenth of the total budget. Only one-tenth of the money the State spends on criminal justice is allocated for the judicial branch. Together, law enforcement, corrections, and juvenile systems make up the other nine-tenths. Innovation is the key to future breakthroughs in the war on crime.

Law Enforcement: Law enforcement officers play an essential role in the criminal justice system. Municipal officers, county officials and state police function as first responders to crime and as guardians of our communities, protecting us from and deterring crime at the same time. Sheriffs and deputies typically serve warrants, manage jails and correction facilities, and provide security for courthouses, judges and staff. Pressure is brought to bear on the law enforcement community for keeping crime numbers down, solving crime where it does exist, and closing cases.

The Judicial Branch: Another major part of the criminal justice system is Georgia's judiciary. There are three branches of government, nationally and at the state level. They are the Executive, Legislative, and Judicial. The executive branch does the day-to-day work of governance, applying the law through officials appointed by the governor. The legislative branch makes the laws through our elected representatives, while the judiciary interprets and applies these laws to the facts of individual cases. The important point here is that judges must be independent enough to make decisions without reservations about who may like or dislike the result. We have a hierarchy of courts in Georgia, from the State Supreme Court to the Court of Appeals to the trial courts and specialized lower courts.

The state's highest court is the Supreme Court of Georgia, which accepts appeals only on petition for certiorari. The Supreme Court also has exclusive appellate jurisdiction over unusual cases like constitutional cases, election contests, and the death penalty.

The Georgia Court of Appeals is a 12-member court, and hears cases in panels of three. The Court of Appeals hears all cases not reserved to the Georgia Supreme Court, and typically functions as a court of last resort in over 80% of Georgia cases. The decisions made by the Court of Appeals are final decisions, unless the Georgia Supreme Court accepts a cert. petition for review. As the busiest state appellate court in the nation, the National Center of State Courts tracks such courts nationwide and has designated the Court of Appeals of Georgia. The caseload at the Court of Appeals is very heavy. In 2004, there were 2,394 cases filed in our Court as a result of parties to the lawsuit alleging errors committed at the trial level below. The Court hears both civil and criminal cases.

A large part of those appeals – just under 50%, in fact – are from guilty pleas or verdicts in criminal cases. A criminal defendant has the *right* to a direct appeal from his or her conviction, even if only to challenge the sufficiency of the evidence against him. In most cases, the Court of Appeals is the *only* court to review these appeals, and thus plays an important part in protecting us all from overzealous police and prosecutors.

The Court hears appeals in all kinds of criminal cases, including voluntary manslaughter, rape, kidnapping, aggravated assault, burglary, robbery, and theft. The court also reviews decisions of the juvenile courts involving delinquency, child custody, and parental rights, and a variety of civil cases on appeal, of course, from multimillion-dollar corporate cases to those involving slip-and-fall injuries and property boundary-line disputes.

Initially, most criminal cases start out in the superior courts of our state, which are courts of general jurisdiction. There are 159 superior courts, one in each Georgian county. The juvenile courts of our state have exclusive jurisdiction in cases involving delinquent, unruly, and deprived children. Each county also has one of these courts.

There are also state courts which function as trial courts, as well as probate and magistrate courts, which have jurisdiction to deal with special areas of the law, such as wills and estates and small claims.

The Bar: Georgia's Attorneys: As you know, for better or for worse, our society works out many of its most important problems in the courtroom. A great lawyer, the late Johnnie Cochran, once said that the color of justice is green. I work hard each day to make sure that this is *not* the case in my court. It takes more than the judges presiding over cases, however, to ensure fairness in the system.

The landmark 1963 U.S. Supreme Court case of *Gideon v. Wainwright* held that defendants in state courts have the right to counsel in every criminal case, just as defendants in federal courts had since 1938. The point is that every defendant in America, and in Georgia, has a constitutional right to appointed counsel if he is indigent and accused of a crime. The defense attorneys who represent those accused of crimes in Georgia and the prosecutors representing the State have the responsibility of insuring fairness and accountability in our system of criminal justice. Without their hard work, neither defendants nor victims would get the justice they deserve.

The Georgia Department of Corrections: There are currently more than 49,000 inmates in Georgia's prisons – the sixth largest correctional population in the country. Maintaining each inmate costs over $17,000 a year, for a total cost of well over $800 million in 2004. Over half of Georgia's inmates have only a 10th grade education or less, were raised with no father at home, have a high incidence of alcohol addiction and drug abuse, and were previously incarcerated (or recidivist). Forty-five percent of those incarcerated have been convicted of a crime of violence.

These statistics are worth pondering. It is plain that building and staffing prisons is one principal activity of our state government, amounting to over 5% of its total budget, as well as a major expense for county governments throughout Georgia. And it is equally obvious that the people incarcerated in state and county prisons tend to be undereducated, with all the ills that traditionally accompany this handicap, such as substance abuse and exposure to family violence.

The cost and importance of this correctional function makes it imperative that officials elected to administer state corrections are held to high standards of conduct and achievement. The true key to corrections is to rehabilitate and educate. Incarceration alone leads to recidivism and more incarceration. Programs that help people re-enter society as productive human beings can transform ex-convicts and the lives of the people around them.

However high aspirations may be, there are signs of trouble in the state corrections system. Sometimes we hear about shocking individual incidents, such as the one reported a few days ago. In the Union City jail, a woman arrested on drug charges and awaiting arraignment was stripped, strapped to a chair, and left exposed to male prisoners and guards for hours on end. Nightmare scenarios like this one are rare, and the female jailer responsible for this treatment, which involved nine separate violations of jail policy, was fired a few days later. But our jails seem at times to fall sway to an entire culture of neglect and abuse.

In a letter published just this week in the Fulton County Daily Report, a prominent defense attorney writes about the hours he has spent waiting to see clients at Fulton County's Rice Street jail, only to be told that they cannot be located or taken to court for a hearing. Behind the alarming headlines, however, there are also encouraging signs of change, as in the Department of Correction's Certified Family Violence Intervention Program. The purpose of this important initiative is to help individuals take responsibility for their emotions, and thereby to bring an end to the cycles of violence that destroy families, generation after generation.

Another hopeful sign is the expansion of programs that assist those who are brought into the criminal justice system as the result of substance abuse or mental illness. The Community-Based Problem-Solving Criminal Justice Initiative, first funded by the federal government in 1984, is one example of such a program, now attracting the participation of the Georgia Municipal Association. This initiative welcomes citizens into the process of changing the criminal justice system, inviting their participation in advisory boards, community projects, and courts designed especially to handle cases involving drug treatment, mental health, domestic violence, and re-entry into the community. Creative initiatives like these, not more or larger jails, point the way to a brighter future when *they attack crime at its origins.*

Unfortunately, the reality is that educational and community programs like these are the first to be cut when times are hard. When such programs fall under the budget axe, we increase the likelihood that our criminal justice system becomes a system of warehousing criminals. Though obviously necessary, we should turn to punishment and incarceration only when it is too late for other, more effective interventions. Unless we all take responsibility for participating in and defending innovative solutions, we will have little basis for complaint about the intractable nature of crime and punishment in Georgia.

Of Particular Concern - Juvenile Justice: Anyone concerned about fighting crime before it happens must be interested in the juvenile justice system, the place where we as a society try to help endangered children in danger of being overwhelmed by violence and abuse in all its forms. Juveniles in our justice system are of particular concern to me because a substantial percentage of these youthful offenders go on to commit crimes as adults. We must more effectively rehabilitate these children to make sure that they do not re-appear in the system somewhere down the road.

According to the Department of Juvenile Justice, over 22,000 juveniles were admitted into youth detention centers in Georgia in 2003, mostly for property-related crimes such as burglary and theft. Fifty-four percent of these were African-American males. State funding for juvenile facilities and programs reached over $281 million in 2004 – a large sum, to be sure, but only one quarter of the amount devoted to the adult criminal population.

Part of the answer is to ensure that appropriate punishment and effective rehabilitation happen the first time around, when there is still a substantial chance that the child can make a change in his life. The last thing we want is for juveniles to languish in jail for six months or more without being brought to trial, as happened to more than 50 children last year. The General Assembly has taken a small step in the form of a new law requiring that indictments be brought within 180 days. But we surely want to take larger steps as well: to *examine* the factors surrounding the first offense in order to give these children *a second chance, but one conditioned on change.* Only then can we begin to make a difference in the lives of our juvenile offenders.

Even more effective is to *prevent juvenile crime before it starts.* This means that education in our state needs to be improved in such a way that it provides a safety net for our children at risks, who may not come from stable homes and who often live in poverty. Many have come to the call of improving education in Georgia, but so much more needs to be done. In response to Georgia's failing grade in education, Charter Schools have been created as an innovative alternative to low-performing traditional public schools. These charter schools continue to be the subject of debate, however, and it is too early to determine what long-term effects they will have on education in Georgia.

As for our public schools, we must reward our best teachers with better pay and more respect, and weed out those teachers who don't respect the importance of the profession. We must also rebuild confidence in our educational system. Education needs to be held in higher esteem by the public.

If we can prevent many of our children from falling through the cracks of our educational system, then we can begin to see a reduction in the number of juvenile offenders. The earlier in life they are given a fair chance, the more likely they are to become productive citizens.

Possible Solutions to Persistent Problems: African Americans now hold leadership positions in Georgia politics and law enforcement. Many prosecutors and defense attorneys are also members of the black community. The fact remains, however, that there are a disproportionate number of African-American men in Georgia's prisons. In 2003, 64% of the 2003 Georgia prison population was nonwhite, although whites constitute a majority in this state.

These sad statistics must change. Taken with my earlier observation that a disproportionate number of incarcerated offenders are recidivists, the statistical majority of the prison population consists of what Dr. Du Bois called the "submerged tenth" of the African-

American community, locked in a longstanding cycle of poverty, ignorance, violence, substance abuse, and mental illness.

These tragic facts resonate all the more here at Clark Atlanta University, Dr. Du Bois' academic home for nearly half a century. Early in his career, Dr. Du Bois speculated that the cultural and political leadership of African-American society, his so-called "Talented Tenth," might allow all African Americans to overcome the historical legacy of educational and economic discrimination. As the president of the NAACP commented on the occasion of Dr. Du Bois's retirement from Atlanta University in 1944, however, the "Talented Tenth" was one of Dr. Du Bois's many ideas that were far ahead of their time, "raising hopes for change" which, though "they may be comprehended in a hundred years," could not prevail in thc Jim Crow South.

Today, citizens of all races play an important role in the criminal justice system. Crime prevention means more than participating in a neighborhood watch, however. It requires action *outside* the criminal justice system to stop crime long before it happens.

After many years of work in the criminal justice system, I believe that the most powerful answers lie in giving our children the right start: putting them on a high road of morality and knowledge that passes by the criminal justice system altogether, even as we secure justice for both victims and defendants.

The African-American community can best address the serious issues posed by the criminal justice system by giving children the tools and skills they need to prevail in our society. It is time for all of us to move beyond critiques of the system as racist, beyond complaints about severity of sentences or adequacy of legal representation. We need leaders who reflect our values, and who are accountable for their actions as public servants.

Creation of an Urban Family Court

Judge Thelma Wyatt Cummings Moore

Transformation of the justice system is an enormous undertaking. A paramount tenet may be that the justice system traditionally exists to preserve the status quo. Therefore, change requires focus, tenacity and a righteous cause.

One such righteous cause has been the creation of the Family Court. It is clear that our nation's courts were not designed to address the needs of families in crisis. Rather, they are typically designed to preside over criminal prosecutions and civil adversarial disputes. Why should the resolution of family issues be adversarial in matters of dissolutions, child custody, child support, or legitimation? These matters affect the best interests of families and children at their most personal level and at their most vulnerable. Yet, family disputes have been traditionally calendared, tried and disposed of in the same manner as adversarial cases. This results in intense hostility and trauma for families and children.

Innovative Family Courts approach family crises entirely differently by removing the adversarial process and replacing it with a mediation model where husbands, wives, parents and others involved are *empowered* to frame their own resolution of the issues. This empowerment yields a more satisfying result. Parties are assured that the best possible outcome has been achieved; the "winner take all" atmosphere is eliminated.

In a "winner take all" atmosphere, orders, judgments and decrees were often repeatedly challenged. Motions for reconsideration were filed. Parties still encountered arguments and disputes over issues. Motions for contempt were filed. Delays in court proceedings were necessitated by intense squabbling. Tempers ran high. Hostilities were fiercely exhibited. Children caught in the middle of these scenarios were subjected to unhealthy emotions or worse, physical trauma which could scar them for a lifetime. There were no services to evaluate and monitor the emotional toll taken on the family.

The Family Court was born out of these realizations. The Family Court Mission addresses the basic complications of the traditional adversarial method of handling family disputes:

To provide a speedy, certain, comprehensive, non-adversarial approach to the judicial resolution of multiple family problems and disputes while more systematically and effectively addressing the interests of children and the family unit.

The Need: In assessing the need for a Family Court, one need only look at the litigants, their attorneys, the number of cases, the high-strung emotions, and the delay in disposition of the cases. Delay is especially harrowing in resolving family disputes. Delay occasions uncertainty in knowing where a family will live, what school a child will attend, and the resources a family has to meet basic needs, all issues which are fundamental to existence.

The need is especially poignant in the eyes of children of divorce. The tipping point for me came when a case I tried was particularly touching and traumatic. All parties, including the husband, wife and two young children were prescribed Prozac. During one divorce hearing, I received a call from the husband's psychiatrist. The psychiatrist indicated to me that he did not want to breach psychiatrist-patient confidentiality; however, he needed to inform me that the husband was suicidal and that he would not recommend that he be allowed visitation with the two children.

The intensity of that case, together with my experience in other cases over a considerable time on the bench, convinced me that the courts need a specialized approach in handling family law cases. I knew that I would have benefited in the "Prozac" case from a professional evaluation of the parties and the children involved, in order to make better decisions affecting their future. That realization had developed over years of handling increasingly complex emotional scenarios which domestic cases present. Delays in adjudicating such cases only exacerbated hostile feelings which were certain to transfer to any children involved. Serendipitously, the former Chief Judge of the Superior Court of Fulton County, the Honorable Isaac Jenrette, encouraged me to create the Family Court.

The Method: In effectuating institutional change, one knows that one cannot do it alone. There must be a consensus, a community buy-in to the need, the concepts, the approach and the ultimate solution. Together with my Staff Attorney, Ms. Angel Wheeler, I designed an approach of calling together judges, attorneys practicing in the family law area, leaders of the bench and bar, public and private agencies dealing with the welfare of families and children, elected officials, counselors, mental health professionals, juvenile justice professionals, prosecutors, defenders and other interested persons to meet to discuss this monumental change from court business as usual in family disputes to *therapeutic justice* for families.

We called regular meetings over a period of two years as we framed the design of our Family Court. We started with a framework which I designed together with my Law Clerk to allow for focus on the issue. Input was gained through respect for each point of view with a buy-in from the majority. Ultimately, we were able to frame our Goals and Objectives. They are as follows:

Objective A: One Family-One Judge: The Family Court addresses and adjudicates all issues affecting the same family in a single court system with emphasis on the best interests of children affected by legal proceedings and others not having a direct voice in the legal proceedings affecting them. Under Georgia's court system, numerous courts have sometimes unique and overlapping jurisdiction over family matters and matters dealing with domestic violence or juvenile issues. Decisions are likely to be conflicting, disparate, delayed and fragmented without regard to the total needs of the family unit. Creation of a system where all cases are brought before one judge for disposition allows for consistency and comprehensiveness in dealing with the needs of the family, most especially the children. Thus, under the new Family Court, all cases involving child support, child custody, legitimation, paternity, visitation, termination of parental rights, adoption and adult and minor guardianship, garnishment, juvenile issues and domestic violence are to be consolidated in the Family Court from respective jurisdictions in the Superior, State, Juvenile, Magistrate, Probate and Municipal Courts. The Family Court will then assume coordinated judicial oversight and case management to insure the prompt and appropriate resolution of issues affecting the family. The same court is assigned to hear all matters involving the same family, thus allowing the Family Court Judge to focus exclusively on the constant metamorphosis of laws and legislation related to family law issues and preventing litigants from moving through a system seeking different judges and rulings on the same fundamental problem The "one judge-one family" organization helps to eliminate delay and inconsistencies in judicial decision-making while also empowering families to seek resolutions and compromises in their own best interests.

Objective B: Training: The Family Court must have trained and experienced judges, staff, professionals and volunteers who have a genuine interest in resolving family conflicts. Family court judges and staff are to have the highest level of expertise, including familiarity with related disciplines, such as psychology and child development. Attorneys, staff and volunteers must undergo special training, including planned programs of instruction in psychology, family dynamics, child development, non-adversarial techniques and working with diverse populations.

Objective C: Accessibility and Coordination of Cases: The Family Court is user-friendly and accessible to the public. A system that allows all cases to be screened and coordinated at the time of filing was established to promote earlier, more effective resolution of family issues. Not only is there an earlier review of cases, but a state-of-the-art case management system is employed to insure that cases do not stagnate. This component of the project required copious input from the Family Law bar and reference to cutting edge case management systems to insure speedy, comprehensive management of family law cases.

In conjunction with this objective, a centerpiece of the Family Court is to allow accessibility for all persons. Previously, many indigent persons could not obtain court intervention and relief due to barriers of attorneys' fees, court costs, as well as lack of basic knowledge of how to proceed. The *Family Law Information Center* is the most innovative component of the Family Court effort and one which touches the lives of the general community. The FLIC, as it is called, affords all persons the opportunity to review packets of information on family law issues and to obtain direction from an Atlanta Legal Aid staffer on which information may be most appropriate to meet that individual's concerns. Packets are available at a minimal fee (in the range of two dollars each), which fee may even be waived if a person is deemed a pauper. Furthermore, such information is available on-line for download. The FLIC in no way conflicts with attorneys' pool of clients, for FLIC clients are generally those who would not otherwise be able to afford legal services at all. Moreover, Atlanta Legal Aid staffers are careful not to give legal advice. Persons precede *pro se* with the attendant pitfalls, but with the advantage of proven petitions, affidavits and other documents. Judges recognize pro se litigants and are pleased with the upgraded documents which comport with known legal requirements.

Another component of access to the courts is that of public education seminars on such issues as child support, child custody, legitimation, name changes and parenting. Community organizations can take advantage of a wealth of information to share with those needing and desiring the know-how to secure their legal rights.

Objective D: Reduction in Case Processing Time: The Family Court shortens the time previously required for the litigation of family disputes by monitoring processes to ensure that families' needs are identified and met in a timely and consistent manner. Cases are calendared within a 30 day time-frame for an initial conference with a judicial officer. Thereafter, cases are scheduled for 60 and 120 day hearings. In the interim, case managers, mediators, the staff psychologist and other professionals review and refer the case to address specific family needs.

Objective E: Services: The Family Court design includes a variety of services: mediation, counseling, children services and parental education to evaluate the needs of each family and to reduce the use of forced resolution through the litigation process. Family Court utilizes services provided by victim advocates, child advocates, guardians, mental health advocates, substance abuse counselors, anger management counselors, mediators and negotiators, social workers, interpreters and specialized support groups, as well as referral to emergency financial assistance and protective housing.

One aspect of the Family Court which has yet to be addressed is that of a child care facility for children whose parents are in court. The purpose of this component is to remove children from the courtroom arena while recognizing the court's and community's role in securing safe childcare. The concept applies to all court proceedings: civil, criminal and domestic as well as childcare for jurors' children. This facility was to have been available to jurors to insure that the broadest possible pool of jurors could be utilized, negating the necessity of striking jurors because of their childcare responsibilities and limitations. This piece of the project was never completed although there are models in other states, specifically in Missouri, Washington State and New York State.

Objective F: Intervention by Professionals, Volunteers and the Community: The Family Court expedites the intervention of social service professionals by sorting out issues early on and directing families to the services they need. Coordination of such social services is designed to conserve scant public resources and to avoid multiple and inconsistent demands placed on agencies and families. Access to professional and community services has expedited the legal process by allowing the judge to craft the most appropriate solution to the family's problems while affording families the opportunity to participate in the outcome of their legal disputes and to work through disagreements in a non-combative manner.

The Process: Gaining Community, Judicial, And Legislative Support: Even after formulating the plan for the Family Court, it was necessary to obtain the legal authorization to proceed. State constitutions and statutes specify jurisdictions of various classes of courts. Thus, our proposal to unify cases under the "One Judge-One Family" concept required special legislation

Our first task was to obtain approval of the judges of the Superior Court, our trial court of general jurisdiction, which has authority over domestic cases. Next we obtained the approval of the Atlanta Bar Association, having already worked with its Family Law Division in drafting the plan for the court. Required approval was also necessary from the Georgia Bar Association, its various committees and finally, its Board of Governors. The Judicial Council of Georgia, comprised of Chief and Administrative Judges of the various level courts, chaired by the Chief Justice of Georgia gave its imprimatur to the project, as did the Georgia Supreme Court itself. Meanwhile, numerous letters of support were solicited and received from elected officials, community and educational organizations, public and private agencies. The Atlanta Constitution published several articles on the project and published an editorial recommending passage of the bill. Chief Justice Robert Benham urged passage of the legislation creating the Family Court in his State of the Judiciary address. The salutary effect of working with these individuals, officials and organizations throughout the process engendered the strong support needed to go to the legislature. Finally, our bill for creation of the Family Court was put before the legislature, beginning with its various committees, Judiciary, Appropriations, Rules, and so forth before heading to the floors of the House and the Senate. State Representative Bob Holmes supported us and was very instrumental in shepherding the bill through the legislature. The Family Court Bill passed both Houses and was signed by the Governor creating the Fulton County Family Court on July 1, 1998. The legislation has since been renewed in 2005 for an additional term.

Conclusion: Family Courts employ methods for dealing with the unique need of families. The primary beneficiaries of the Family Court are children. Too often, child custody, child support and visitation disputes are prolonged because of the nature of our justice system. If we can offer early intervention, children may be shielded from some of the hostilities and bitterness which result from the adversarial system. Piecemeal justice from the complex overlay of courts in many jurisdictions is counterproductive to assessing families' needs as a whole. Moreover, the Family Law Information Center addresses the needs of many families which have never had access to the justice system due to lack of knowledge or to finances.

The two-year process of creating the family court was, indeed, a rewarding one in transforming the system of justice on behalf of families, most especially the children. While we undertook a grassroots effort in our jurisdiction, Family Courts in other states have been created by legislative or judicial fiat from the top down. Whatever method is employed, one thing is for certain: Family Courts' new approaches offer rays of hope in providing therapeutic justice to strengthen the family and the community.

Treatment Courts of Madison County, Alabama

Judge Lynn Sherrod

The Treatment Courts of Madison County began with the inaugural session of the Family Drug Court (dependency court) in April 2002 followed by the introduction of an Adult Drug Court (criminal offenders) in October 2003. Mental Health Court was added in 2004, and 2005 has seen the expansion of therapeutic jurisprudence into the local juvenile court system. The Madison County Family-Focused Drug court was developed and implemented under the direction of District Court Judge M. Lynn Sherrod. The Court operates in partnership with the Madison County Departments of Human Resources and the Madison County Mental Health Center, District Attorney, Huntsville City Schools and Madison County School System, the National Children's Advocacy Center and numerous specialized community service providers.

A system assessment showed that an exceptionally large number of child abuse/neglect and criminal cases are alcohol or drug related. Thus, the Court concluded that in order to meet the needs of these families, a multi-disciplinary team concept with agencies that service similar clientele might help to stop the underlying cycle of victimization. To that end, the Family Drug Court is designed to assist all the partnering agencies in meeting their individual service time clocks and promote healthy families.

The emergence of these new courts in Madison County reflects the growing recognition that the traditional tools of our justice system, jail, probation, and foster care have not stemmed the wave of domestic violence, crime and generational cycles of drug abuse. Record numbers of individuals were incarcerated, and children were removed from their families to such an extent that the foster care resources were nearing exhaustion. Yet, the neighborhoods seemed to grow even further unstable, and children continued to be victimized by family and care givers.

After more than a dozen years in the legal arena, as a lawyer, prosecutor and as a judge, I realized I was seeing whole families. Many of the young people were very blasé about going to jail and time in the detention facility seemed preferable to home. In addition, the court's criminal dockets were inundated with drug cases. The drug related offenses were so time-consuming it allowed little time and fewer resources to adjudicate other serious and more often violent crimes. The Drug Court is designed to intervene with intensive substance abuse treatment; legal accountability (i.e. reunification or termination of parental rights in compliance with the Adoption and Safe Families Act, 1997 guidelines) and ancillary resources needed to ensure permanent lifestyle change. This is provided under intensive judicial monitoring, which enhances treatment efforts, child safety and compliance with the case plan.

For Madison County the development of the treatment courts has been the most significant judicial initiative in decades. Each court serves a different population, but the goals are consistent:

- Help people become clean and sober.
- Help people remain clean and sober.
- Reunite families.

The Madison County Treatment Courts has adopted the Ten Key Components promo- gated by the National Association of Drug Court Professionals (NADCP, 1997) as our court model. These Ten Components have been the basis of the treatment court development.

Defining Drug Courts: The Key Components:

1. Drug Courts integrate alcohol and other drug treatment services with justice system case processing.
2. Using a non-adversarial approach, prosecution and defense counsel promote public safety while protecting participants' due process rights.
3. Eligible participants are identified early and promptly placed in the Drug Court program.
4. Drug Courts provide access to a continuum of alcohol, drug, and other related treatment and rehabilitation services.
5. Abstinence is monitored by frequent alcohol and other drug testing.
6. A coordinated strategy governs Drug Court responses to participant's compliance.
7. Ongoing judicial interaction with each Drug Court participant is essential.
8. Monitoring and evaluation measure the achievement of program goals and gauge effectiveness.
9. Continuing interdisciplinary education promotes effective Drug Court planning, implementation, and operations.
10. Forging partnership among Drug Courts, public agencies, and community-based organizations generates local support and enhances Drug Court effectiveness.

Family Drug Court: The Madison County Family Drug Court became operational in April 2002 as the first family dependency court in Alabama. The first family dependency court nationwide opened in 1994 in Reno, Nevada. The Family Drug Court is devoted to dependency cases involving abuse or neglect where substance abuse has been identified as a primary contributing factor putting the children at risk. The stated purpose is to protect the safety and welfare of children while helping parents acquire the tools they need to become clean and sober, to stay clean and sober, and to become responsible caregivers. The legal basis of the program is derived from the duty and responsibility of the Department of Human

Resources (DHR) and the Juvenile Court system to protect children. The failure of the parent to protect a child provides for procedures for referrals of complaints and allegations of dependency to DHR for investigation, reports, recommendations and procedures whereby children may be committed to the care of the Department. If the Court establishes adjudication of dependency, the parent can voluntarily agree to enter Family Drug Court but must also contract to comply with the terms and conditions of Family Drug Court. Furthermore, the participant agrees to the imposition of immediate consequences for failure to abide by the requirements of the program. This enforces accountability and establishes a system of meaningful motivation for the parent.

The Court facilitated the development of an interdisciplinary team that works collaboratively to assess the family's situation and to develop an individualized case plan that addresses the needs of both the children and the parents. Consistent with the Adoption and Safe Families Act of 1997 (ASFA) guidelines the children are provided quick access to permanency and the parents receive a viable opportunity to achieve sobriety, and a chance to raise their children in a safe and nurturing home.

> *I met the M family in open court. The father brought the five children, each less than six years of age to court for their mother's sentencing on 30+ counts of issuing worthless checks.I believe he thought the presence of the children would somehow mitigate the crimes, and keep his wife from going to jail. The father said he worked construction, and could not care for the children. Since the father had an odor of alcohol, we immediately notified the Department of Human Resources (Child Protective Services). While on Work Release the mother delivered a beautiful baby girl that tested positive for marijuana at birth. In addition to these six children the mother had a seventh child in the custody of a relative. This mother was twenty-four years old. She enrolled in*

Drug Court upon completing her Work Release on the check charges, and the father enrolled soon thereafter. Both parents maintained their sobriety for the eighteen (18) months they were enrolled in Drug Court.

The Family Drug Court Team includes the Court, The Department of Human Resources, The Mental Health Center, The National Children's Advocacy Center, Madison County District Attorney, and the Madison County School System. The team recognized during the development of the program that the complex web of problems facing the families identified as appropriate for Drug Court would only be adequately addressed through a coordinated approach. Since becoming operational, the interdisciplinary team has expanded to include the Huntsville Housing Authority, the faith-based community, vocational rehabilitation and numerous health care providers. Together the team members operate a formal program of early intervention and treatment based on a comprehensive needs assessment and case plan. Participants are required to appear in court once or twice a month, and may attend group meetings three times a week during Phase I.

Attaining affordable treatment for families – especially treatment that is timely, accessible and culturally sensitive has been difficult. Affordable, drug free, housing has been another challenge for the program participants. The drug court social workers do not hesitate to recommend relocation if the situation appear to warrant a change. Living in a community without public transportation has made transportation a key issue.

The Mission Statement of the Family Drug Court: To create, in partnership with community service providers, a continuum of services needed to identify and develop family strengths, and to assess and treat family dysfunction caused by drug or alcohol dependency. To ensure that our approach to fostering healthy homes reflects a commitment to professional collaboration, intensive substance abuse treatment, legal accountability and intervention strategies that focus on the needs of family as a whole.

Vision Statement: Create a safe environment for the re-unification of children with drug-free parents, nurturing homes that are free from abuse and neglect, crime, and detrimental reliance on social services.

Program Design: The target population for the Madison County Family Drug Court Program is substance- abusing parents who are in danger of losing legal and/or physical custody of their minor dependent children due to abuse neglect. In Madison County District Court this is referred to as the "Dependency Case Population": Individuals (parents, custodians, or primary caretakers) that are identified by The Department of Human Resources, and are scheduled to appear before the Court as a result of the filing of a petition of abuse or neglect in a child protection case; or whose children have already been removed due to substance abuse. Participants are male or female and at least 19 years of age. They are residents of Madison County and dwell in the same household with one or more dependant children.

The Madison County Family Drug Court Program is structured using a strength-based model of "therapeutic jurisprudence". This model serves as the primary tool in shifting the court's philosophy, to systemically address the alcohol and drug treatment needs of all family members. The 5 key program components are: I) Voluntary participation in non-adversarial court proceedings; II) Access to immediate drug and alcohol treatment services; III) Prolonged alcohol and drug abstinence, monitored by frequent drug testing and team evaluations; IV) Effective multi-disciplinary case planning; V) Focus on Family as a unit of analysis and course of support.

Drug Court is an eighteen month intensive outpatient/in-patient program: During the first ten weeks, the client attends session three days or evenings per week; during the next twenty weeks, the client attends continuing care and life/parenting skills program sessions, one day or evening per week; upon completion of the 30 week program, the client attends a 42 week continuing care program one day or evening per week.

The primary treatment provider is the New Horizons Recovery Center, the Substance Abuse Treatment Division of the Mental Health Center of Madison County. Cases opened to the Family Drug Court Program are staffed weekly in Court with all interested parties, including, but not limited to the following: Therapist, Judge, Court Referral Officer, Drug Court Coordinator, the Madison County Department of Human Resources, and the Client. In addition, weekly progress letters are mailed to each referral source detailing the client's progress or lack of progress.

The treatment program consists of the following phases: Assessment; Phase I – Treatment; Phase II – Continuing Care and Life/Parenting Skills; Phase III – Aftercare. The assessment is conducted by a master's level clinician to determine if the referred client has a substance abuse/dependency problem and the severity of the problem. The clinician and client then develop a treatment plan based on the client's strengths and needs. The client signs off on the treatment plan verified by their participation in goal development. The treatment plan recommends an effective program of treatment for substance abuse/dependency issues and identifies other treatment issues that may be treated, or the client is referred to other facilities for assessment and treatment. This includes assessing the need for referral to the Mental Health Center of Madison County. All treatment plans are reviewed and updated at least quarterly by the primary therapist. In addition, when a client progresses to his/her next phase in treatment, he/she meets with the therapist to update or develop a new treatment plan.

Cases are staffed weekly in Court by the Drug Court Team. The Drug Court Team is comprised of the following individuals: Drug Court Coordinator; Drug Court Specialist; Treatment Provider; Social Worker; and any other parties involved in the individual treatment plan of each client. A written report is prepared by the Drug Court Specialists detailing the defendant's progress and is presented to the judge on the day of court. Frequency of appearance before the judge will depend upon the phase of treatment in which the client is currently enrolled: Phase I – weekly; Phase II – bi-monthly; Phase III – monthly.

The Madison County Office of Alternative Sentencing and release provides case management services for the Family Drug Court Program. The Drug Court Team monitors cases on a weekly basis.

Family Drug Court participants submit to random/periodic/ reasonable-cause drug screens and/or breath tests to verify abstinence, conducted by New Horizons Recovery Center. These screens are in addition to the drug screens conducted by the Drug Court Specialist.

Participants contact the court daily to determine the color of the day for drug testing. For each compliant event any of the following rewards may be granted: Acknowledgment by Judge; reduced court appearances; reduced urine testing; case called early in court; increased or unsupervised visit with children; reunification with child; an honor roll listing (kept in court); a phase advancement certificate in court; graduation ceremony, including a picture with the Judge. For each noncompliant event, any of the following sanctions may be imposed: Reprimand from the judge; increased court appearances; increased case management; increased intensity in treatment program; reduction in phase of program; if participating in out-patient treatment, a referral to residential treatment; two (2) days in jail the first time with escalating sanctions up to (5) days; recommendation for termination of parental rights.

A key member of the Family Drug Court team is the dedicated social worker. She serves as the case manager, provides transportation as needed, attends all staffings, serves as the court's liaison to the dependency proceeding, makes home visits, occasional drive byes to work sites, schools, performs educational assessments, and makes referrals for all ancillary services including parenting classes.

The Madison County Family Drug Court during its first twenty-four (24) months of operation diverted forty-eight (48) children from the foster care rolls, or children spent less time in foster care than expected. This program has created a centralized referral source for families with substance abuse issues, and facilitates a rapid delivery of services for children at risk for abuse or neglect. Our goals of crime reduction, improved public health, protecting children from abuse and neglect are attainable. Substance abuse is a treatable illness. I look forward to the day when Drug Court is institutionalized into the judicial system.

The Treatment Courts of Madison County
(Comparison of Court Models)

	Adult Drug Court	*Family (dependency) Drug Court*	*Juvenile Drug Court*	*Mental Health Court*
Client	Adult Criminal Offenders	Parents of children at risk for victims of abuse or neglect.	Delinquents	Criminal offenders with diagnosed mental illness.
Type of Proceeding	Criminal	Civil	Juvenile	Criminal
Comprehensive Assessment	Treatment, Job/Skills and Educational needs assessed.	The treatment job/skill, education and health needs of parents are assessed. The health safety and developmental needs of each child is assessed.	The health, safety, and developmental needs of each child are assessed by the Juvenile Probation Officer.	Most participants are known to mental health authorities. Mental health worker makes assessment at the jail.
Family Involvement	Family support is encouraged, but but not included in the case plan.	Nuclear and extended family members are included in case plan.	Parents are parties to the actions.	Extended family is involved in the treatment process.
Treatment	Adult Focused	Required for participants provided for children as appropriate. May be provided to the family as a unit.	Court ordered child and parents.	Focuses on mental illness and developmental disabilities.
Objectives	Adult sobriety and reduce recidivism.	Provide a safe, nurturing, permanent placement for the children.	Juvenile sobriety and reduced recidivism.	Compliance with treatment plan and reduced recidivism.

References

Defining Drug Courts: The Ten Key Components, U.S. Department of Justice, Office of Justice Programs, Drug Court Standards Committee Report (1997).

Looking At A Decade Of Drug Courts, The Drug Court Clearinghouse and Technical Assistance Project, U.S. Department of Justice, Office of Justice Programs (1999).

Huddleston, C. W. III, Freeman-Wilson, Judge (Ret.) Karen and Boone, Donna L., *Painting The Current Picture: A National Report Card on Drug Courts and Other Problem Solving Court Programs In The United States*, Volume I, Number I, National Drug Court Institute (2004).

DISCUSSIONS

Discussion of "Training Pre-Service Teachers to work with Juvenile Delinquents: from Theoretical Implications to Practical Applications" and "Trying Children as Adults in Georgia: Can the Deadly Sins be Forgiven?"

Section I: Pre-Service Teachers to work with Juvenile Delinquents: It is a privilege to serve as a discussant of these great presentations focusing on school violence. Violence has become a serious problem in our schools. Preparing pre-service teachers to help reduce violence in schools is, certainly, a step in the right direction. Let me now briefly summarize the presentation of our three able presenters.

- Homicides involving guns is the leading cause of death of African-American males.
- Children who become violent are not safe in their homes, schools, and communities.
- Post traumatic stress that children experience as either victim or witness to violence results in intrusive imagery, emotional constriction or avoidance, fears of recurrence,

sleep difficulties, disinterest in significant activities, and attention difficulties, all of which interfere with normal development, learning in schools, happy and safe living in the community.

- Increase of violence and vandalism in schools make it necessary to help students and teachers to learn effective ways to deal with conflict.
- High youth crime rate is evident in schools, homes, and community.
- Multiple factors such as family bonding, child abuse, poor parental supervision, inconsistent discipline or harsh discipline may contribute to the escalation of violence.
- Violent and inappropriate actions of a few students disrupt educational programs and services
- Approximately 1000 crimes per 100,000 students were reported in our national public schools.
- Many schools are reporting violent acts occurring in classes, hallways, and playgrounds by 12-17 year old population.
- Some of the early predictors of youth violence are truancy, peer rejection, poor class performance and early dropout.
- Colleges and universities next prepare pre-service teachers as "highly qualified" to teach in diverse class settings, and to provide higher quality and more equitable and accountable classes for poor, minority students, juvenile and youths at risk for violence. The No Child Left Behind Act (NCLB) is designed to ensure that all children have a fair, equal, and significant opportunity to a high quality education.
- The NCLB Act and calls from accreditation bodies have led to changes in the perpetration of pre-service teachers of those at risk for violence and those in juvenile diverse settings.
- Juveniles and other diverse students need teachers who can build on the personal, cultural, social, and physical

strengths students bring to the school, home, and community settings.

- Effective and motivated teachers can accommodate juveniles in a learning setting.
- Teachers must accept the fact that they must work effectively with struggling students.
- The need to specially train pre-service teachers to work with juvenile delinquents is crucial.
- Models for such training were presented, including some discussions of surveys of pre-service teachers before and after training.
- If no child must be left behind, all professions, including pre-service teachers must re-examine how they prepare themselves with appropriate strategies to meet the challenges in diverse classrooms.

Reducing violence in our schools is a challenge to all of us. I am convinced that we have learnt enough material from these presentations that will help us begin to make some difference in our various schools towards reducing violence and making our environment more conducive for learning.

Section II: Trying Children as Adults in Georgia: The future of this great country rests squarely on the shoulders of our youths. I am, therefore, always excited to listen or comment on presentations that deal with important matters concerning our youths. Needless to say that Prof. Howell has done justice to this topic titled: Trying Children as Adults: Can the Deadly Sins be Forgiven? The presentation was concise, straight to the point and very informative. My job as the discussant is to briefly summarize the presentation and proffer some general comments. Let me now start with a summary of the presentation.

- Prior to 1899 most states tried juveniles in the same system and manner as adult offenders.

- In 1899 the concept of juvenile courts design to treat juveniles differently was introduced partly due to the efforts of the juvenile court reform movement. The underlying thinking was that the community was ultimately responsible for ensuring that youths act lawfully. For the youths that fail to act lawfully, the community was to provide the care and nurturing to make such youths correct their unlawful conduct. The state under the doctrine of *parens patrie* was to act in the place of parents and in the best interest of the youths.

- The juvenile court emphasized rehabilitation and not punishment. The process was very informal. The need for due process safeguards, such as right to jury trials, and right to attorneys were not necessary.

In re Gault Ramifications

- The Supreme Courts decision *In re Gault* changed the informality of the juvenile courts. Procedural due process safeguards were introduced into the operations of the juvenile courts; these formalities made juvenile courts operate like adult courts.

- The *In re Winship (1970)* decision extended the requirement of "proof beyond reasonable doubt" to juvenile court proceedings. Additionally, the U.S. Supreme Court's decision in *Breed v. Jones (1975)* applied the double jeopardy ban to juvenile court proceedings.

- The effect of the U.S. Supreme Court's due process decisions was to make juvenile court proceedings seem like adult court proceedings with little concern for individualized treatment and more preference for assembly line processing.

Georgia as a Case Study for Trying Children as Adults

- Georgia like many states has moved to harsher punishments for juvenile offenders.

- Georgia has two mechanisms for transferring juveniles to be tried in Superior Courts: 1). Transfer after a hearing in juvenile court; 2). Automatic transfer by operation of SB440.

- A juvenile court judge may transfer a case after hearing if it was determined that the child was at least 15 years old at the time of the offense or at least 13 years old and committed a delinquent offense punishable by death, or life, or an aggravated battery that results in serious bodily injury to the victim.

- The SB440 Law automatically gives Georgia Supreme Court exclusive jurisdiction over juveniles who are 13 years or older, and found to have committed any of the offenses commonly referred to as the "seven deadly sins", such as: Murder, Voluntary Manslaughter, Rape, Aggravated Sodomy, Aggravated Child Molestation, Aggravated Sexual Battery, Armed Robbery committed with a firearm

- Georgia Supreme Court has rejected all constitutional challenges to the SSB440 Law.

- In Georgia, as in many states, increasing number of children are being tried in adult courts.

- SSB440 offenses may attract a minimum of 10 years without parole in adult prisons or as long as life in prison without parole.

- To worsen matters, the SB440 is disproportionately applied to African-American children.

- Suggests shying away from automatic transfer of youths to the adult courts. Juvenile court judges should be allowed the discretion to determine the youths to be transferred after a hearing.

- Studies show that juveniles tried in adult courts and sentenced to adult institutions display high recidivism rates, are more likely not to be rehabilitated, and likely to be sexually abused in prison.

- The recent U.S. Supreme Court decision in *Roper v. Simmons* holding the execution of juveniles under the age of 13 to be unconstitutional is a welcome development. It may signal the beginning of a return to treating juveniles as juveniles with emphasis on treatment and rehabilitation.

While I agree with the presenter that the U.S. Supreme Court's extension of procedural safeguards to juvenile court proceedings made the proceedings to mirror adult court proceedings, I however, suggest that we must not discount the positives of according juveniles some rights to ensure fairness and cut down on arbitrariness in juvenile proceedings. Such rights as *the right to counsel* in waiver cases *(Kent v. United States-1966)[1]*, *right to due process (In re Gault – 1967)[2]*, requirement of *proof beyond reasonable doubt (In re Winship- 1970)[3]* are in order and should ordinarily not undo the treatment and the rehabilitative trust of the Juvenile Court.[4]

Furthermore, transferring juveniles to be tried in adult courts is generally not a bad idea for heinous crimes. It may serve to deter other juveniles who may be contemplating committing similar acts. The public is certainly in support of such transfers. For example, in one public opinion survey, 62% agreed that a juvenile charged with a serious property crime should be tried as adults; 69% agreed that a juvenile charged with selling illegal drug should be tried as adults; and 87% agreed that a juvenile charged with a serious violent crime should be tried as an adult.

---

[1] Kent v. United States (1966) in the American System of Criminal Justice, George F. Cole and Christopher E. Smith, 2004, 538

[2] Ibid

[3] Ibid

[4] Ruth Triplett, "The Growing Threat: Gangs and Juvenile Offenders", in Americans View Crime and Justice, ed. Timothy J. Flanagan and Denis R. Longmire (Thousand Oaks. Calif.: Sage 1966), 142

Discussion of "Domestic Violence, Law Enforcement, and African-Americans"

Ali Al-Taie

The institution of family is human society's first and most ancient creation. This societal cornerstone plays a dominant, if not the most dominant, role in social cohesion and organization. At the same time, it is subject to societal development in all directions. For a complex range of reasons, which for space concerns cannot be addressed presently, societal changes in the US society have affected this institution, and in consequence, have affected society itself undesirably. By its origins, consequences, and societal response, domestic violence is such an emergent problem in this context. More specifically, the problem of domestic violence impacts more on, and can be found among, those social strata and groups that are most affected by socioeconomic disparity and injustice. In both historical and contemporary dimensions, the Africa-American community comprises such a huge group that has not received justice deserved and has suffered from discrimination.

Researching this same problem, Dr. Joanne V. Rhone has elaborately examined the issues existing in the domestic life of this group. As a scholar of social work, her analysis of domestic violence merits from her theoretical and practical experiences. In this study, she not only traces domestic violence to homes and households, where in principle it exists in the first place, she also locates it in other closely-related domains, the school, and the work place. Further, the author delves into the public policies as well as community responses offered which altogether are adopted to combat this problem. While homegrown responses are not adequate to play a significant part in curbing the social problem of domestic violence, the criminal justice system is targeted for its inadequate response and/or disparity in rendering services needed.

Furthermore, while domestic violence is usually attributed to the male, or thought to be a masculine product only, in this study women too have realistically been given their fair share in the escalation of the problem.

The author invites the parties concerned to join forces to introduce new measures and policies, to reduce the rising tide of domestic violence. Included in this call are the criminal justice system, African-American communities, and Historically Black Colleges and Universities. These parties are expected to address domestic violence oriented towards this minority from external sources, namely society at large, and from within the African-American community itself. Thus, the author seems to suggest that those who do not consider themselves as a part of the solution sought, they may practically become a part of the problem imposed.

Dr. Rhone's study is insightful and has a great potential for publication in a prestigious professional journal. This, in my opinion, should be done successfully after the working paper is developed further and revised. The diverse issues relevantly mentioned in the draft, require further space towards elaboration and exemplification. Because domestic violence is, in essence, a societal problem per se, it should primarily be analyzed sociologically. This approach should by no means prevent the author to pay more attention in this context to another discipline such as social work when a specific focus in this research is deemed necessary. Finally, when it comes to critique of how society at large addresses a given social problem, specific solutions should be pinpointed. Otherwise, social scientists, who are not part of the decision-making process nor the determinants of definite programs for action, should restrict their roles to comprehensive academic analysis only. It seems that inadequate societal and governmental response to social problems and issues, including domestic violence, has encouraged some social scientists operating on academic campuses to play the role of planners and policy makers as well, which even if needed may not look plausible.

Discussion of "The War on Drugs and the African-American Community" and "California's 3 Strikes Law and the Impact of Mandatory Minimum Laws"

Dianne A. Williams

Several meaningful policy implications can be derived from these discussions. Firstly, the increases in bias-motivated actions indicate that the United States may not be moving toward the egalitarian, free-choice, and tolerant society that is boasts to the rest of the world. Secondly, scholars and practitioners all assume that the ultimate goal is a truly "color-blind civil society" that ignores racial and ethnic differences and tries to exist as "one people." But is this utopian vision what this society really wants?

Political economy scholars have long argued that penal practices are directly correlated to a perceived threat from economically marginal and minority populations.[1] [2] [3] They predicted that social control attempts would escalate as the size of black and

---

[1] Jankovic, I., (1977). Labor market and imprisonment. *Crime and Social Justice* 8:17- 31

[2] Michalowski, R. and M. Pearson, (1990). Punishment and social structure at the state level: A cross sectional comparison of 1970 and 1980. *Journal of Research in Crime and Delinquency* 27:52-78

[3] Rusche, G. and O. Kirschheimer, (1939/1968). *Punishment and social structure.* New York: Russell and Russell

other minority populations increased. [4] [5] More recently, researchers have argued that increases in unemployment rates are associated with increases in imprisonment rates even after crime rates are controlled. [6] [7] This trend was identified as far back as 1939. We should therefore, not be surprised by the continued attempt to legally control minority populations.

Studies on California's Three-Strikes law and the national war on drugs are both timely because of the tremendous impact they both have on the black community. General policing policies and the so-called "cracklaw-blacklaw" for example, clearly target African-American communities, and encourage double standards of criminal justice treatment. In fact it is arguable that the "War on Crime" is actually a war on African Americans.

Russell's discussion of *California's Three- Strikes Law and the Impact of Mandatory Minimum Laws* is an outstanding source of empirical data that supports the argument that penal practices are perhaps a method of minority control. It addresses two critically important issues (1) the disproportionate application of the Three-Strikes law to minority populations in California and (2) the long term effect of this disproportionate application on the longevity of minority communities.

The research presented gives a detailed view of the havoc that the Three-Strikes law is wreaking on minority populations in California. However, any discussion of the Three-Strikes law must by necessity, make strong reference to two sub-categories of crime statistics—recidivism and rehabilitation. If parolees and probationers

---

[4] Blalock, H.,(1967). *Toward a Theory of Minority-Group Relations.* New York: John Wiley & Sons.

[5] Jacobs, David and Carmichael, Jason T. (2001). The politics of punishment across time and space: A pooled time-series analysis of imprisonment rates. *Social Forces* 80:61-91

[6] Beckett, K. and B. Western, (2001). Governing social marginality: Welfare, incarceration, and the transformation of state policy. *Punishment and Society* 3:43-59

[7] Greenberg, D. and V. West, (2001). State prison populations and their growth, 1971-1991. *Criminology* 39:615-653

are properly rehabilitated, the rates or recidivism would fall and the likelihood of a second or third 'strike' would be slim.

The data presented is strongly supported by other research such as that done by the Little Hoover Commission, which reports that the recidivism rate in California is 67% - almost double the national average of 35%. [8] This all but guarantees the success of the Three-Strikes law. Since most of the other states do not have Three-Strikes, the validity of the deterrent effect is also an issue, not to mention the fundamental question of fairness in the application of the law.

Russell also noted that the third felony that triggers the automatic sentence, very often is a relatively minor one. A life sentence for such a crime is arguably "cruel and unusual". This raises the constitutional question of whether the punishment violates the Eighth Amendment because it is "grossly disproportionate" to the severity of the crime committed. The Supreme Court, although divided, decided the punishment was not cruel and unusual and did not violate any Eight Amendment right. In a pair of 5-4 rulings, the court said the constitutional ban on cruel and unusual punishment is not violated by sentences at the outer limits of the 1994 law and that California is entitled to decide that criminals who can't or won't obey the law should be separated from society.[9]

Opponents of the Three-Strikes law claim that these laws give criminals no chance to rehabilitate and redeem themselves and, as the presenter's statistical analysis clearly shows, recidivism has not been reduced by the presence of such laws. Moreover, the general reduction in crime, when and where it has occurred, is perhaps due to effective policing, rather than to harsh sentencing.

Proponents, on the other hand, argue that the fundamental purpose of the criminal justice system is to protect the rights and the safety of law-abiding citizens. Citizens cannot be protected by "revolving door justice", which allows criminals back on the street

---

[8] Little Hoover Commission (1998). Beyond Bars: Correctional Reforms to Lower Prison Costs and Reduce Crime. CA: Author

[9] Ewing V. California (01-6978) 538 US 11 (2003)

after repeat offenses. The Three-Strikes laws remove repeat offenders from society, and prevent them from committing further crimes. They also argue that rehabilitation is highly unlikely for recidivists. Someone who has committed three felonies is not likely to reform; rather, it is the destiny of the recidivist to keep committing crimes.

Additionally, proponents of the Three-Strikes law argue that since its passage the recidivism rate of parolees who are returning to prison because of the commission of a new crime (as opposed to a parole violation) has dropped by nearly 25% while in the three years prior to passage of the law the recidivism rate increased by almost 4%.[10] What these proponents did not consider was the significant number of parolees who are leaving California. The number of parolees leaving the state is significantly greater than the number of parolees from other jurisdictions who are entering the state. This striking turnaround started in 1994 when, for the first time more parolees left the state than entered since 1976. This trend has continued and in 1997 more than 1,000 net parolees left California.[11] If the most serious offenders leave the state then it stands to reason that the crime rate would fall and give the misleading impression that the Three-Strikes law works.

There is no denying that one of the fundamental principles of criminal justice is that the punishment should fit the crime and the penalty for the crime should be clear and certain. But as Blain argues is his discussion of *The War on Drugs and the African-American Community*, this fundamental principle is abandoned when a life sentence is automatically imposed for a third felony - whether that felony is serious and violent, or minor and non-violent. Since many crimes carry only one possible sentence, it follows that the sentence will not always correspond to the seriousness of the offence.

---

[10] Greenwood, P. W. and A. Hawken, (2002). *An Assessment of the Effects of California's Three Strikes Law*. Los Angeles, California: Greenwood & Associates
[11] California's District Attorney's Association (2004). *Prosecutor's Perspective on California's Three Strikes Law*. CA: Author

Notwithstanding this, protagonists argue that the three strikes law is in effect, ex post facto law: that is, criminal sentences can take into account - as first and second strikes - crimes that were committed before the law was passed. Moreover, the imposition of mandatory maximum sentences because of past history constitutes "double jeopardy" in that criminals are being punished again for crimes for which they have already served time.

Russell also makes mention of the fact that judges who have historically had discretionary powers when sentencing criminals have lost this power to prosecutors. Traditionally, judges have recognized that sentencing should take into account the circumstances of the crime, the character of the criminal, and the amount of harm caused by the crime. Not only has, mandatory sentencing robbed judges of this discretionary power, but the Three-strikes law has transferred unlimited power to prosecutors who now have discretion to throw out 'strikes' for selected offenders.

Another issue that is highlighted in the study presented is the significant impact of the Three-Strikes law on the children of prisoners. Although the impact on the minority community is unmistakable, and the law is noticeably harsher on minorities, is it fair to blame the law makers when the parents made the initial decision to choose a life of crime by committing the first felony, then by committing a second felony and then a third?

Finally, Russell mentions of the 2000 election approval of Proposition 36. This requires first-and second-time drug possession offenders to receive drug treatment instead of being incarcerated and also gives third-time offenders who have been paroled or released for five years an opportunity to received treatment instead of the 25-years-to-life prison sentence.

We can make two assumptions about Proposition 36. On the one hand we can assume that Proposition 36 has been implemented successfully and recidivism is a result of the unwillingness of minorities to participate in drug treatment programs. Or, we can assume that prosecutors are unwilling to make the option of drug treatment available to minorities. The statistical analysis presented tells the story.

According to the Department of Justice's 2003 prison statistics, one in every one hundred and forty U.S. residents is incarcerated.[12] This has changed our communities and the labor pool so much that even the current administration has had to revisit criminal justice policy reform. There are rumors that a White House endorsed bipartisan legislation called, the Second Chance Act of 2004 is floating around somewhere in Washington.[13] This bill is supposed to acknowledge how difficult it is for formerly incarcerated people to find work upon release, and if passed is expected to review laws that keep people from receiving federal financial aid or state licenses for work if they have been convicted of a drug-related crime. If this Act is passed and properly implemented, we can expect dramatic, positive changes especially within minority communities.

The central theme of both Blain's and Russell's discussions is that incarceration is not an acceptable way to alter behavior except at a very minor level. Obviously, we cannot continue to employ the same strategies and policies that we've utilized in the past. So any discussion of Sentencing Reform and the Black Community must focus on feasible recommendations for dealing effectively with the problem.

Within our own communities we must increase the availability and use of alternative sanctions for nonviolent drug offenders including, but not limited to, the use of special drug courts in which addicted offenders are given the opportunity to complete court-supervised substance abuse treatment instead of being sentenced to prison.

The black community must take the initiative to increase the availability of substance abuse treatment and prevention outreach in the community as well as in jails and prisons. We must fight to redirect law enforcement and prosecution resources to emphasize the arrest, prosecution, and incarceration of importers,

---

[12] Harrison, P.M. and A.J. Beck, (2004). *Prisoners in 2003.* Washington, D.C.: U.S. Department of Justice, Bureau of Justice Statistics.

[13] Senate Bill No. 2789 (2004). *The Second Chance Act 2004: Community Safety through Recidivism Prevention.* 108th Congress-2d Session

manufacturers, and major distributors, e.g., drug king pins, rather than low level offenders and street level retail dealers. And finally, we must fight for the elimination of different sentencing structures for powder cocaine and crack cocaine, drugs that are pharmacologically identical but marketed in a different form.

Current an ongoing statistical data support this argument. This does not mean, however, that incarceration should not be considered from the standpoint of effective crime prevention. However, until crime can be totally eradicated, only effective and meaningful rehabilitation programs will lower recidivism. Harsher and longer punishment will not. This was clearly pointed out in the November, 2003, Little Hoover Commission Report, where California's single minded focus on punishment was described as a 5.2-billion-dollar-a-year-failure.

ABOUT THE CONTRIBUTORS

Ali Al-Taie is Associate Professor of Sociology and Chairman Department of Social Sciences at Shaw University. He earned his doctorate from the University of Oklahoma, and joined went to Shaw in 1989. He established the Department of Social Sciences and later restructured it into College of Social Sciences. He designed the Shaw University's Institute of Social Justice and Policy Studies (ISJPS). Dr. Al-Taie has published works in English, Arabic, and Farsi/Persian. He has publication in progress include: *The Sociology of Collective Identity* (Planned as Textbook) and *The Arabs of Al-Ahwaz (Iran): A Socio-historical Approach*

Lucinda Barron is Coordinator of the Special Education Program at South Carolina State University. Dr. Barron has twenty years of public school experience in special education. In addition, she has served as a school psychologist and school counselor. Her "real life" experiences in the public schools helped her to better prepare pre-service teachers to work with diverse students. Since Dr. Barron has been in higher education, she has been the recipient of the "Teacher of the Year" award from her department.

Michael Blain is the Director of Public Policy at Drug Policy Alliance. He is a graduate of the University of Maryland and a former Soros Fellow. As the Director of the Office of Public Policy, Michael supervises and directs the Alliance's lobbying efforts in 12 states. He combines the lobbying power of the Alliance with existing grassroots movements in states to create campaigns to enact sensible drug policy reforms. Michael has been a key player in drug policy initiatives in Texas, Maryland, and Alabama that have resulted in 10 new pieces of legislative reform. Michael's organizing efforts have resulted in the formation of two new advocacy organizations in Texas and Alabama that are focused on ending the drug war, the Alabama and the Texas Justice Network, alliances of formerly incarcerated people and their family members. He is part of a highly developed nationwide network of formerly incarcerated people, their family members, and communities of color. His advocacy work has been featured on the *Tavis Smiley Show*, in *Corrections Today*, the *New York Times*, the *Washington Post*, and the *Baltimore Sun*. In June of 2004 Michael was given an Exemplary Leadership Award by the Black Caucus in Maryland for the passage of HB 295.

Helen Brantley is Coordinator of Technology/Assessment at South Carolina State University. Dr. Brantley received her BS in Elementary Education from New York University and her MA, MED and Ph.D. from Columbia University in New York City. She is responsible for workshops and disseminating assessment and technology information in reports to the university staff. She has written proposals and received funds from the Family and Community Violence Prevention Program of the U.S. Office of Minority Health. Dr. Brantley has organized over fifty workshops and made presentations at the national, state and local levels, written several book chapters and articles and authored Behavior *Modification of Thinking and Test-Taking Strategies.*

Sutham Cheurprakobkit is Associate Professor of Criminal Justice in the Department of Sociology, Geography, Anthropology, and Criminal Justice at Kennesaw State University. He was a police officer for three years in Bangkok, Thailand and a police instructor for one year at the National Police Cadet Academy in Thailand. He earned his master's degree in Criminal Justice from University of Alabama at Birmingham in 1989 and his Ph.D. in Criminal Justice from Sam Houston State University in 1996. His research interests include comparative policing, community policing, police and minorities, computer crime, and web-based education. He has received 5 research grants and has published 25 refereed articles and 3 book chapters.

Obie Clayton, Jr. is Professor and Chair of the Sociology Department at Morehouse College. He is the former Executive Director of the Morehouse Research Institute and Project Director of the New Minority Male Consortium for the Study of Male Health funded by the Office of Minority Health. He is currently President of the Mid-South Sociological Association. His areas of research include crime and deviance over the life course, urban inequality and family formation. He has published widely and edited *An American Dilemma Revisited: Race Relations in a Changing World*, Russell Sage Foundation (1996) and most recently, *African-American Fathers and Families*, Russell Sage Foundation (2003). Dr. Clayton earned his B.A. in Sociology and Religion at Millsaps College and the Ph.D. in Sociology from Emory University.

Judge Thelma Wyatt Cummings-Moore is the first woman to serve as Chief Judge of the Superior Court of Fulton County. Judge Moore earned a Bachelor's Degree from the University of California at Los Angeles. She earned her Doctor of Jurisprudence with Distinction at Emory University. Judge Moore previously served on the Atlanta Municipal Court and the City Court of Atlanta, and was the first African-American woman to serve on the State Court of Georgia. From 1996-1998, Judge Moore conceived and spearheaded the creation of a unified "Family Court" and Family Law Information Center to resolve multiple family disputes while coordinating therapeutic services for families. She has served as an adjunct professor of criminal law and legal ethics at Morris Brown College and a lecturer in contemporary judicial issues at Clark Atlanta University and Emory University School of Law. She has published legal articles in the *Howard University Law Journal*, the *Georgia State Bar Journal*, the *Emory Law Journal* and in the book *Black Judges in America*. She has recently published a book, *Living with a Passion*. She has participated in legal seminars and research missions on substance abuse in the United States, Africa, Asia, Caribbean and Europe. Judge Moore serves on the Board of Governors of the Joint Center for Political & Economic Studies and the Board of the National Center for State Courts. She is the former Chair of the Judicial Council of the National Bar Association. Judge Moore has received over 175 awards and recognitions and has been given the keys to the cities of Chicago, Huntsville, Alabama and Gainesville, Florida. Among her many awards are: the 2001 William H. Rehnquist Award for Judicial Excellence, the "Outstanding Georgia Citizen Award" the 2004 President's Award, induction into the Gate City Bar Association Hall of Fame (2003), Pacesetter Award from the Georgia Legislative Black Caucus (2003), and the 2001 Sojourner Truth Award from the Negro Business and Professional Women. In 2000, the Fulton County Commission declared a Judge Thelma Wyatt Cummings Moore Day in recognition of her tireless service and lasting contributions.

Alan J. Dreher is Assistant Chief of Atlanta Police Department (APD). He holds a Bachelor of Science degree from the George Mason University and a Masters of Science degree from the Johns Hopkins University. He spent 23 years with the Washington, DC Police Department prior to his arrival in Atlanta where he served in various capacities including Homicide Division Commander, Intelligence Division Commander, Violent Crimes and Gang Task Force Commander, and ultimately the Commanding Officer of the First District, which encompasses the Capitol, the White House, and the Downtown Business District. At APD, Assistant Chief Dreher oversees the daily operations of the Department, including the Field Operations Division, Criminal Investigations Division, and the Support Services Division. He is an active member The International Association of Chiefs of Police, The Major Cities Chiefs Association, Police Executive Research Forum, Atlanta Metropol Incorporated, National Organization of Black Law Enforcement Executives, and the Georgia Association of Chiefs of Police. He has served on the Executive Board of The FBI National Academy Associations Washington, DC.

Gale 'Sky' Edeawo is the Director and founder of Project Welcome Home, a service for incarcerated women female ex-offenders who want to change their lifestyle for the better. She received an associate degree from Los Angeles City College. In 2001 she visited Chatman County Sheriff's Detention Center to mentor female inmates which led her a few female inmates, which motivated her to start a service for female ex-offenders that could assist them once they returned to society, Project Welcome Home. She teaches life skills stressing motivation and high self esteem among the women. "Sky" serves as a mentor at the Savannah Runaway Shelter, and is a freelance writer who has won several awards for her writing.

George E. Hicks is Associate Professor and Coordinator of the Elementary Education Program at South Carolina State University. Dr. Hicks has worked twenty-five years in public schools, as a teacher (12 years), assistant principal (1 year), and elementary principal (12 years). The public school experience has enriched Dr. Hicks' teaching as he works with pre-service teachers at the collegiate level to prepare them to work with the youth of today. Dr. Hicks has been the recipient of the "Teacher of the Year" award from his department.

Amy Howell joined the Southern Juvenile Defender Center (SJDC) in 2002 as an Equal Justice Works Fellow, and following her fellowship remained with SJDC to continue her work. Ms. Howell manages the activities of SJDC focusing on the development of research-based policy and systemic improvements for youth involved with the juvenile or criminal justice system. Ms. Howell has assisted courts in developing protocols for pre-trial mental health assessment, detention alternative policies, and public education on the juvenile justice system. She has published several articles, including a comprehensive manual regarding holistic legal representation of youth in the juvenile justice system, *Representing the Whole Child: A Juvenile Defender Training Manual*. Ms. Howell also serves as legal counsel for youth with disabilities in juvenile court and school disciplinary proceedings. Previously, Ms. Howell taught elementary school in North Carolina. Ms. Howell received her BA from Connecticut College and her JD from The Temple University James E. Beasley School of Law.

Ryan Scott King is a Research Associate with The Sentencing Project in Washington, DC. His research specialization is the American correctional system, with a particular concentration on the radiating effects of incarceration upon individuals, families and the community at large. His most recent work is an analysis of the localized impact of felony disenfranchisement laws in Atlanta, GA. Past research has included a national profile of life sentences, an analysis of the economic effects of sitting a prison in a rural community, a study of the effect of Three-Strikes laws on the prison population, and a statistical profile of state prison inmates incarcerated on drug charges. Areas of research interest include felony disenfranchisement, sentencing legislation, incarceration and crime rates, drug policy, and the nexus of class, race and incarceration. Mr. King has appeared in the *Associated Press, New York Times*, *Washington Post*, and *USA Today* as well as in a number of local print media. In addition, he has appeared on local and national talk radio programs to discuss sentencing and corrections issues, including NPR's *The Tavis Smiley Show* and *Talk of the Nation*.

Chief Thetus Knox is first female, African-American Chief of Police of Riverdale City. She is a graduate of Clark College, the FBI National Academy, the Southern Police Institute, and the Police Executive Research Forum Senior Management Institute for Police Training. She spent 32 years as a law enforcement officer and manages a 54-person department that serves a population of over 13,000 citizens. She was the first female in the history of the Atlanta Police Department to serve as a Field Patrol Sergeant and; the first female to serve as a Section Commander of the Criminal Investigations Division; one of the first females to serve as the Deputy Chief of the Field Operations Division. She retired from the department after 31 years as Deputy Chief of the Support Services Division. While in the Atlanta Police Department she implemented the Bicycle and Foot Patrols, as well as spearheaded the opening three mini-precincts in an effort to strengthen the relationship between the police and the community. Chief Knox is a member of Atlanta Metropol, the National Organization of Black Law Enforcement Executives, the International Association of Police Chiefs and the FBI National Academy Associates.

Michael Mears is the Director of the Georgia Public Defender Standards Council. Prior to his appointment to the Georgia Public Defender Standards Council, Michael was the Director of the Multi-County Public Defender Office. He has served as partner-in-charge of litigation for the law firm of McCurdy & Candler. He has personally served as lead trial counsel in over 60 death penalty cases since 1984. In addition to serving as trial counsel, Michael has authored numerous articles and books including *A Brief History of The Georgia Indigent Defense Counsel, Twenty-Five Years of Struggle to Provide Adequate Counsel for The Poor*, and *The Death Penalty in Georgia - A Modern History, 1970 -2000*. He is also a regular contributor to the Mercer Law School Law Review on death penalty law updates. In 1994 Michael was awarded the Indigent Defense Award for Service by the Georgia Indigent Defense Council. He has been instrumental in helping to develop policies, procedures and guidelines which govern the provision of indigent defense services in Georgia. Michael is a graduate of the Mississippi State University where he received his Bachelors Degree and his Master of Arts Degree. Michael served in the United States Navy in Vietnam and in the Middle East. He is a graduate of the University of Georgia School of Law (Class of 1977). Michael served as the Mayor of the City of Decatur, Georgia from 1985 until 1993. Michael is currently the Vice-Chairperson of the State

Bar's Indigent Defense Committee and has served as Chairperson of the State Bar of Georgia's Criminal Law Section.

Judge Yvette Miller is a judge in the Georgia Court of Appeals. She earned her B.A. degree cum laude form Mercer University, her law degree from Walter F. George University School of La, LL.M in litigation from Emory and Masters of Laws in Judicial Process from the University of Virginia's School of Law. In 1999, was appointed the first African-American woman and the 65th judge to serve on the Georgia Court of Appeals by Governor Roy Barnes. And in November 2000, she was elected statewide to the Court of Appeals without opposition. In 1992 the then Governor Miller appointed her as the first African-American, first woman, and the youngest person ever to serve as Director/Judge of the Appellate Division on the State Board of Workers' Compensation. Judge Miller was appointed by Governor Miller to the State Court of Fulton County and was reelected in 1998. Judge Miller was one of the first female prosecutors in Fulton County and was a Senior Associate Counsel at MARTA. She has received numerous awards and special recognitions for her professional and civic service, such as a leading judge in the country in the 2001 Edition of *Black Judges In America.* Judge Miller has also been recognized for her numerous achievements in *Who's Who in Black Atlanta* from 2001-2004. Consecutively from 1991 to 2004, she was designated by the *Georgia Informer* as one of "Georgia's Top 50 Influential Black Women." She is a member of several bar association including the Atlanta Bar, the Gate City Bar, GAWL, and GABWA. She serves on boards of several organizations such as the National Alliance for the Mentally Ill, Kids' Chance, Inc, etc.

Saliba D. Mukoro is an Associate Professor and Chair of the Criminal Justice Department, Mississippi Valley State University. He holds a Bachelor of Science Degree in Criminology and Corrections, a Master of Arts Degree in Criminology and Corrections, and a Doctorate Degree in Criminal Justice from Sam Houston State University, Huntsville Texas. He taught at Grambling

State University as a graduate faculty for 3 years. Served as a military officer in the Nigerian Army for 17 years where he held both infantry and Law Enforcement command positions, including serving as commanding officer of a Military Police (MP) battalion. His research interests include Law Enforcement in the Developing Nations and Disproportionate Minority Confinement (DMC)

Komanduri S. Murty, Professor and Chair of Sociology and Criminal Justice at Clark Atlanta University, received his Ph.D. from Mississippi State University in 1984. He is the author or co-author of more than 45 book chapters and articles, which have appeared in numerous books and journals, including the *Encyclopedia of American Prisons.* Also, he has co-authored three books including *Voices From Prison: An Ethnographic Study of Black Male Prisoners.* He is the principal investigator and director of a community crime prevention project, *Project Redirection,* funded by Fulton County since 1985. He has received a certificate of leadership for distinguished commitment to community service and an appreciation award from the Association of International Affairs in 1995. He is also the 2005 recipient of the *Aldrich Macmillan Award* in overall achievement. Finally, he has been listed in *Who's Who Among America's Teachers, Who's Who Among Asian Americans, and Who's Who in the South and Southwest.*

Sampson Ike Oli is a Professor and Head of the Department of Criminal Justice at Bethune-Cookman College, Dr. Oli received the LL.B and B.L. law degrees from the University of Nigeria and Nigeria Law School respectively. He earned MA degrees in Criminal Justice, Research and Criminology from State University of New Your, Albany, and John Jay College, of Criminal Justice, New York. His M.PH and Ph.D. degrees were earned from John Jay College of Criminal Justice in the City University of New York system. He is a member of the Academy of Criminal Justice Sciences, the Southern Criminal Justice Association, and the International Association of Correctional Officers. Dr. Oli is currently engaged in writing two books *Introduction to Florida Criminal Law* and

Crime and Social Control: Lessons from Africa. Dr. Oli is actively involved in community affairs and is a member of the Dayton Beach Investment Council, the Pan African Awareness Associations, the Central Florida Association of Black Attorneys, and the Daytona Beach Branch of the NAACP.

Joanne V. Rhone is Professor and Assistant Dean of the Whitney M. Young, Jr. School of Social Work at Clark Atlanta University. She is a graduate of Grambling State University (B.S. Degree); Atlanta University (M.S.W.); Union Institute and University (Ph.D. Degree). Dr. Rhone's research and presentation interest is in the area of gerontology, women and children's mental health, domestic violence, and policy issues related to African-American children and families. She has traveled extensively; completed Fulbright research and lectureships in Egypt, and Indonesia; served as Principal Investigator for research/service grants focused on domestic violence and community health; and made scholarly presentations at local, state, national, and international conferences. Presently, Dr. Rhone teaches social welfare policies and health/mental health courses in the Master of social work program and social policy courses in the doctoral program in the School of Social Work.

Judge Martha Lynn Sherrod is judge of Madison County, Alabama, Drug Courts. She received her Doctor of Jurisprudence degree from the University of Houston, Houston, Texas. Judge Sherrod was appointed District Judge in 1999, and was re-elected in 2000. She is the first African-American to win an at-large election in North Alabama. Before joining the State Court, Judge Sherrod served as Presiding Municipal Judge, Assistant District Attorney and private practitioner in Madison County and taught criminal justice at Alabama A&M University. She helped developed the first Family Drug Court, the sixth Adult Drug Court, and a Juvenile Drug Court in Alabama. In response to an increase in traffic accidents involving young drivers, she has taken Alive at 25 Defensive Driving, a defensive driving, program into the local high schools. Judge Sherrod is Chair-Elect of the Judicial Council of the National Bar Association, Vice President of the National African-American Drug Policy Coalition, a member of the Task Force on Diversity of the Alabama State Bar Association and a sub-committee chair on the Alabama Supreme Court's Task Force on State Drug Court Policy.

Diane Williams is a Criminal Justice professor in North Carolina. She is a Certified Criminal Justice Specialist and a board member of Triad Alternatives for Change (a non profit organization with a focus on the rehabilitation of first time offenders). Her areas of specialty are Race and the Criminal Justice System and the Death Penalty. She is a member of the Academy of Criminal Justice Sciences and the American Society of Criminologists.